THE LAW SCHOOL - GLOBAL ISSUES, LOCAL QUESTIONS

The Law School - Global Issues, Local Questions

Edited by
FIONA COWNIE

Routledge
Taylor & Francis Group
LONDON AND NEW YORK

First published 1999 by Dartmouth and Ashgate Publishing

Reissued 2018 by Routledge
2 Park Square, Milton Park, Abingdon, Oxon OX14 4RN
711 Third Avenue, New York, NY 10017, USA

Routledge is an imprint of the Taylor & Francis Group, an informa business

A Library of Congress record exists under LC control number: 98047262

ISBN 13: 978-1-138-34507-2 (hbk)
ISBN 13: 978-0-429-43811-0 (ebk)

Contents

List of Contributors

Anthony Bradney
Senior Lecturer in Law, University of Leicester.

Roger Brownsword
Professor of Law, University of Sheffield.

Fiona Cownie
Senior Lecturer in Law, University of Leicester.

John Flood
Professor of Law, University of Westminster.

Andrew Goldsmith
Professor of Law, Flinders University.

Joy Hillyer
Research Director, College of Law.

René Laperrière
Professor of Law, Université de Québec a Montreal.

Vittorio Olgiati
Professor of Law, University of Urbino.

Claude Thomasset
Professor of Law, Université de Québec a Montreal.

Julian Webb
Professor of Law, University of Westminster.

Foreword

This collection of essays about legal education arises out of the work of the International Sociology Association's Research Committee on the Sociology of Law. The Committee's Working Group on the Legal Professions, convened by Professor Bill Felstiner, Distinguished Research Professor at the University of Wales, Cardiff, has a number of sub groups, of which the group researching into legal education is one. This is the first collection of that group's research to be published; preparatory discussions and planning took place at Peyresq, in France, and we are very grateful to Mady Smets-Hennekine and the Peyresq Centre d'Art International for their support of our work.

The members of this group come from all over the world. Their discussions have led to the realisation that while legal education is carried out differently in different jurisdictions, there are many issues which are of common concern to legal educators, wherever they come from. *Global Issues, Local Questions* is thus written by contributors who write from their own perspective, but who have chosen to write about topics of general interest, casting new light on the discussions and debates within legal education which are taking place in many different jurisdictions.

In the past the study of legal education in all its forms has commonly been a subject that has been neglected and marginalised. Legal academics have pursued research in substantive areas (whether from doctrinal, socio-legal or critical legal perspectives), but have often denigrated work done by others who have been interested in legal education. These essays are an illustration of the consequences of the ever-increasing professionalisation of legal education research throughout the world which has resulted in a greater self-awareness and a realisation that what we are and what we do as legal educationalists can neither be ignored nor entirely divorced from our research and scholarship in more traditional areas of concern.

The publication of this collection of essays is the first stage of an extended comparative examination of legal education in which this group of scholars is engaged. At this stage, I would like to thank Anthony Berry, computer officer in the Faculty of Law at the University of Leicester, for his assistance with the technical aspects of producing this volume.

FIONA COWNIE
Convenor, Legal Education Sub-Group,
Research Committee on the Sociology of Law
Working Group on the Legal Professions.

Foreword

1 Liberalising Legal Education

ANTHONY BRADNEY

Introduction

The most striking feature in the debate about the nature of university legal education in the common-law world has been the existence of dichotomies dividing the starting position espoused by the various writers who have taken part in that debate. Those who favour vocational education have confronted those who prefer academic education, those who see law teaching in terms of skills training have argued with those who see law teaching as the teaching of knowledge and those who see legal education as being about inculcating doctrine have been attacked by practically everybody else. Many writers have regretted the existence of these fundamental divisions in the debate, arguing that they are in fact illusory (Bright, 1991, p. 19). The divisions have, nevertheless, remained and authors have continued to take sides. Yet, through all these divisions, one unifying element runs. Most law lecturers, and most writers concerned with university legal education, are agreed in thinking that such education is a liberal education. Some think that a university legal education is just a liberal education, some think that it is both a liberal education and also some other form of education, but they are generally united in thinking that it is a liberal education.

In a survey of British university law lecturers MacFarlane, Jeeves and Boon found that when asked to indicate what they thought was the most important part of their teaching 74 per cent gave the top score to teaching general intellectual skills. MacFarlane, Jeeves and Boon concluded that '[t]he results of the survey overall indicate a strong bias [in academics in university law schools] towards liberal educational objectives...' (MacFarlane, Jeeves and Boon, 1987, p. 836). This bias towards liberal educational objectives can be found demonstrated in unlikely places and is not confined to Great Britain. Critical Legal Studies, with its denial of the importance of, or existence of the rule of law, is not an obvious place to find support for the notion of a liberal education. Yet in the exchange of correspondence published in the Journal of Legal Education which followed Carrington's attack on those teaching 'legal nihilism' Fiss, who has been associated with the Critical Legal Studies

Movement and who disagreed with Carrington's argument, espoused the liberal position that

> Law professors are not paid to train lawyers, but to study law and to teach their students what they happen to discover. The law school you and I are talking about is an integral part of the university, and by virtue of that membership and all the commitments it entails must be pure in its academic obligations.
> (Martin, 1985, p.26)

Equally, Carrington himself, whilst seeing the university law school as being a professional school devoted to teaching people to be lawyers, thus espousing vocational education, also said in a letter to Fiss '...I have no argument with your assertion that law students may be helped to encounter those who doubt law exists or who doubt that the legal profession has a morally defensible role in our polity' (Martin, 1985, p. 25); a position which could be characterised as indicating a belief in the value of a liberal education.

The prevalence of a belief in the value of liberal education should not be exaggerated. Not all law lecturers would accept the notion of the value of a liberal education. However, even when the notion is criticised the opposing position is often intended to build on what are seen as being valuable elements inherent in ideas of a liberal education whilst disregarding those elements that are damaging either to society or to the individual student. Thus, for example, Thomson, in rejecting the 'liberal arts' model of education also wrote that

> [t]he critical legal movement...identifies with the first great and brilliant theme of the Enlightenment: the belief in the potential of thought to cut through humanly produced distortions and illusions...and to see this as a precondition for human emancipation.
> (Thomson, 1990, p. 191)

The belief that university legal education is, at least in part, a form of liberal education has recently received strong institutional support in England and Wales in the shape of 'The First Report on Legal Education and Training' produced by the Lord Chancellor's Advisory Committee of Legal Education (ACLEC). This recommended, inter alia, that the law degree 'should stand as an independent liberal education in the discipline of law, not tied to any specific vocation' (ACLEC, 1996, p. 57). However, this apparently happy coincidence of official recognition of the desirability of university legal education being a liberal education with the desire on the part of lecturers to approach it in this manner makes pressing the question what does it mean to say that legal education is, or should be, liberal education? In what way does legal education become liberal?

Liberal Education

The notion of liberal education is neither specific to law nor to university education. Its focus begins with the proposition that education is an education for life and that life is not solely concerned with material or utilitarian matters. In his introductory lecture as Professor of Latin at University College, London A.E. Housman argued

> Existence is not itself a good thing, that we should spend a lifetime securing its necessaries: a life spent, however victoriously, in securing the necessaries of life is no more than an elaborate furnishing and decoration of apartments for the reception of a guest who is never come. Our business here is not to live, but to live happily.
> (Housman, 1961, p. 7)

Traditionally the idea of liberal education has involved both an acceptance of the Aristotelian view of the individual as being inherently curious and the Enlightenment view that individuals can comprehend, and through comprehension control, the world. Barnett has said that a dominant, if conservative view, of liberal education has seen such education as being about 'allowing to unfold characteristics of reason and independence which lie naturally within the individual' (Barnett, 1990, p. 190). This has been seen as being valuable both for the individual and for the state.

> The advanced study of the human sciences involves attempting to realise the aims of the practical Enlightenment (ie Kant's injunction not to learn by rote what others have thought but to think for oneself): it contributes to the formation of intellectually and morally responsible citizens.
> (Davies, 1996, p. 24)

It pursues a form of knowledge which is both useful for the individual and for society at large.

> ...the knowledge that Newman values as worth possessing for its own sake, for what it is, is best described as that sort of knowledge which allows human beings to understand themselves; whether that be in terms of their past, their culture, their morality or their relation to the natural world. Pursuit of this knowledge produces two great benefits for both the individuals who study and for the society of which they are part...it initiates students both into their own traditions and into a wider civilisation...
> (Bousfield, 1996, p. 68)

Helpful as they are, analyses of this type describe liberal education in terms of what should be achieved rather than the manner in which that might be done. If legal education is to be liberal education it must allow the student to develop their independence of thinking and it must inculcate into the student true knowledge which is worth possessing for its own sake. But what is that knowledge to be and how is this to be done? Seeking an answer to these questions in the available literature that concerns itself with liberal education would be a futile exercise in an essay of this type. The range of literature is too vast and its content too quarrelsome to allow for any clear suggestions. Instead this essay will look more specifically at the work of F.R. Leavis and see to what extent his ideas can help in searching for the way in which legal education can be turned into a liberal education.

Leavis and Liberal Education

The work of Leavis is not chosen randomly from the corpus of material on liberal education. Leavis has both the advantage that his ideas about liberal education have been highly influential within the academy in general and that his own discipline, literature, is one which is in many ways similar to that of law since they both tend to be text oriented subjects.

Leavis' most important contributions to the debate about liberal education are found in his essays 'The Idea of a University' and 'A Sketch for an 'English School', both of which were collected in his book 'Education and the University' (Leavis, 1948a).[1] In these essays Leavis argues that '[t]he problem [for liberal education] is to produce specialists who are in touch with a humane centre, and to produce a centre for them to be in touch with...'

(Leavis, 1948a, p. 28). Leavis thus identifies liberal education not just with the student who is learning but with the culture that the student is learning. Liberal education's job is to contribute to the development of both (Doyle, 1989, pp. 95-98). For the student Leavis sees literature as being a way of building both sensitivity and sensibility.

> The essential discipline of an English School is the literary-critical...It trains, in a way no other discipline can, intelligence and sensibility together, cultivating a sensitiveness and precision of response and a delicate integrity of intelligence - intelligence that integrates as well as analyses and must have pertinacity and staying power as well as delicacy.
> (Leavis, 1948a, p.34)

Sensibility here is, for Leavis, an important concept, lying at the centre of what makes an education liberal. Education is not simply about training an enquiring and empirical mind. It is not solely about producing that which can rehearse, disassemble and analyse the most recondite facts. To do that is of value but 'there must be training of intelligence that is at the same time a training of sensibility; a discipline of thought that is at the same time a discipline in scrupulous sensitiveness of response to delicate organizations of feeling, sensation and imagery' (Leavis, 1948a, p.38). It is in the combination of high intelligence and precise, delicate emotional response that, for Leavis, a liberal education is to be found (Wyatt, 1990, p. 76). Marianne, sensibility in Austen's *Sense and Sensibility*, looks for 'that spirit, that fire, which at once announce virtue and intelligence' (Austen, 1969, p. 51) in a person's character.[2] Similarly, in an appreciation of Wordsworth, Leavis looks for and approves 'spontaneity' in Wordsworth's writing but this spontaneity 'involves no cult of the instinctive and primitive at the expense of the rational and civilised; it is the spontaneity supervening upon complex development, a spontaneity engaging an advanced and delicate organization' (Leavis, 1934, pp. 245-246). For Leavis sensibility, experience, expression and intelligence are so intertwined that a failure in one will necessarily be a failure in all. Thus in his review of Max Eastman's book *The Literary Mind* he writes

> Mr Eastman's defect of sensibility is a defect of intelligence. This becomes plain if we say that he lacks fineness of perception...What we diagnose in expression, as inadequacy in the use of words, goes back to in adequacy behind the words, an inadequacy of experience.

(Leavis, 1932, p. 22)

In Leavis' writing the personal response of the student to the text studied is very much to the fore whilst factual learning is decried.

> Literary history, as a matter of 'facts about' and accepted critical (or quasi-critical) description and commentary, is a worthless acquisition; worthless for the student who cannot as a critic - that is as an intelligent and discerning reader - make a personal approach to the essential data of the literary historian, the works of literature (an approach is personal or it is nothing...
> (Leavis, 1948a, p. 68)

Leavis' insistence on the priority of individual sensibility should not be taken to indicate an acceptance of the validity of mere subjectivity in reading. The text was both the starting point and the end point for Leavis. In his response to Ezra Pound's book *How to Read* Leavis wrote '[e]verything must start from the training of sensibility' (Leavis, 1948a, p. 120) but that training in sensibility involved began with a close attention to texts.

> It should, by continual insistence and varied exercise in analysis, be enforced that literature is made of words, and that everything worth saying in criticism of verse and prose can be related to judgements concerning particular arrangements of words on the page.
> (Leavis, 1948a, p. 120)

Leavis largely discounted the importance of anything which lay outside the text when looking at a particular poem, play or novel (Leavis, 1953). '[E]verything done by the artist and experienced by the reader is done and experienced here, here and here at an advancing point in a sequence of words...' (Leavis, 1948a, p. 121). But that close textual observation is done in the service of an attempt at an appreciation of value (Leavis, 1945, p. 55; Leavis, 1948a, p. 35). Literature, for Leavis, was a vehicle for considering values which lay at the heart of the individual and society; a vehicle which gave the reader access to observations and arguments not to be found in other sources.

> ...the sociologist can't learn what D.H. Lawrence has to teach about the problems of modern civilized man without being a more intelligent critic than any professional literary guide he is likely to find. Nor, without being an original critic, adverted and sensitized by experience and the habit of

> critical analysis, can the social psychologist learn what Conrad has to teach about the social nature of the individual's 'reality'.
> (Leavis, 1962b, pp. 193-194)

Whilst passionately concerned with culture Leavis was also intensely individualistic. Praising an essay by Eliot about Blake, Leavis writes that Eliot

> stresses in Blake that rare capacity to recognize and seize in his art the personal thisness of his experience which is the mark of creative genius - that thisness in which significance inheres.
> (Leavis, 1982, p. 3)

The text for Leavis is vital but it is vital for the reader's realization of themselves and the culture they are living in. That realization is to be achieved by a personal confrontation with literature. Thus he writes '[o]ne judges a poem by Marvell...out of one's personal living' (Leavis, 1953, p. 176). However, once again mere subjectivity in judgement is rejected. '[O]ur judgements ought to come from an impersonal centre in us...' (Leavis, 1948b, p. 100). Judgement, moreover, is not only to be sustained by repeated reference to the objective text; it is always a judgement addressed to others, to which, if they have an appropriate sensibility, they should respond.

> A judgement is a real judgement, or it is nothing. It must, that is, be a sincere personal judgement; but it aspires to be more than personal. Essentially it has the form: 'This is so, is it not?'
> (Leavis, 1951, p. 227)

Sensibility is to be trained by a consideration of the sensibilities of the great novelists, poets and dramatists mirrored in their work. But more than this a liberal education, a training of both intellect and sensibility, is to be achieved by a reading of those who can combine

> the power of giving concrete definition to (that is, of seizing and evoking in words and rhythms) feelings and apprehensions - the focal core with the elusive aura - that have seemed to him [the writer] peculiarly significant elements in his most private experience,
> (Leavis, 1969, p. 115)

with 'the power of searching and sustained thought' (Leavis, 1969, p. 115). In reading these works the student will be led to reflect on fundamental questions of value and choice for '[t]he problems of a poet that are worth any intensity of study are the problems of a man - one open to being profoundly disturbed by experience, and capable of a troubled soul...' (Leavis, 1982, p. 7).

Liberal Education and Legal Education

How, if we are to follow Leavis, is a legal education to be a liberal education? Legal education, like the study of literature, remains primarily an education based upon texts. New forms of scholarship have supplemented and in some cases supplanted pure doctrinal analysis but, nevertheless, the life of the law for the large part remains a life of books. For a Leavisite liberal education the question is, how do we approach those books? More precisely the question is, what would we wish our students to get out of those books?

Cramton has argued that

> If legal education is to be a form of graduate liberal education, if lawyering is to be more than advocacy, both teaching and practice need to be infused with a delight in conversation on important questions carried on with both hopefulness and humility.
> (Cramton, 1986, p. 8)

It is this which gives the key to the beginnings of a Leavisite, liberal, legal education. For each student, whether they are a law student or any other kind of student, the most important question is how they should relate to other individuals, to communities, to society and to the state. In his inaugural lecture, Bankowski states '[m]y endeavours have always been to try to see how one can lead a good life; to be able to encounter people and deal with them honestly' (Bankowski, 1996, p. 26). If a student's education does not contribute to them answering this question it is not a liberal education. Such an education is intended to make students better citizens, or perhaps more properly better persons, not better lawyers (Brownsword, 1992, p. 48). How this is to be done in a Leavisite manner can be shown by reference to standard legal material.

A typical legal text is Lord Atkin's statement about a person's liability for negligence in Donoghue v Stevenson.

> The liability for negligence, whether you style it such or treat it as in other systems as a species of 'culpa', is no doubt based upon a general public sentiment of moral wrongdoing for which the offender must pay. But acts or omissions which any moral code would censure cannot in the practical world be treated so as to give a right to every person injured by them to demand relief. In this way rules of law arise which limit the range of complaints and the extent of their remedy. The rule that you are to love your neighbour becomes in law: You must not injure your neighbour, and the lawyers' question: Who is my neighbour? receives a restricted reply. You must take reasonable care to avoid acts or omissions which you can reasonably foresee would be likely to injure your neighbour. Who then, in law, is my neighbour? The answer seems to be persons who are so closely and directly affected by my act that I ought reasonably to have them in contemplation as being so affected when I am directing my mind to the acts or omissions which are called in question.
> (Donoghue v Stevenson [1932] AC 562 at p. 580)

Generations of law students have studied this passage, analysed it and no doubt, in some cases, memorised it. Textbooks on tort usually cite some or all of it and analysis in the textbook will repeatedly return to the passage. But what are students expected to take from this text? Jones' *Textbook on Torts*, now in its fifth edition in ten years, provides an illustrative answer. Having quoted the passage above Jones goes on to observe

> The test [for a person's duty of care], then, is reasonable foresight of harm to persons whom it is foreseeable are likely to be harmed by my carelessness. As a principle of liability this statement is too wide, because it is not true, even today, that in all circumstances the infliction of foreseeable damage is actionable in negligence. The whole point of the 'duty problem' is to determine when foreseeable damage is actionable.
> (Jones, 1996, p. 27)

There then follows a lengthy analysis of the effect of subsequent judgements on what we can glean, by way of legal rule and legal principle, from Lord Atkin's initial starting point. Much of this fits squarely within what Leavis would have understood to be a liberal education. Students are referred to precise passages in judgements and Jones attempts to discern how principles either underlie, or can be drawn out of, the historical development of cases through a relatively close reading of the language of the judgements. Implicit in the analysis is a presumption that the student will attempt a personal understanding based upon their own close attention to what judges have written in their judgements. In this little could be closer to Leavis' approach to literature than the doctrinal lawyer's approach to judgements and statutes. But it is in what is sought in the close analysis of the text that the doctrinal lawyer differs from Leavis and, in so doing, falls far short of offering a liberal education. Jones' concern is with what the legal rule is. His is essentially a factual question; albeit a factual question of a particularly erudite and complex form. Leavis looked for an appreciation of sensibility and value in the text. The doctrinal lawyer is typically concerned with positivist questions about legal rules which are understood as being separated from issues of value. In this the doctrinal lawyer differs not only from Leavis but also from the originator of this particular text, Lord Atkin himself.

Lord Atkin understood law to offer the student precisely the tuition in value that Leavis sought. In a lecture on the educational value of law Lord Atkin said

> I myself am of the strongest opinion that an educational subject derives an enormous claim to be considered if, in addition to acting as a mental gymnastic, it at the same time has a bearing upon character and discipline and training. And I think it is impossible to forget that as far as the law is concerned, it is perpetually laying before the student standards of conduct which are standards of conduct which it is desirable to have maintained in the social state.
> (Atkin, 1932, p. 30)

Lord Atkin's own words suggest immediate Leavisite reflections on the nature of a modern understanding about the relationship between individual and individual and individual and society.

A Leavisite consideration of Lord Atkin's text might take the following form. The powerful trope in Lord Atkin's judgement in Donoghue v Stevenson is Christianity; more specifically, the parable of the good Samaritan and the Christian answer to the question, for whom am I responsible? It is in considering this standard of conduct offered in the text that the doctrinal lawyer's approach can be supplemented and a liberal education begun. For most legal scholars familiarity with the passage, and the doctrinal lawyer's insistence on searching for a legal rule, has dimmed the sense of moral shock that should attend Lord Atkin's use of that trope. In drawing attention to the parable of the Good Samaritan Lord Atkin expects assent to its message. The reference is there not just for aesthetic or stylistic reasons. It is intended to add powerful, persuasive rhetorical force to his argument. If one agrees with Lord Atkin's judgement one is, impliedly, siding with Christianity; and this in an era when being a good Christian was regarded as being more unreservedly a desirable thing than is the case in contemporary society. Yet the notion of legal liability that Lord Atkin describes is far removed from the values incorporated in the parable. On close observation the legal sensibility that Lord Atkin portrays is one which is both crude and vulgar. As Lord Diplock later said in a much quoted passage in Dorset Yacht Co v Home Office, and as Windeyer J noted in another much cited passage in Hargrave v Goldman, the priest and the Levite in the parable of the Good Samaritan would incur no legal liability for their neglect under the principles of negligence laid down in Donoghue v Stevenson.[3] Reference in Lord Atkin's judgement to a grand, heroic ideal leads to a limited legal liability that is morally squalid and tawdry (albeit a liability slightly less squalid and slightly less tawdry than that which went before Lord Atkin's judgement). If one accepts the message of the Good Samaritan how can one live one's life according to the principles of liability annunciated by Lord Atkin? Beginning from a high point of Christian rhetoric, which calls upon one to aid not merely one's neighbour but one's enemy, Lord Atkin, a convinced and dedicated member of the Church of Wales (Lewis, 1987, p. 20), confines a legal duty of care to a relatively circumscribed and narrow section of an individual's life. The contradiction in this is redoubled by the fact that Christ originally used the parable as an answer to a lawyer's question, 'what shall I do to inherit eternal life?' (Luke X: 25).

Lord Templeman, commenting on developments in the law of negligence after the House of Lord's decision in Anns v Merton London Borough Council, said

> a fashionable plaintiff [now] alleges negligence. The pleadings assume that we are all neighbours now, Pharisees and Samaritans alike, that foreseeability is a reflection of hindsight and that for every mischance in an accident-prone world someone solvent must be liable in damages.
> (CBS Songs Ltd v Amstrad Consumer Electronics plc [1988] 2 All ER 484 at p. 497)

Yet such a development, surprising and unwelcome as it is to Lord Templeman, is closer to the principles of the Good Samaritan than Donoghue v Stevenson and is closer to the original understanding of the Christian message. John Donne's well-known words

> Any Man's *death* diminishes *me* because I am involved in *Mankinde*; And therefore never send to know for whom the *bell* tolls; It tolls for *thee*. (Donne, 1987, p. 124)

are no more than a crisper restatement of Christ's original message and that message is restated not only in Christ's telling of the Good Samaritan parable but also in Paul's understanding of the early Church's own unity.

> For as the body is one, and hath many members, and all the members of that one body, being many, are one body: so also *is* Christ.
> For by one spirit are well baptized into one body, whether *we be* Jews or Gentiles, whether *we be* bond or free; and have all made to drink into one spirit.
> For the body is not one member, but many.
> If the foot shall say, because I am not the hand, I am not the body; is it therefore not of the body?
> And if the ear shall say, because I am not the eye, I am not of the body; is it therefore not of the body?
> If the whole body *were* an eye, where *were* hearing? If the whole *were* hearing, where *were* the smelling?
> But now hath God set the members every one of them in the body, as it hath pleased him.
> And if they were all one member, where *were* the body?
> But now *are they* many members, yet but one body.
> And the eye cannot say unto the hand, I have no need of thee: nor again the hand to the feet, I have no need of you.
> Nay, much more those members of the body, which seem more feeble, are necessary:
> And those *members* of the body, which we think less honourable, upon these we bestow more abundant honour; and our uncomely *parts* have more abundant comeliness.
> For our comely *parts* have no need: but God hath tempered the body together, having given more abundant honour to that *part which lacked:*
> *That there should be no schism in the body; but* that the members should have the same care one for another.
> And whether one member suffer, all the members suffer with it;

or one member be honoured, all the members rejoice with it.
For ye are the body of Christ, and members in particular.
(1 Corinthians 12: 12-27)

Both ways of reciting the Christian message celebrate a morality of responsibility and unity that runs beyond an individual's connection with family, community, common religious creed, society or even state. There is a baseness in Lord Atkin's argument and in the happy acceptance of his argument by lawyers. Lord Atkin's judgement is not, as he writes in his judgement, a 'restricted' response to the Christian message; it is a direct but unacknowledged dissent from that message. To suggest, as Lord Atkin does, that 'acts or omissions which *any* moral code would censure cannot in a practical world be treated so as to give a right to every person injured by them to demand relief' raises the question, what kind of meaning do these moral codes have in they have so little life in the world at large?[4] It is understandable that acts or omissions which some moral codes condemn will not lead to legal liability in a pluralistic and morally hesitant world; a swift movement from acts or omissions condemned by all moral codes to limited legal liability is an entirely different matter. It is in considering this gulf between the moral image prayed in aid Donoghue v Stevenson and the legal principle which results and in considering what this might say about law, lawyers and modern society that a liberal education begins.

Four points in this illustrative example of the possibility of a Leavisite liberal legal education need emphasis. First, the concern in the reading of Lord Atkin's judgement is a concern with value and not, more narrowly, a concern about morality or politics. It is, in Leavis' language, a concern with sensibility. It cannot be subsumed simply into a debate about political or ethical codes. It remains personal and individual. It remains a concern with a student's subjective response which must imply a concern with how their reading of Lord Atkin's judgement will affect the way in which they live their lives. Lord Atkin is not attempting to enunciate a new moral code. Analysing such codes in their pure theoretical form is helpful in understanding our connection with the world. But considering the way in which people like Lord Atkin work out their own moral responses, albeit unsystematically, is also useful. This is so in the case of literature (Welleck and Warren, 1963, p. 115). It can be so in the case of legal judgements. Secondly, the above is exactly a reading of Lord Atkin's judgement. It pays precise attention to language and the nuances of words. It is solidly grounded in attention to the text of the judgement. It attempts to offer both the precision and the sensitivity of reading and response that Leavis sought. Thirdly, what is of interest is the dissonance between the Christian values to which Lord Atkin aspired and the legal reality which he was willing to accept and the way in which he was willing to use language to persuade his readers to accept that dissonance. This tripartite relationship remains of interest even if one does not accept the validity of Christian values. It is how values, 'the practical world' and language collides that is important. Finally, a legal education becomes liberal by having this kind of analysis added to that which went before. A legal education still needs at times to be technical; it still needs to be an education in, or an education about, law. (A quite separate question is whether or not doctrinal analysis can ever produce a worthwhile analysis of the content of legal rules.)

Liberal Education, Imperialism, Patriarchy and Hierarchy

As was noted earlier Leavis saw liberal education not just in terms of what it did for the student but also in terms of its task in creating or preserving the culture that the student was inculcated into (Wyatt, 1990, p. 88, Mulhern, 1981, p. 117). Liberal education was both there to preserve 'the humane centre' and there to tell the student what 'the humane centre' was (Leavis, 1948a, p. 28). The notion of 'the humane centre' was of particular importance to Leavis' philosophy of education. Leavis sought a critical response from his students. However, a critical response can become, all too easily, merely a subjective response. A response which is solely subjective, which is validated entirely by the fact that it is a genuine personal response, allows of no conversation. This is what the person says and there is no more to be said about it than that. Such subjectivity is, intellectually, not necessarily inappropriate. Steiner, writing about the difficulties of translating poetry into another language, has argued that such difficulties 'implicates even rudimentary acts of linguistic exchange' (Steiner, 1970, p. 22). In seeking the precision of meaning that we find in poetry, and in seeking to translate that precision from one language to another, we learn that finding equivalence between even one word in one language and one word in another may be impossible. But, if this is so, can there be equivalence between one person's understanding of one word in any language and another person's understanding of that self-same word? And if that equivalence in understanding cannot be found how is conversation possible? How far can we communicate with anyone other than ourselves? It may be true to say that 'man is...unhappily trapped in a language game of which he knows nothing' (Welleck, 1982, p. 6). We may overvalue the advantages and indeed the possibility of conversation. The Chinese novelist Xianling may be correct in concluding '[i]n the end, I can only tell myself what I say' (Xianling, 1991, p. 135). Subjective response may be all there is or, at least, we may not be able to fully communicate, and thus fully debate, our response. However, academic discourse in universities has always presumed, through the conventions of lectures, tutorials and seminars, the possibility of conversation and community (Davies, 1996, p. 27; Feldman, 1989, p. 516), even if that conversation leads us to the conclusion that we have either nothing to say to each other or no way in which to say it. Thus it is not surprising that Leavis sought from students a critical judgement which took the form of saying 'this is so, is it not?' (Leavis, 1951, p. 227). In part he could achieve this by demanding that the critical response played close attention to the words of the text. 'The humane centre' was another way of providing a cultural focus that ensured critical responses were capable of engaging with each other. Critical judgements from individuals had to engage with the stipulated humane centre if in Leavis' view they were to be valid.

Whilst the purpose of 'the humane centre' can easily be understood it does create problems for the idea of a liberal education. The idea of a humane centre, a culture which liberal education tries to protect, can be taken to imply a static body of texts which constitute that culture or centre which must be preserved and taught. Alldridge has already written about the possible problems generated by applying this type of Leavisite view of liberal education to legal education.

> The view of a highly traditionalist school of English teaching, associated with F.R. Leavis, is that there is a canon of great literature exposure to which in some way makes the students better people (perhaps because the canon embodies and promulgates great values?), and that this is why students should study and be examined upon D.H. Lawrence, but not J.R.R. Tolkein or Raymond Chandler, although similar mind-honing exercises in exposition and interpretation could be set...I suggest that there is no text without having been exposed to which a student could definitely be said not to have studied

> criminal law...
> (Alldridge, 1990, p. 41)

If a culture, legal or otherwise, is defined and limited by a small number of set texts which must be studied the range of responses from readers is reduced. Reading stands in danger of becoming ritual as students are asked to consider books already 'known' to be 'great'. Personal judgements by neophyte readers are difficult to make and come only hesitantly. New students look at the words of the texts but see the only the patina of critical judgement that has already glossed the works. Equally, if study is only of 'great works', then swathes of work which deal with small but important issues not debated in the central texts are lost from sight. However, it is not clear that this limited idea of what constitutes a culture does in fact represent Leavis' view. In *The Great Tradition* Leavis identified the great English novelists as being Austen, Eliot, James and Conrad and then added '[t]he view, I suppose, will be confidently attributed to me that, except Jane Austen, George Eliot, James, and Conrad, there are no novelists in English worth reading' (Leavis, 1962a, p. 9). In fact he wrote widely about English novelists and poets who were outside his great tradition. Not everything, in Leavis' estimation, was worth reading but far from everything outside the great tradition was cast aside. Only Leavis' reputation, not his writing, would give cause for centring legal education on a select and immutable body of judgements known to constitute the centre of legal culture.

Even if 'the humane centre' is not simply and solely 'the great tradition' the notion still creates problems for a practice of liberal legal education. Leavis both seeks to instil in students a particular culture and sees an understanding of that culture as being something which only a minority can aspire to (Leavis, 1948, p. 16 and p. 17, Leavis, 1982, pp. 160-161). What that culture was is a matter of some debate. King argues that Leavis reflects and encourages a particular moment in English cultural history.

> Along with the shift in cultural values came a redefinition of the tradition of English literature. The attention given to the literary criticism of F.R. Leavis, with its emphasis on moral seriousness, the realistic portrayal of life, English lower-middle-class non-conformity, and the notion of a provincial England - in contrast to an international, metropolitan or cosmopolitan - cultural tradition was taken up by many young writers, critics and students as standing for the essential England in contrast to the superficial elite values of the

> wealthy, the expensive public schools and the London literary establishment. Similarly the 'cosmopolitan' writings of Yeats, Eliot and other 'modernists' were increasingly seen as foreign, non-British, French or American influenced, the opposite of those who understood what English life and literature are really about. The displacement of Henry James and TS Eliot as English writers was followed by the creation of an 'authentic' English tradition based on such writers as Arnold Bennett, H.G. Wells, William Empson, Robert Graves and Thomas Hardy. The novels of John Wain and the poetry of Philip Larkin and Donald Davie concerned provincial life in the Midlands and the north of England.
> (King, 1980, pp. 216-217)

However, whilst King sees Leavis as leading to a muddy, middle-class, Midlands value system Mulhern sees the matter somewhat differently, perceiving older elite values reasserting themselves in Leavis.

> In attacking industrialism and commerce, the historic destruction of an older order and the despoilation of its natural setting, the now pervasive spirit of 'mechanism' and calculative rationality, the progressive atrophy of organic wholeness in individuals and in society, the *Scrutiny* group continued a line that included Cobbet and Shelley, Carlyle and Lawrence. In propounding the idea of a disinterested clerisy centred on literature and capable of guiding the moral life of an aberrant society, they resumed the argument initiated by Coleridge and brought to classical maturity by Arnold.
> (Mulhern, 1981, p. 306)

Whichever view is taken, it is clear that Leavis' view of culture is exclusionary; there are things that are in the English tradition and things that are not. It is the things that are in the tradition that constitute the culture that is to be taught. Moreover, those things that are in the culture are thought by Leavis to be inherently valuable and, in some way, inherently good. Study of such things was, for Leavis, redemptive (Evans, 1993, p. 131). Leavis intends to teach an English way of doing things and intends to teach an English way that does not include the way of all those who are in fact English (Eagleton, 1983, p. 37, MacKillop, 1995, p. 241). Applying Leavis' ideas to English legal education would imply the identification of, and the teaching of the value of, an English legal culture.

For a cosmopolitan university law school aspiring, because it is an intellectual meritocracy (Young, 1961, p. 60), to draw staff and students from a wide range of ethnic, national and cultural backgrounds, Leavis' attitude is deeply problematic. Whilst in most cases a legal education will be a legal education in one national legal culture, in English law or French law or whatever, it would be the antithesis of a liberal education for that to imply that the education should involve inculcating into the student values pre-set in that legal culture. Part of the essence of liberalism is that it avoids imposing value choices on individuals except that it forbids value choices that individuals would like to make which would negate the ability of other individuals to make value choices (Rawls, 1988, p. 262). Liberalism insists on an arena of tolerance for the choices of others but goes no further. Similarly, liberal education is predicated on the student's consideration of values but does not involve an insistence on the priority of any particular values except the value of considering values and allowing others the freedom to do the same. This is not to say that particular values cannot be espoused in a particular educational programme and even put forward has having foundational truth. But for there to be a liberal education it must be for each student to decide whether or not things put forward do indeed have foundational truth. In a liberal education there is for the student an academic freedom to decide not what they study but what they believe about what they study. (A freedom which is bounded by the conventions of rational response capable of explanation and defence in conversation noted above.) It is exactly of the essence of a liberal, legal education that a student, in considering the values of a legal culture, might reject them in whole or part. A central objection to Carrington's rejection of the teaching of 'legal nihilism' in the law school was the imposition of values implied by his approach (Carrington, 1984). A similar objection could be made to the stance of Kronman (Kronman, 1981).

It follows from the above that a liberal legal education should always involve giving the student those materials that are necessary to help them reflect upon the values of the culture. Studying Lord Atkin's judgement in Donoghue v Stevenson immediately involves students in looking both at the Christian values that Lord Atkin refers to as well as to the more prosaic or utilitarian values that are implicit in his view of what law should do. These values have to be drawn out and compared. This comparative aspect is important. It is assessing what values are present in a particular example of an individual legal culture and in looking at alternative values available that the student's education proceeds. And it is in the fact that a programme explicitly attends to this process of comparison by the student and makes it central to the education that the education becomes truly liberal.

Leavis' insistence on the minority nature of university education raises a second difficulty for the practice of a Leavisite liberal legal education. Leavis wrote that

> ...it is disastrous to let a country's educational arrangements be determined, or even affected, by the assumption that a high intellectual standard can be attained by more than a small minority.
> (Leavis, 1982, pp. 160-161)

Leavis' view is that, in Eagleton's words, 'the overwhelming social majority...[are] morally callous, humanly banal and imaginatively bankrupt' (Eagleton, 1983, p. 34). This dictum can be interpreted in one of two ways. The first is that this is an historical and empirical observation that no culture has ever managed to educate to a high level, in the Leavisite sense of education, anything other than a very small percentage of its population; that therefore to date most people have been callous, banal and bankrupt. Taken in this sense there is at least an arguable case for Leavis' position which is compatible with the pursuit of liberal education. Human history is not replete with examples of societies which have been ethical successes. When people's life have not been nasty, brutish and short they have usually been unconsidered in their manner and uncaring of others. In such a climate an educational strategy of seeking to 'build a public and foster a minority', of trying to encourage the very culture the education is trying to teach within those most immediately responsive to that culture, may offer the greatest chances of success (MacKillop, 1995, p. 208). This approach is not incompatible with the pursuit of a liberal education. It does not forbid the possibility of an education in a very different kind of future society which involves everybody and which has as its aim a humane life lived by all. It does not suggest that past failure dictates future failure or that history suggests caste divisions and Brahmic leadership within types of human nature.

However, following a second interpretation, Leavis' contention could be seen as meaning that most people will never, whatever their economic and social circumstances, be able to be educated to a high level; that they are, intrinsically, callous, banal and bankrupt. In this second sense, Leavis' argument about the minority nature of education strikes at the essence of liberalism and thus liberal education. It suggests a vision of a society where the position of Platonic Guardians is pre-ordained. Individual choices are circumscribed by their position in society. People simply are what they are and the majority are morally and intellectually inferior. Which interpretation Leavis would have put on his position is a matter of some doubt and may have changed as he grew older (Eagleton, 1983, p. 43). What is more important than Leavis' own view on this matter is the fact that his view about the minority nature of culture is severable from his view that education was education in sensibility and value. For a liberal legal education this severing is necessary. It is Leavis' views on the practice of reading that are important not his views on who can take part in that practice.

One final problem for a Leavisite liberal education lies in Leavis' rejection of the use of theory in helping to tutor student's responses to material studied. Welleck's comment on Leavis' book *Revaluation*, 'I could wish that you had stated your assumptions more explicitly and defended them systematically' (Welleck, 1937, p. 376), could properly be applied to all Leavis' writing.

The practice of Leavisite criticism in British university English departments has, in some cases, demonstrated the dangers of his abandonment of theory. It has shown that the close reading of texts, unmediated by any theoretical structure in analysing the response, can lead to a hierarchical educational setting where a lecturer's dictat that true sensibility will see merit in the particular text in question controls students by the assertion of power rather than the use of argument (Evans, 1993, p. 132). Without a theoretical background against which to place response students struggle to judge what it is that is true and that which is merely said to be true by those in authority. Notwithstanding Leavis' objection to theory in the practice of criticism in assessing literature a student's task, and indeed any reader's task, is to 'translate his experience of literature into intellectual terms, assimilate it to a coherent scheme which must be rational if it is to be knowledge' (Welleck and Warren, 1973, p. 15). In this sense the approach must be theoretical. At the same time the approach must be an approach to literature and, if a Leavisite approach is taken, an approach to issues of value in literature. As Belsey notes, Leavis' concern was with the possibility of a critical response being diminished by a concern with issues of theory. She is right to note that, despite his rejection of theory, Leavis' own work was infused with an unexplored theoretical background (Belsey, 1980, pp. 11-13). Nevertheless Leavis' highlighting of the importance of the student's response to a text is not unimportant. In a liberal education in literature the focus of the student's concern remains literature, remains Cramton's 'important questions', not technical questions of theory.

The question of the place of theory in education has a particular resonance in legal education. University legal education in the common-law world has commonly been aggressively atheoretical and anti-intellectual (Wilson, 1987, p. 819). The use of Leavis in constructing a liberal legal education might seem to give comfort to these tendencies. It is certainly true that Leavis, like any other writer, has to be used with care. Not everything that he held to be true is useful in constructing a liberal legal education. The complete rejection of theory is not merely unacceptable but impossible. The only choice is between explicit attention to theory and the unattended presence of theory. To be a liberal education a legal education needs to be more than a Leavisite liberal education and needs to include an education in theory. The reading of texts with close attention to the language in order to uncover and explore the underlying issues of value being pursued in the judgements needs to take place alongside other sustained theoretical study of the way in which law contributes to society and the way in which we come to assess questions of value. How individuals struggle to come to terms with question of values and the pure and often highly technical discussion of the language games of value systems are both important. But Leavis is right in arguing that education should not concentrate being an education in theory to the exclusion of everything else. Wilson has noted that when dealing with theoretical issues there is a

> noticeable tendency amongst some legal scholars to concentrate on what were originally presented as preliminaries to such an extent that the general effect has been centrifugal and what began as a preliminary study has ended up as study for its own sake with little direct relation to law.
> (Wilson, 1987, p. 825)

Wittgenstein, in discussing technical questions of philosophy, sought not to prevent people thinking about issues that could not be approached via philosophy nor to persuade them to think only about these technical issues but to teach them that philosophy would be of limited help in dealing with some issues (Monk, 1990, pp. 410-411). Attention to theory, for Wittgenstein, does not mean that theory becomes all. Similarly, even when he errs about the importance of theory, Leavis is helpful in reminding us that in legal education it is not, in the final analysis, theory that we are concerned with but with matters of relationship and connection.

Conclusion

The widespread acceptance of the value of liberal education amongst legal academics probably rests in part on a lack of understanding of what such an education entails. For many liberal education may be no more than an opposition; liberal education, for them, is not vocational education, not what professional lawyer's associations have a business in dictating, not what a previous generation of legal academics were engaged in. Vaunting a belief in the value of liberal education may serve the same political purpose that the creation of the textbook tradition did in the past. It enables the academy to separate itself from other bodies that would seek to control it (Sugarman, 1986). It gives it a separate source of power and legitimation. It is certainly true that some of those who espouse law as a liberal education then immediately give that education most illiberal characteristics. Thus, for example, the same ACLEC report that suggested the law degree should be a liberal education not tied to any particular vocation had already insisted that legal education necessarily involved students learning the importance of the rule of law (ACLEC, 1996, p. 24). Precluding law students, and presumably legal academics, from assenting to the whole host of philosophies that have either denied the desirability of, or the possibility of, the rule of law does not seem to be the most obvious way of pursuing a liberal education. Nevertheless, to see the espousal by university law schools of liberal education as being mere rhetoric is to misrepresent the strength of the feeling, if not the understanding, that this declaration represents. University law schools do have a sense of their own agenda. Where official reports do not reflect that agenda they are quietly ignored. Law schools both believe in, and know very little about, liberal education. As they come to know more so their curricula will be changed to accommodate that new knowledge.

Notes

1. Other contributions include *English Literature in Our Time and the University* (Leavis, 1969); *The Living Principle* (Leavis, 1975) and 'The Great Books and Liberal Education' and 'Believing in the University', both published in *The Critic as Anti-Philosopher* (Leavis, 1982).
2. Leavis begins The Great Tradition with the pronouncement '[t]he great English novelists are Jane Austen, George Eliot, Henry James and Joseph Conrad...' (Leavis, 1962a, p. 9). There is thus good reason for using her description of sensibility to explain Leavis' ideas.
3. Dorset Yacht Co v Home Office [1940] 1004 at p.1060, Hargrave v Goldman (1963) 110 CLR at p. 66.
4. Donoghue v Stevenson [1932] AC 562 at p. 580.

References

ACLEC (1996), *The First Report on Legal Education*, The Lord Chancellor's Department, London.

Alldridge, P. (1990), 'What's wrong with the traditional Criminal Law course?', *Legal Studies*, vol. 10, pp. 38-62.

Atkin, Lord (1932), 'Law as an Educational Subject', *Journal of the Society of Public Teachers of Law*, pp. 27-31.

Bankowski, Z. (1996), 'Law, Love and Computers', *The Edinburgh Law Review*, pp. 25-42.

Barnett, R. (1990), 'The Idea of Higher Education', Society for Research into Higher Education and the Open University Press, Buckingham.

Belsey, C. (1980), *Critical Practice*, Methuen, London.

Bousfield, A. (1996), 'The voice of liberal learning: is there still room for the "Idea of a University" in 1996?', in Brecher, B., Fleischmann, O. and Halliday, J. (eds), *The University in a Liberal State*, Avebury, Aldershot.

Bright, S. (1991), 'What, and How, Should We Be Teaching?', *The Law Teacher*, vol. 25, pp. 11-25.

Brownsword, R. (1992), 'Teaching Contract: A Liberal Agenda', in Birks, P. (ed), *Examining the Law Syllabus: The Core*, Oxford University Press, Oxford.

Carrington, P. (1984), 'Of Law and the River', *Journal of Legal Education*, vol. 34, pp. 222-228.

Cramton, R. (1986), 'Demystifying Legal Scholarship', *Georgetown Law Journal*, vol. 75, pp. 1-17.

Davies, M. (1996), 'University culture or intellectual culture?', in Brecher, B., Fleischmann,

O. and Halliday, J. (eds), *The University in a Liberal State*, Avebury, Aldershot.

Donne, J. (1987), 'Seventeenth Meditation', in Donne, J., *Selected Prose*, Penguin Books, Harmondsworth.

Doyle, B. (1989), *English and Englishness*, Routledge, London.

Eagleton, T. (1983), *Literary Theory: An Introduction*, Basil Blackwell, Oxford.

Evans, C. (1993), *English People*, Open University Press, Buckingham.

Feldman, D. (1989), 'The Nature of Legal Scholarship', *Modern Law Review*, vol. 52, pp. 498-517.

Housman, A. E. (1961), 'Introductory Essay', in Housman, A. E., *Selected Prose*, Cambridge University Press, London.

Jones, M. (1996), *Textbook on Torts*, Blackstone Press, London.

King, B. (1980), *The New English Literatures*, Macmillan, London.

Kronman, A. (1981), 'Legal Scholarship and Moral Education', *Yale Law Journal*, vol. 90, pp. 955-969.

Leavis, F.R. (1932), 'The Literary Imagination', *Scrutiny*, vol. I, pp. 20-32.

Leavis, F.R. (1934), 'Wordsworth', *Scrutiny*, vol. III, pp. 234-257.

Leavis, F.R. (1945), '"Thought" and "Emotional Quality": Notes in the Analysis of Poetry', *Scrutiny*, vol. XIII, pp. 53-71.

Leavis, F.R. (1948a), *Education and the University*, 2nd edition, Chatto and Windus, London.

Leavis, F.R. (1948b), 'Henry James and the Function of Criticism', *Scrutiny*, vol. XV, pp. 98-104.

Leavis, F.R. (1951), 'Mr Pryce-Jones, the British Council and British Culture', *Scrutiny*, vol. XVIII, pp. 224-228.

Leavis, F.R. (1953), 'The Responsible Critic', *Scrutiny*, vol. XIX, pp. 162-183.

Leavis, F.R. (1962a), *The Great Tradition*, Penguin Books, Harmondsworth.

Leavis, F.R. (1962b), *The Common Pursuit*, Penguin Books, Harmondsworth.

Leavis, F.R. (1969), *English Literature in Our Time and the University*, Chatto and Windus, London.

Leavis, F.R. (1975), *The Living Principle*, Chatto and Windus, London.

Leavis, F.R. (1982), *The Critic as Anti-Philosopher*, Chatto and Windus, London.

Lewis, G. (1987), *Lord Atkin*, Butterworths, London.

MacFarlane, J., Jeeves, M. and Boon, A. (1987), 'Education for Life or for Work?', 137, *New Law Journal*, pp. 835-836.

MacKillop, I. (1995), *A Life in Criticism*, Allen Lane, The Penguin Press, London.

Martin, P. (1985), '"Of Law and the River", and of Nihilism and Academic Freedom', 35, *Journal of Legal Education*, pp.1-26.

Monly, R. (1990), *Ludwig Wittgenstein: The Duty of Genius*, Jonathan Cape, London.

Mulhern, F. (1981), *The Moment of 'Scrutiny'*, Verso, London.

Rawls, J. (1988), 'The Priority of Right and Ideas of the Good', *Philosophy and Public Affairs*, Vol. 17, pp. 251-276.

Steiner, G. (1970), *Poem into Poem*, Penguin Books, Harmondsworth.

Sugarman, D. (1986), 'Legal Theory, the Common Law Mind and the Making of the Textbook Tradition', in Twining, W. (ed), *Legal Theory and Common Law*, Basil Blackwell, Oxford.

Thomson, A. (1990), 'Critical Legal Education', in Fitzgerald, P. and Hunt, A. (eds), *Critical Legal Studies*, Basil Blackwell, Oxford.

Welleck, R. (1937), 'Literary Criticism and Philosophy', *Scrutiny*, vol. V, pp. 375-383.

Welleck, R. (1983), *The Attack on Literature and Other Essays*, The Harvester Press, Brighton.

Welleck, R. and Warren, A. (1973), *Theory of Literature*, Penguin Books, Harmondsworth.

Wilson, G. (1987), 'English Legal Scholarship', *Modern Law Review*, vol. 50, pp. 818-854.

Wyatt, J. (1990), *Commitment to Higher Education*, Society for Research into Higher Education and the Open University Press, Buckingham.

Xianling, Z. (1991), *Getting Used to Dying*, William Collins, London.

Young, M. (1961), *The Rise of the Meritocracy*, Penguin Books, Harmondsworth.

2 Law Schools for Lawyers, Citizens, and People

ROGER BROWNSWORD

Introduction

Some years ago, at a series of seminars exploring the teaching of the core subjects of the law syllabus, Peter Birks (1992) suggested that, whilst there are many different conceptions of law school education, it is surely common ground that we all aspire to producing really good lawyers. Unobjectionable though this may sound, my instinct was that this articulation of our aspirations did not quite reflect either descriptively or, more importantly, prescriptivelymy sense of the law school mission. In an attempt to correct the emphasis of Birks's remark, I suggested that the law school mission should be conceived of in terms of producing really good citizens (Brownsword, 1992: 48). To some extent, I am ready to concede that the dichotomy between really good lawyers and really good citizens is strained (see Collins, 1992: 41). Nevertheless, if we have to choose between expressing the mission of a law school in terms of good lawyers or good citizens, I continue to prefer the latter.

In the present paper, I want to revisit this idea of law schools for citizens (which I will also refer to as the 'liberal project') from two angles. First, I want to relate this idea to the new vision of legal education (and the accompanying conception of law schools) that we find in ACLEC's *First Report on Legal Education and Training* (ACLEC,1996). Secondly, I want to assess the viability of the liberal project in the light of the expansion of the law school population (which is one expression of the idea of law schools for people) and the narrowing of government funding for research (in the wake of RAE96).

This revisitation generates an assessment that has both a positive and a negative thrust. The positive thrust is that ACLEC has presented theacademic community with a quite remarkably enlightened view of the function of law schools (which, as ACLEC sees it, should be released from their traditional role as initial stage vocational trainers for the legal profession, to become free-standing liberal academies where all manner of people can engage in independent and critical thinking). However, the negative thrust is that the academic community not only lacks the resources to carry through ACLEC's thinking, but also it is divided in such a way that this opportunity to open a new and exciting chapter in legal education is unlikely to be grasped. On the one hand, ACLEC's proposals must reckon with those academic lawyers (quite possibly aided and abetted by various sectors of the legal profession) who remain wedded to the idea that the principal function of law schools is to ensure that students clock up plenty of doctrinal miles. On the other hand, significant parts of the academic body that might otherwise have been expected to back ACLEC's vision are likely to find themselves increasingly disabled from doing so and, against a background of severe pressure on resources, the key disabling factors, I suggest, are the separation of funding for teaching and funding for research, together with the devaluation of research activity that does not qualify for entry in research assessment exercises (the upshot of which is that the academic community is in the process of being divided into 'teachers without research obligations or funding for research' and 'researcher/publishers with limited teaching obligations').

What, then, is the shape of the future? The worrying prognosis that emerges from these reflections is that ACLEC's vision even if it got the green light from the profession is unlikely to be realised. This is because, in teaching-led law schools, academics will not be resourced in a way that enables them to respond to the liberal mission while, in research-led law schools, research-active academics who could respond to this mission will have other priorities (sometimes personal, sometimes institutional), particularly the production of published work that will attract income in the next round of research selectivity.

The Law School Mission: Law for Citizens

The idea that law schools should aim to produce really good citizens presupposes a law school with a number of distinctive features. The model that I have in mind is that of the 'liberal' law school (cf Brownsword, 1996a). The essence of this model can be captured in the following four features:

(i) In the most general terms the mission of the law school (in both its teaching and its research activities) is to work towards an understanding of the phenomenon, or practice, of law.

(ii) The project of understanding law implies (a) a pervasive inquiring approach (a pervasive concern with questions of evaluation, explanation, and so on) and (b) a willingness to follow lines of inquiry into disciplines that contribute to our appreciation of law (generally, see Adams and Brownsword, 1992).

(iii) Law school discourse should be what Roberto Unger (1996: 8) describes as 'a sustained conversation about our [socio-economic and political] arrangements'. As a result of participating in this conversation, at the point of graduation, students should have the capacity to engage in rational debate about issues arising in and around the practice of law, including the capacity to form their own independent judgments on such matters.

(iv) Although there is no standard way in which the liberal model should be implemented (in principle, it could be instantiated in many different forms), it is a *sine qua non* of this project that law school academics, whether in their role as teachers or as researchers, should act as exemplars of the inquiring approach.

The concession that there is no standard way in which the liberal model must be implemented, does not entail that we cannot check that a law school is on the right track. But, how might we confirm that the paper commitments expressed in a liberal mission are actually being put into practice? First, we might check whether students engage with the material actively (whether the material be doctrinal or theoretical), or whether the student experience is one of merely passive learning. As Dawn Oliver (1996: 143) has put it:

> Teachers should be concerned to ensure that the learning experience of students is active not passive, recognising that understanding is more important than rote learning of material, that depth is more important than breadth, that superficial learning is not desirable, and that students should acquire research skills and skills of analysis, synthesis, and so on.

Secondly, we might check whether law school discourse is limited to doctrinal exposition and rehearsal. For, whatever else the liberal mission implies, it is clear that the legal imagination has seized up if supposedly 'critical analysis' never gets beyond first base familiarity with doctrine.

Nevertheless, the concession that the liberal model can be instantiated in more than one way raises some difficult questions about the extent to which structure and progression is implicit in this model. In the case of the black-letter model, we might say that there is structure in the sense that students are taken through doctrinal foundations before being offered non-foundational options. And, we might argue that that this is progressive in the sense that students build incrementally on their core doctrinal knowledge. Against this, though, the sceptical view is that, once the ground rules of doctrinal manipulation have been mastered, although the student's doctrinal knowledge base is broadened, there is little progression essentially the same black-letter exercise being repeated time after time but with varying doctrinal content. On this view, although there is a steep learning curve in the first year of law study, the black-letter degree is not truly progressive from there on. If a law school takes the liberal model seriously, one of the first tasks is to address questions of structure and progression. Such an academy must ask whether, within this model, there are analogues of the foundational (or core) subjects that we find in the black-letter curriculum; and, if so, what these subjects are. It must ask whether there should be a collective understanding about the sequence in which different kinds of inquiries are opened up, or whether it is to be left to individuals to take an inquiring approach to their subjects in whatever way they see fit. It must ask whether students are expected to have attained certain levels of competence at various staging points through the degree programme, or whether it is enough that, at graduation, students have the capacity for critical citizenship. These are not easy questions and there is no reason to think that each law school would answer the questions in the same way.

Before I leave the abstract idea of the liberal project, is it possible to be any clearer about the aspiration to produce really good citizens? In very general terms, the liberal legal education seeks to prepare the graduate for intelligent participation in the politico-legal life of the community. As Tony Bradney (1996: 153) (drawing on Mill) puts it, the aim is not so much to produce skilful lawyers as 'capable and cultivated human beings'human beings who, in Hugh Collins' (1992: 41) words 'have a critical and reflective attitude towards the institutions of society'. In a sense, the mode of active learning inculcated as a student is continued after graduation in the broader community, enabling law graduates to participate in the debates about community purpose, policy and principle that form the agenda of their time whether (to take some topical issues) these are debates about the incorporation of a bill of rights (and associated questions concerning the constitutional relationship between the Executive and the Judiciary), about a woman's right to have access to her deceased spouse's frozen sperm (coincidentally, the Court of Appeal handed down its decision on Diane Blood's application on the same day that this paper was presented), or about the implications of a risk-averse society developing a culture of litigation, and so on. None of this presupposes that liberally-educated law graduates will be 'good citizens' in the sense that they will take a particular party line in politico-legal debates, or even that they will be conscientious in supporting the ordinary democratic processes associated with representative government. However, it does presuppose that 'the law' will hold no mystery for these graduates and that they will be capable of making a rational assessment of the arguments relating to debates arising in and around the practice of law.

ACLEC and the Liberal Mission

How well does ACLEC's vision of the law degree fit with the liberal mission that I have just outlined? The short answer is that the fit is very close. And, with due apologies to those who are entirely familiar with the ACLEC vision, let me briefly pick out the salient features of ACLEC's model.

Having reviewed the changing needs of legal practice (especially the need for the practitioners of the C21 to have generic skills and understanding, enabling them to be flexible yet capable of specialisation), ACLEC sets out five requirements for legal education and training. These requirements are: intellectual integrity and independence of mind; core knowledge; contextual knowledge; legal values; and professional skills (para 2.4). Of these five requirements, ACLEC sees the first as being definitive of *degree level* education; and the second, third, and fourth requirements as particularly the concern of *law* degree programmes. To these requirements, ACLEC subsequently (para 4.4) adds a range of transferable intellectual skills, before making its landmark recommendation (para. 4.6) that 'the degree course should stand as an independent liberal education in the discipline of law, not tied to any specific vocation'. We can see how closely ACLEC's vision of legal education corresponds to the liberal mission by considering each of the basic law degree requirements identified by ACLEC.

First, for ACLEC, the requirement of intellectual integrity and independence of mind is applicable to degree level education itself. In other words, degree level work generically presupposes critical and reflective processing of material. Indeed, ACLEC says that 'a liberal and humane education implies that students are engaged in active rather than passive learning' (para 2.2) and it repeats Dawn Oliver's (1994: 78) elaboration of the emphasis on understanding that comes with a liberal education (para. 4.4). Thus:

> A liberal education will have as an aim that students should not merely *know or know how to* but *understand* why things are as they are and how they could be different...

Suffice it to say that this is entirely in line with my liberal approach and that I share ACLEC's view of the essence of a degree, whether it be a straight law, mixed law, or non-law degree.

Secondly, according to ACLEC, core knowledge of legal principles and lawyers' analytical and conceptual skills is something that law degrees must offer. ACLEC, however, is commendably alert to the risk of licensing the professional bodies to prescribe too large a core, or to prescribe it in too detailed a manner (2.12). Moreover, not only does ACLEC weaken the remarks that it earlier made in its Consultation Paper (ACLEC, 1994) about a sufficiency of core knowledge (para. 4.5), it continues to put the emphasis on general outcomes rather than detailed inputs and it recommends that law schools should be left to decide which areas of law are to be studied (para. 4.19). Although we must always allow for some tension between the liberal mission and the interests of professional legal bodies, ACLEC takes a remarkably robust view in defence of the liberal mission.

Thirdly, we come to contextual knowledge, by which ACLEC means 'an appreciation of the law's social, economic, political, philosophical, moral and cultural contexts' (para. 2.4). Such perspectives, ACLEC thinks, can be given by law degrees, mixed degrees, or even non-law degrees. Despite ACLEC's heroic stand against the creeping core, we might sense a lingering assumption that the essence of a *law* degree is that it offers core doctrinal knowledge. If this is the assumption, then I want to oppose it by saying that the essence of a *law* degree is that it takes the practice of law (including legal doctrine) as its cognitive focus. This might be no more than a difference of emphasis but it gives the contextual content a place of equal importance to that of legal doctrine and, crucially, on the liberal view, context and doctrine both have their place in the curriculum because they are part of the practice that we are trying to understand. To the extent that this is no more than a difference of emphasis and, in a strong culture of inquiry, I see no problem with anchoring understanding to legal doctrine. However, in a culture where the dissemination of information dominates over inquiry, we must be careful that ACLEC's sound intentions are not misapplied either as an excuse to privilege black-letter exposition or as an invitation to take students in descriptive mode through an eclectic patchwork of doctrinal and theoretical materials (cf Farmer, 1995).

Finally, and importantly, we come to the emphasis that ACLEC gives to legal values. As we have seen, ACLEC includes an appreciation of the moral context within its specification of contextual awareness. However, it goes some way beyond this in emphasising the importance of legal values. According to ACLEC (para. 2.4):

> This means a commitment to the rule of law, to justice, fairness and high ethical standards, to acquiring and improving professional skills, to representing clients without fear or favour, to promoting equality of opportunity, and to ensuring that adequate legal services are provided to those who cannot afford to pay for them.

In its Illustrative Statement of Outcomes, this broad statement is expressed a little less expansively as 'including a commitment to the rule of law, to justice, fairness and high ethical standards.' (ACLEC, 1996, p.72). On the face of it, ACLEC's liberal vision is not simply one of active inquiry and the quest for understanding (liberalism in approach) but also one of a law programme inscribed with particular value commitments (Liberalism in political, moral and legal values, as it were). If we take our lead from the liberal approach, there are two levels at which such an inscription of Liberal values gives rise to concern.

At one level, let us suppose that ACLEC's intention is that a commitment to the rule of law, justice, and fairness and the like, should be written into the law school mission in no more than formal terms. This involves a commitment to the legitimacy of all facets of the practice of law but, recognising that the rule of law, justice, and fairness are contested concepts, the material particulars of the commitment are open to debatein the case of the rule of law, for example, the formal commitment leaves it open to debate the material details of procedural due process and, indeed, it remains open to debate whether due process carries with it any substantive constraints on legitimate governance. Although such a commitment is weak, it is nevertheless too strong for someone who wants to argue for an amoralist view (that is, for someone who wants to argue, not that x rather than y is legitimate, but that any kind of concern with questions of legitimacy is inappropriate). If the law school is to encourage critical inquiry, the coherence of amoralism and its implications are issues that simply cannot be excluded (cf Kronman, 1981).

At another level, let us suppose that ACLEC's intention is that its commitment to legal values should carry a particular substance, that particular conceptions of the rule of law, justice and fairness should be instilled in law students. If this were the case, our concern would deepen rapidly, for a mission of this kind would not only stifle debate and active learning, it would involve a fundamental challenge to the liberal idealwhich has no core commitments other than to free and open inquiry (and, to similar effect, see Bradney, elsewhere in this book).

Yet, if we detect a tension in ACLEC purporting to follow a liberal educational approach at the same time that it apparently advocates an unquestioning commitment to Liberal legal values, is there not equally something odd about espousing a liberal approach without also insisting that students should be educated in the virtues of Liberalism? In short, how far is it possible for practitioners of the liberal approach to avoid leading their students into Liberalism? For instance, can this be avoided where:

(i) they (i.e. liberal law teachers) maintain that understanding law presupposes an understanding of politics (and, indeed, vice versa, cf Lewis (1996): 131 et seq); or
(ii) they personally subscribe to the values of Liberalism; or
(iii) they see the whole purpose of the law school as preparing students for citizenship within a rule of law democracy; or
(iv) they consider that a liberal approach would be tolerated only within a Liberal Democracy, and thus they accept that a positive valuation of the liberal model entails a positive valuation of Liberal Democracy?

I see no problem with (i). To be sure, an understanding of politics involves a level of literacy such that engagement with the values of Liberalism is almost unavoidable. However, so long as the engagement is critical, so long as students form their own independent judgments, there is a clear separation between the liberal approach and a commitment to Liberalism. Much the same applies to (ii) although it must be conceded that a liberal approach might be more difficult to sustain where a teacher is also a writer whose published views on a particular matter (such as the virtues of Liberalism) are well-known to students. Greater difficulty might be thought to arise in relation to (iii) because, without a prevailing rule of law democracy, the law school preparation for citizenship would be pretty hollow although, no doubt, committed Liberals would hope that a liberal education would encourage students to see the virtues of a Liberal polity and to work towards that end. In principle, (iv) gives rise to no difficulty, being no more than a contingent argument in favour of Liberalisman argument to be assessed along with others and not at all the same as the *uncritical* inculcation of Liberalism. It is true that, in practice, some (even many) students are likely to accept the premise in this argument and, thus, accept the (Liberal) conclusion. However, the key point in relation to both (iii) and (iv) is that, whilst the liberal approach cannot (and must not) guarantee that students will graduate as committed Liberals, it cannot guarantee that they will not become convinced that a Liberal politico-legal system has the best credentials.

To draw these threads together, the essential ground rules of the liberal approach are that all claims are contestable, that all are invited to participate in the debates, that all voices are equally respected, and that the only force that prevails is that of the better argument (cf Habermas, 1970; Outhwaite, 1994: 40). For practical pedagogic purposes, some claims may have to be treated as provisionally correct; but any provisional beliefs must be reviewable. To insulate any set of beliefs against challenge obstructs the development of a constructively critical relationship with students (cf. Goodrich, 1996, esp. at 64) and it is incompatible with the liberal mission. If there is a contradiction in ACLEC's thinking, it is in assuming that a liberal approach can incorporate an unchallengeable Liberal political agenda; and, if there is a paradox in the liberal approach itself, it is that its proponents must accept that some graduates may leave the law school convinced that Liberalism (and perhaps a liberal law school mission) is a thoroughly bad idea.

The Liberal Law School Mission: Post RAE96

Although the precise funding implications of RAE96 are not yet known, we can be confident that they will serve only to sharpen the distinction between the three classes of law school (the research-led, the middle order with some funding for research, and the teaching-led with little or no funding for research: cf Griffith, 1995). To some extent, however, the funding details following RAE96 are of secondary importance to the changes in law school culture already brought about by research selectivity. The most important of these changes are: the hardening of the association between research and publication (without publication an academic lawyer is no longer regarded as research-active); and the dividing of teachers from (and against) researchers (i.e. the creation of two pools of academic lawyers, the 'mere teachers' and the 'researcher/publishers'). Never has the culture been better represented by slogans such as 'publish or perish', or 'those who can publish, those who cannot teach'. Predictably, such a culture creates all sorts of tensions (and hierarchies) within law schools but, most importantly for present purposes, *it militates against the fulfilment of the liberal mission.*

The liberal mission, as we have seen, requires a culture of inquiry, in which teachers act as exemplars of the inquiring mind. We can quibble about how we use the word 'research' indeed, we *should* quibble about this but what the liberal mission presupposes is that teachers are also researchers in the sense that they constantly quest after a better understanding of their subject (to similar effect, see Welch, 1995, and Oliver 1994 at 79 ('the aspect of research-based teaching which most enhances student learning...is to do with exposure to the enthusiaism, research skills, insights and originality of the teacher-researcher as a role model'). In the case of law, we can be quite confident that such a quest is a lifetime endeavour. To do this, teachers need time to read and reflect, much of which time might not be easily cashable as material to discharge lecture or class obligations. For example, an academic who spends six months reading a major work of political philosophy (e.g. Rawls, 1972, or Nozick, 1974) and the critical commentaries, or who grapples with the latest monograph dealing with the frontiers of Property Law, may find that they have relatively little material that they can put in their lectures. If, by contrast, that same academic had spent the same time reading a couple of leading textbooks, before you know it, they would have a full set of (largely) expository lecture notes. The moral of this is clear: if teachers are not resourced to research, they will become second-class members of the academic community, and their priority will be to get up to speed on the doctrinal basics rather than to contribute to the liberal mission.

The division between teachers and researcher/publishers is also problematic on the researcher/publisher side. If teaching is regarded as a matter of 'getting across the basics', and if many academics are not researcher/publishers, there will be all sorts of pressures for researcher/publishers to distance themselves from 'simple' teaching activities and those who could teach to the liberal mission will end up doing other things (especially working with postgraduate students and teaching their research specialisms to late-stage undergraduates).

The fate of the liberal mission lies neither with those who are innovative in teaching methods, nor with those who are prolific publishers. Rather it lies in the hands of those academic lawyers for whom the quest to understand law is a way of life, and it is a way of life that informs their practice in both the lecture theatre and, if they publish, in the law reviews. Worryingly, the RAE is one element in a context that tends to diminish this group, on the one side, pulling teacher/researchers (who publish only occasionally) into teaching only work and, on the other side, pulling them into publishing at all costs and, of course, in some cases, driving such persons out of academic life altogether.

Law for the People

If law schools are for citizens, does this not mean that they are also for the people? Unless we are to take the elitist view (to which I do not subscribe) that only a fraction of the population is capable of gaining from a liberal legal education, it does indeed have this implication. And the figures cited by ACLEC (in Tables 1 and 2), showing the increasing number of law school admissions and graduations from the mid-80s to the mid-90s, are to be welcomed. However, an expanding law school population is not an unconditional good and a major caveat needs to be entered before we celebrate this development.

It is quite clear that, in global terms, the expansion of law student numbers has not been matched by central government resources for the law schools. So much so that Phil Harris's (1997) survey indicates that a 50%

increase in student numbers between 1992 and 1996 has been accompanied by an increase of a mere 3% in academic staff. When we set the selective funding of research in this overall context of contraction of resources, we must question whether the student experience is one worth having. To put the point bluntly, the fact that ever-increasing numbers enter law school is a reason to be cheerful only if the liberal mission is delivered. If, rather than delivering the liberal mission, law schools deliver a dead-weight of doctrine, graduates will leave even less able to assume the responsibilities of critical citizenship than they were at the point of entry.

To this sobering thought it might be objected that the outcome of the HEFCE Teaching Quality Assessment of the law schools was relatively encouraging, for some 28% of the English law schools were judged excellent, and the vast majority were rated satisfactory. Moreover, the HEFCE Subject Overview Report for law (HEFCE, 1994) often suggests the employment of liberal criteria. For example, the Report frequently evaluates teaching quality by reference to whether students were encouraged to take an independent, critical, and analytical approach (see e.g. paras. 6, 19, 20, 48, and 50(b)). Even so, given that it was a cornerstone of HEFCE's methodology that the quality judgment must be relative to each law school's own mission (which, as the Report recognises in para. 6, might be "black-letter', contextual or practice-oriented'; and see, further, Oliver 1994), given the dynamics of assessment visits, and given the deepening pressure on resources since 1993-94, it surely would be unsafe to treat the general approbation of the assessors as confirmation that the liberal mission is being delivered satisfactorily in most places (cf Brownsword, 1994). The truly sobering thought, I suggest, is to imagine a teaching quality team working its way through the law schools with just two questions in mind: first, whether the liberal mission is alive and well; and, secondly, whether the infrastructure is in place for the ACLEC vision of law school education to be put into effect.

Before we leave the idea of law schools for the people, it is worth repeating that the liberal mission offers an arena for politico-legal debate without aligning itself with any particular substantive manifesto. When ACLEC talks expansively about the inculcation of legal values, it refers *inter alia* to the promotion of equality of opportunity and to the need to secure access to justice (para. 2.4). Under the rubric of 'law schools for the people' it might be tempting to take such rhetoric as a prescription for radical lawyeringlaw *for*, rather than *against*, the people (cf. Lefcourt, 1971). However, as should be clear by now, this is a temptation to be resisted by the liberal. Whether the political values are those of the New Right or the Old Left, whether the politics are those of privilege or redistribution, the liberal law school must maintain a neutral position. Of course, disinterest in this sense does not signify a lack of interest. To the contrary, one of the questions that a liberal approach certainly should address is how far legal interventions are able to transform (for the better) the daily lives of the great mass of people (and in particular disadvantaged sectors). Here, much of the socio-legal literature would suggest some fairly disquieting answers (cf Brownsword, 1996b). However, the task of the liberal law school is not so much to teach these answers or some other answers, but to keep on asking the questions in the light of the answers that we currently have.

Conclusion

ACLEC could scarcely have expressed stronger support for the liberal mission. It goes wrong, in my view, in seeking to inculcate Liberal values as part of the mission; but, in all other respects, ACLEC's vision of the law school of the C21 is progressive and enlightened and it should be vigorously supported.

Against ACLEC, however, some powerful forces are at work, not least in the law schools themselves, where the division between teachers and researcher/publishers seems destined to become even sharper after RAE96. But, it would not be right to blame it all on the RAE. Even before the RAE, there was plenty of resistance to curriculum innovation that threatened the privileged position of doctrinal exposition. Accordingly, despite ACLEC's best efforts and intentions, it is on the cards that the liberal project will be compromised by a mutually reinforcing combination of (a) the actual and perceived requirements of the legal profession for doctrinal knowledge and (b) the persistence in law schools (for a variety of reasonsindividual comfort, habit, textbook style, stretched resources, staff turnover, perceived constraints of modularisation etc.) of a subject-based black-letter curriculum.

In an age of greater selectivity, the liberal mission gives us an important focus for our law school priorities. To borrow once again from Roberto Unger (1996: 20):

> [Legal analysis or, in the present context, the law school] must elect the citizenry as its primary and ultimate interlocutor. It must imagine its work to be that of informing the conversation in a democracy about its present and alternative futures.

To rise to this challenge, which is both exciting and exacting, the law schools should take a collective stand. They should discourage teaching without research and publication without research as they should seek to preserve and encourage teaching with research and research with publication. ACLEC largely sends out the right messages; Government largely sends out the wrong messages; the critical question is which messages the academic community really wants to hear and endeavour to act upon.

References

ACLEC (1994), 'The Lord Chancellor's Advisory Committee on Legal Education and Conduct Review of Legal Education: The Initial Stage' (Consultation Paper), Lord Chancellor's Department, London.

ACLEC (1996), 'The First Report on Legal Education and Training', Lord Chancellor's Department, London.

Adams, J. and Brownsword, R. (1992), *Understanding Law*, Harper Collins, London, reprinted 1996: Sweet and Maxwell, London.

Birks, P. (ed) (1992), *Examining the Law Syllabus: The Core*, Oxford University Press, Oxford.

Bradney, A.G.D. (1996), 'The Quality of Teaching Quality Assessment in English Law Schools', 30, *The Law Teacher*, 150.

Bradney, Anthony (1999), 'Liberalising Legal Education', in F. Cownie (ed), *The Law School-Global Issues, Local Questions*, Ashgate, Aldershot.

Brownsword, R. (1992), 'Teaching Contract: A Liberal Agenda' in P. Birks (ed), *Examining the Law Syllabus: The Core*, Oxford University Press, Oxford, p.42.

Brownsword, R. (1994), 'Teaching Quality Assessment in Law Schools: A Cause for Concern?', 21, *Journal of Law and Society*, 529.

Brownsword, R. (1996a), 'Where Are all the Law Schools Going?', 30, *The Law Teacher*, 1.

Brownsword, Roger (1996b), 'From Co-operative Contracting to a Contract of Co-operation' in D. Campbell and P. Vincent-Jones (eds), *Contract and Economic Organisation*, Dartmouth, Aldershot.

Collins, H. (1992), 'Aims of Teaching the Law of Contract', in P. Birks (ed), *Examining the Law Syllabus: The Core*, Oxford University Press, Oxford, p.14.

Farmer, L. (1995), 'Bringing Cinderella to the Ball: Teaching Criminal Law in Context', 58, *Modern Law Review*, 756.

Goodrich, P. (1996), 'Of Blackstone's Tower: Metaphors of Distance and Histories of the English Law School', in P. Birks (ed), *Pressing Problems in the Law, Vol 2: What are Law Schools For?*, Oxford University Press, Oxford, p.59.

Griffith, J. (1995), Research Assessment, Council for Academic Freedom and Academic Standards, London.

Habermas, J. (1970), 'Toward a Theory of Communicative Competence', in H.P. Dreitzel (ed.), *Recent Sociology No. 2*, Macmillan, New York, p.114.

Harris, P. (1997), 'The Way We Are Now: The Law School Survey' (paper presented at SLSA Conference, 'The Shape of Things to Come', IALS, London, February 6, 1997).

HEFCE (1994), 'Subject Overview Report: Quality Assessment of Law 1993-94', HEFCE, Bristol.

Kronman, A. T. (1981), 'Foreword: Legal Scholarship and Moral Education', 90, *Yale Law Journal*, 955.

Lefcourt, R. (1971), *Law Against the People: Essays to Demystify Law, Order, and the Courts*, Random House, New York.

Lewis, N. D. (1996), *Choice and the Legal Order: Rising above Politics*, Butterworths, London.

Nozick, R. (1974), *Anarchy, State, and Utopia*, Basil Blackwell, Oxford.

Oliver, D. (1994), 'Teaching and Learning Law: Pressures on the Liberal Law Degree', in Peter Birks (ed), *Reviewing Legal Education*, Oxford University Press, Oxford, p.77.

Oliver, D. (1996), 'The Integration of Teaching and Research in the Law Department', 30, *The Law Teacher*, 133.

Outhwaite, W. (1994), *Habermas: A Critical Introduction*, Polity Press, Cambridge.

Rawls, J. (1972), *A Theory of Justice*, Oxford University Press, London.

Unger, R. M. (1996), 'Legal Analysis as Institutional Imagination', 59, *Modern Law Review*, 1.

Welch, R. (1995), 'Rise of the Managerial Cadre', The Times Higher Educational Supplement (June 16).

3 Searching for Theory in Teaching Law

FIONA COWNIE[1]

The Status of Teaching in Academia

Traditionally, three areas of activity go to make up the academic job: research, teaching and administration. While British academics have been noted for their strong attachment to the idea that teaching and research are closely linked (Halsey, 1992, p.176), research has long been perceived as the most valuable and prestigious activity carried out by academics: promotion, status and peer approval has traditionally been correlated with research output. Some data about academics would appear to suggest that they regard teaching as an important and valuable activity; a majority of respondents to Halsey's 1989 survey (and an especially large majority in what were then polytechnics) continued to disagree with the assertion put to them that 'an academic's first loyalty should be to research in his or her discipline: the teaching of students and the running of the institution should come second'. They also agreed that 'promotion in academic life is too dependent on published work and too little on devotion to teaching' (Halsey, 1992, p.187). However, Halsey also noted that there was a clearly perceptible shift towards greater research orientation in both polytechnics and old universities (Halsey, 1992, p.185).

As between teaching and research, then, research continues to be the dominant activity within universities. The pre-eminence of research is, in part, related to the high status which it is afforded by academic institutions and the academics within them. For academics, the most important ingredient of attaining status is not power, but reputation. The ingredients of a good reputation vary from discipline to discipline, but generally a good reputation involves strong identification with the discipline, coupled with a concern to preserve and enhance its public reputation as much as one's own (Becher and Kogan, 1992, p.112). Research attitudes and performance are strongly associated with entering the professoriate. Professors are more than twice as likely to give priority to research as non-professorial academics. They are also almost twice as likely to value teaching and research equally as distinct from being orientated towards teaching as compared with other ranks (Halsey, 1992, p.207). Becher and Kogan argue that teaching does not go entirely unrewarded, but the teaching function is undervalued, for two main reasons. Firstly, academics' concern with reputation is focused on contributing to and promoting their discipline. The leading practitioners in the field usually achieve their pre-eminence because of the energies they devote to achieving a reputation. Few have much creative energy left over to devote to teaching, and thus do not portray it as an activity of comparable significance. Those who are the most influential members of the peer group are not perceived as regarding teaching as a serious intellectual task. The second reason that teaching is undervalued, according to Becher and Kogan, is that teaching has traditionally been regarded as a private activity; the quality of interaction between an academic and their students is perceived as very personal. Competence as a teacher therefore, has not traditionally been easy to assess, especially in contrast with research, whose products are usually in the public domain. External pressures such as teaching quality assessment and appraisal schemes may cause this to change in the future, but in their view it is likely that the academic's fundamental loyalty will continue to be to the advancement of knowledge and that teaching will not be seen as of prime importance (Becher and Kogan, 1992, pp.114-15).

The secondary status of teaching, as opposed to research, is true not only of the UK, but also in other Common Law jurisdictions; Dunkin and Precians report an American study surveying a large quantity of the U.S. literature on the relationship between teaching and research which concluded very firmly that 'Teaching is a significant activity for many academics, but it does not bring national recognition and esteem' (Dunkin and Precians, 1994, p.85).[2] Dunkin's own work in Australia came to very much the same conclusion (Dunkin, 1991). In Canada, Johnston paints a similar picture, including in his analysis reference to a whole body of work which comes to the conclusion that universities are not only bad for teaching, but hostile to it (Johnston, 1991, p.111). Johnston's work has been challenged by O'Neill, who points out that not all academics are promoted solely on the basis of their research, nor is it true to say that all academics are actively engaged in research (O'Neill, 1991). O'Neill's comments are clearly applicable outside the specifically Canadian context in which he made them. However, it remains the case that the overwhelming weight of the evidence supports the view that research is more highly valued than teaching within universities throughout the Common Law world.

In the UK the traditional emphasis on research has been reinforced, in recent times, by the periodic Research Assessment Exercises carried out by the Higher Education Funding Councils. Departments are under constant pressure to achieve the much-coveted '5' rating, and there is consequent pressure on individual academics to produce an almost constant flow of research. Since this is in a context of diminishing resources, where there are a myriad of other pressures on their time, including large numbers of students, in the new world of 'mass higher education' it is unsurprising that many academics accept without question that teaching pales into insignificance as compared with research.

The place of teaching and research within the university, and the relationship between those two activities, has been the subject of endless debate stretching from Newman's seminal Victorian work *The Idea of a University* (Newman, 1987), through Clark Kerr's *Uses of a University*, published in 1963 (Kerr, 1963) to more modern works such as Peter Scott's *The Meaning of Mass Higher Education* (Scott, 1995) and collections such as Smith and Webster's *Postmodern University* (Smith and Webster, 1997). I have argued elsewhere that the essence, or hallmark, of a university is the contribution it has made to the advancement of knowledge, and that in this tradition, where knowledge is pursued for its own sake, teaching is secondary to research (Bradney and Cownie, 1996, p.18). In applying these ideas specifically to law schools, Bradney has argued that law schools must remain academic in nature, and not seek to satisfy the short-term goals of the legal profession, thus implying a commitment, above all, to legal research (Bradney, 1992, p.18). But acknowledging the importance of research, and its priority as an activity within the university, and therefore within law schools, does not inevitably mean that teaching should be consigned to the intellectual wilderness.

Academic Attitudes?

To say that teaching is less valuable than research is a relative statement. It does not mean that the activity of teaching is totally lacking in value, nor that it is in fact a non-intellectual activity. In her critical examination of some of the most common assumptions about teaching which are made in higher education, Weimer looks at the belief that teaching requires no training and no ongoing development. She argues that lack of knowledge about teaching produces academics who

> ...do not know how they teach, understand why they teach as they do, or see how such self-insight might improve their practice...Most know they teach as they were taught, but beyond that they have no articulate philosophy of education, and no clear understanding of the premises and assumptions that reside implicitly in policies and practices...used to govern instructional transactions.
> (Weimer, 1997, p.54)

How would those same academics regard someone who adopted such an approach to their substantive subject? It does not take a wild leap of imagination to foresee the outright condemnation which would be heaped upon the poor unfortunate who professed to be an academic, but whose knowledge of their subject was so limited. Yet many academics appear to be content to take this attitude to teaching. Teaching is less valued than research, as Weimer observes, not because research actually *is* a more intellectually rigorous activity, but because the intellectual complexity of teaching is almost completely unknown within academia (Weimer, 1997).

It appears to be very common for academics to take a very pragmatic and uninformed approach to teaching. In this respect, legal academics do not appear to behave differently to their colleagues in other disciplines. Anecdotal evidence appears to play a large part in the construction of many lectures and tutorials, as lecturers turn to their own experience as undergraduates to guide them in designing lectures, or borrow tutorial sheets from colleagues in order to cut and paste them for their own courses. Conscientious preparation for teaching appears to demand that one be up-to-date as regards the latest research in the area, or the latest Court of Appeal pronouncement, but little thought is given to any but the most basic of the pedagogic aspects of teaching. As Feinman and Feldman say:

> Most legal educators are anti-intellectual about the area of their primary professional concern: the content and method of legal education. This anti-

> intellectualism is characterised by an unwillingness to reflect on the goals of legal education, the content of the curriculum, the methods of teaching and the abilities of law graduates to practise law competently. At most law schools, the purposes and methods of teaching are regarded as unfruitful, if not unfit, topics of conversation.
> (Feinman and Feldman, 1985, p.875)

The complacency of legal academics as regards their teaching responsibilities has been reinforced in the U.K. by the teaching quality exercise (TQA), which is the responsibility of the Higher Education Funding Councils.[3] As a result of the TQA, the vast majority of law schools were confirmed in their belief that their teaching was satisfactory, while a sizeable proportion were rated as excellent (HEFCE, 1994b). However, the exercise was regarded with some disquiet within the academic community, even by those who were involved as assessors; '...the HEFCE tried to pretend that it was possible, during a two-and-a-half day visitation, for a group of enthusiastic amateurs, after a couple of days' formal instruction, to come to a considered and apparently definitive view about the quality [of teaching]' (Alderman, 1996, p.188). One putative law assessor resigned after undergoing the training for assessors and published an open letter enumerating the failures, as he saw them, of the HEFCE system (Allen, 1993). One of the actual law assessors wrote an extended critique of the whole process in the Journal of Law and Society, expressing doubts about the ability of any quality assessment linked to funding to do anything other than dividing the academic community and devaluing the currency of law school education (Brownsword, 1994, p.530). In the course of that article, Roger Brownsword went on to express concerns about the ability of the methodology used in the assessments to promote fair, reliable and useful judgements (Brownsword, 1994, p. 530ff). These are fundamental issues, and the doubts expressed confirm one's view of that exercise as wholly inadequate, especially when it is realised that in not one of the reports is there any mention of educational theory, that the assessors themselves were not required to have any knowledge of educational theory and that it went virtually unremarked that this is also true of the vast majority of those whom they were assessing. It is no great comfort to contemplate the revised methodology for carrying out assessments which HEFCE has put in place in response not only to widespread consultation within the higher education sector, but also to the independent evaluation of the methodology used in the TQA which was carried out by the Centre for Higher Education Studies (CHES) at the Institute of Education in the University of London (Barnett et al, 1994). As a result of its soundings, HEFCE issued a revised methodology for TQA, inaugurated in 1995 (HEFCE, 1994a). However, there is still no mention of philosophy or theory of education, either in relation to the assessors nor in relation to those who are to be assessed, and many of the criticisms of the original methodology remain valid (Bradney, 1996).

Ignorance about the intellectual content of teaching is also reflected in the research output of legal academics. Academic writing about law teaching is not a mainstream activity among legal academics: a perusal of articles published in the last five years in any of the leading general law journals will reveal that few are about legal education at all, and of those even less focus specifically on teaching matters, as opposed to policy. Looking at the specialist journals on legal education, the *The Law Teacher* is alone amongst British law journals in confining itself to legal education, though *The Web Journal of Current Legal Issues* has a legal education section.[4] As far as educational theory is concerned, it has a mixed history, even in the pages of the specialist journals; theory is only really beginning to establish itself as a major concern of writers in the field.

It is not true to say, however, that legal academics have no interest in teaching. Many of the articles in *The Law Teacher* focus on the practice of teaching, and occasionally such articles appear in the pages of the general law journals. Neither is it true to say there is no research which engages with the idea of educational theory and law teaching (see for example Webb and Maughan, 1996, MacFarlane, 1992). However, apart from such honourable exceptions, it is nevertheless true that, 'It would appear that much of the work of law teachers appears to rely on rules of thumb, based on, at times, anecdotal and impressionistic evidence rather than on explicitly designed theoretical models which draw on...hard rigorous analysis...' (Le Brun and Johnston, 1994).

Teaching as an Intellectual Pursuit

If legal academics are to justify their place in the academy, they cannot approach teaching on the basis of ignorance. They should take teaching seriously, and that involves familiarity with the relevant research literature. As Feinman and Feldman put it:

> This notion that we must be as concerned about the intellectual integrity of our learning theory as about our legal theory traditionally has not held sway in law schools. Law professors have long believed that educational theorists are either charlatans or primitives. That belief is arrogant and anti-intellectual. (Feinman and Feldman, 1985, p.895)

For an academic to be 'anti-intellectual' is surely a contradiction in terms. It is in the very nature of being an academic, belonging to the academy, that all of one's life is conducted in the light of reasoned argument. Being an academic is not something which you can turn on and off. The idea that one is intellectually rigorous about one's research, but completely unintellectual about teaching should be totally unacceptable.

Arguments that the attitude of legal academics towards teaching needs to change, and in particular that it needs to be more intellectual, are not new. As long ago as 1935 Karl Llewellyn wrote an article in the Columbia Law Review entitled 'On What Is Wrong With So-Called Legal Education' (Llewellyn, 1935). This was a wide-ranging critique of the university law schools with which he was familiar - Columbia, Harvard and Yale. Apart from discussing the failure of law schools to equip law students to deal with law in context, and in particular its political and social context, Llewellyn also urges law teachers to address the 'whole self' of the student. Teaching students to 'think like a lawyer' is only part of the task of the university law school; it is also necessary to integrate the human and artistic with the legal. Asking law teachers to fulfil all these objectives is, Llewllyn admits, bound to be met with a whole bundle of excuses as to why this is not possible; lack of resources, lack of time, lack of ...almost everything is likely to be called in aid to explain why it is not possible to fulfil any more demanding objectives of legal education. Nothing daunted, Llewellyn proposes a number of 'methods' which could be adopted to improve legal education in the ways he is suggesting. One of his main methods is the suggestion that law teachers should move towards a theory of teaching:

> About the law, we have taken thought; and then about the judge. About the lawyer, we are beginning to. About our own procedures, no. Each man for himself. Teachers are born, not made... as to *method* of teaching - there we

> balk at communication, we balk at analysis. This is idiocy, plain and drooling. (Llewellyn, 1935, pp. 676-677)

Surely, in a university, of all places, there can be no acceptance of idiocy. The credibility of the university, as a place of scholarship and learning, as an academy in the Aristotelian sense, is undermined to the extent to which idiocy and ignorance are tolerated with regard to any of its activities.

Taking Teaching Seriously

The ignorance of law teachers about teaching does not stem from the paucity of advice and information available. There is a large literature of 'teaching manuals' and 'how to..' books. Many writers about teaching in law schools have concentrated on what can broadly be termed teaching skills or techniques: how to improve lectures, more interesting things to do in tutorials, the purposes and varieties of assessments (Taylor, 1993). The approaches taken vary widely, from the banal and boring to the sophisticated and stimulating. An interesting example of the more interesting work of this type is Jennifer Rosato's discussion of using games to enrich her teaching. A number of educational theorists, including Dewey and Piaget, have extolled play as a way of learning. Games have been used in clinical legal education for some time, but Rosato argues that gaming can be used throughout the law school curriculum, seeing benefits in terms of increased motivation, as well as the possibility, in some cases, of increased knowledge (Rosato, 1995, p. 568ff). While skills such as devising games, or 'snowballing' are very useful, and they can in themselves be used to improve teaching and learning, there is a danger that these 'tricks' come to be accepted as the *totality* of knowledge about teaching (Weimer, 1997). However, knowledge of techniques alone is not enough; teaching must be grounded in theory, not just skills, just as with substantive law it is insufficient to know merely how to look up a case or what the ratio is; one must understand the place of theory in contract or in torts.

The kind of theory with which legal academics ought to be familiar in relation to their teaching can broadly be divided into philosophy of education and education theory. Philosophy of education includes work on the nature of education itself, its purpose and place in society. Education theory includes the work of cognitive psychologists, interested in how humans understand, reason and comprehend; it also encompasses the work of educationalists who are interested in learning theories and in particular in the relations between students, learning and teaching (see Le Brun and Johnstone, 1994, chapter 2).

Philosophy of education offers insights which provide a broad background to the purpose of education. It enables consideration of questions not only about why we teach, but also about how we should teach in order to be more effective. It allows us to consider the process of education from different perspectives - the student's, the teacher's, even to think of education as a political act. It is not the purpose of this article to set out a comprehensive syllabus for the education of university law lecturers, but in order to illustrate the arguments I am making, I include some examples. I begin with the work of John Dewey, one of the few educational theorists whose name may be familiar to those whose research interests do not include legal education.

Dewey's ideas were developed in America during the early years of the twentieth century.[5] An educational experience for Dewey is one in which a mental connection is made between what a person does and what happens in consequence. Then '...doing becomes a trying : an experiment with the world to find out what it is like; the undergoing becomes instruction...' (Dewey, 1916, p.40). Education therefore consists of the cumulative and unending acquisition, combination and reorganisation of educative experiences which he called 'growth'. Growth means that new experiences should cause people to reconsider, recast and revamp old experiences, so the educational process is a 'continual reorganisation, reconstruction and transformation of experience' (Dewey, 1916, p.40). Learning is therefore an active process, arising out of personal experience in working on a problem; it is necessary for the student, in order to learn, to be like an explorer, mapping unknown territory, making sense of the new land for him/her self. It is vital, in Dewey's view, that students should learn for themselves, and not merely be told things by their instuctors. In order to overcome the difference between the artificial problems which might be posed in an educational setting and the real ones encountered in everyday life, Dewey argued that the everyday experiences of students should be used as '...the intellectual starting point for moving out into the unknown ...' (Dewey, 1916, p.212). Familiarity with Dewey's work, and that of other educationalists who have been influenced by him, could enable law teachers to consider their own teaching activities in a new light. If persuaded by Dewey's ideas, legal academics might question the extent to which law students learn by doing, and if they do, how this might affect the delivery of law courses.

In the same way, studying philosophy of education might involve looking at the work of radical educationalists, such as Paolo Freire. Freire was a Brazilian educationalist, whose work was firmly rooted in the South American context, and widely used in literacy campaigns in Brazil. However, it is universal in its appeal, and has much to offer in widely differing educational situations. Freire's most famous work is *Pedagogy of the Oppressed*, published in 1972 (Freire, 1974). In it, he discusses the humanising nature of the intellectual enterprise, emphasising the way in which thought can open the way to a new future. His basic assumption is that a person's ontological vocation is to act upon his or her world, and in doing so to change it, moving towards new possibilities of a fuller and richer life, both individually and collectively.

> It is only when the oppressed find the oppressor out and become involved in the organised struggle for their liberation that they begin to believe in themselves. This discovery cannot be purely intellectual, but must involve action; nor can it be limited to mere activism, but must include serious reflection: only then will it be a praxis...Attempting to liberate the oppressed without their reflective participation in the act of liberation is to treat them as objects which must be saved from a burning building; it is to lead them into the populist pitfall and transform them into masses which can be manipulated. At all stages of their liberation, the oppressed must see themselves as men engaged in the ontological and historical vocation of becoming more fully human.
> (Freire, 1974, p.41)

Freire argues that every human being, no matter how 'ignorant' is capable of looking critically at their world, and with the proper academic tools, can gradually perceive his or her personal and social reality, and deal critically with it; 'The pedagogy of the oppressed is an instrument for their critical discovery that both they and their oppressors are instruments of dehumanisation' (Freire, 1974, p.28).

Education as a means by which people deal critically and creatively with reality is not something whose relevance is confined to South America; it is the essence of the enterprise in which all teachers are engaged, and is as relevant to the philosophy of education in a university as anywhere else. Consideration of Freire's ideas might lead law teachers to be more aware of the transformative possibilities of education, to question whether the content of their teaching encourages those transformative possibilities, and if not, whether it should. From the evidence which is available, it seems that few academics think about their teaching in this way at all; yet as members of the academy, surely thinking, informed by relevant theories, is what academics are supposed to be good at.

The amount of educational philosophy available to law teachers is vast; these examples merely serve to emphasise that such theories are not just remote and abstract concepts which are removed from the daily activities which go on in a law school. The whole point of knowing more about philosophy of education is that it should inform the daily lives of law teachers and students. Like all educational experiences, knowledge of theory is a transformative experience, leading one, in many cases, to do things differently (and in a superior way) from that which went before.

Empirical evidence that knowledge of educational theory is transformative in this sense is provided by research carried out by Halliday and Soden in relation to a professional development course which they devised specifically for lecturers in higher education (Halliday and Soden, 1998). 'In designing the course, the authors tried to address both the concern that teacher education programmes often lack a substantive theoretical basis, and the well documented problem that professional knowledge is resistant to any substantial restructuring' (Halliday and Soden, 1998, p.22). The course provided by Halliday and Soden introduced participants to the disciplines of psychology. sociology and philosophy. They were then asked to try to re-interpret their practice in the light of insights gained from the course; their progress was assessed in terms of the theoretical sophistication of their justifications for what they chose to do with their students in their classes.The researchers then depicted at four points in the course the progress of the participants towards being able to integrate theoretically justifiable ideas into justifications for their actions. At the beginning of the course, the justifications provided were very limited, revealing a negligible understanding of learning theory; at this stage only one person on the course (out of a total of 11) moved beyond personal beliefs and assertions. However, by the fifth month of the course, all the participants drew on theories justifying their practices (Halliday and Soden, 1998, p.29).

This level of integration between teaching practice and educational theory should be the norm for all academics. As far as legal academics are concerned, it is important to realise that the relationship between teaching and educational theory suggested here *is* an integral one. I am not talking about an optional extra or an add-on; this is not 'law and politics' or 'law and geography', but law teaching suffused with pedagogic theory, in the same way that an academic approach to the law of contract or the law of property should be suffused with relevant theory.

Education Theory

Although I have up to now concentrated on urging law teachers to become familiar with what might best be described as the philosophy of education, familiarity with educational theory is equally important. It is this type of theory which has made most impact on the field of legal education to date, with writers applying the work of a variety of educational thinkers to law teaching. One of the most influential authors in this field has been D. A. Kolb whose experiential learning theory has been used by a number of authors (Kolb, 1984).[6] Of these, Caroline Maughan's contribution to the collection she has edited with Julian Webb, *Teaching Lawyers' Skills*, is especially noteworthy in the current context, because its whole purpose is to explain exactly how this theory can be applied in law teaching (Maughan, 1996).

In her essay, entitled 'Learning how to Learn: the Skills Developer's Guide to Experiential Learning' Maughan emphasises that experiential learning theory is not just concerned with the acquisition of skill, but also involves learners taking control of their learning in a way which enables them to understand themselves better as learners. It is a lifelong, holistic process which integrates knowledge, skills, attitudes and values, integrating thinking, feeling, perceiving and behaving (Maughan, 1996, p.69). Kolb's theory builds on the work of, among others, Dewey; experience therefore plays a central part in the learning experience, but there are strong cognitive frameworks as well.

Kolb wished to reconcile potentially conflicting modes of adapting to the world, in particular concrete experience and abstract conceptualisation, and action and reflection. Learning is seen as a process of tensions and conflicts, the resolution of which will lead to personal growth and creativity (Maughan, 1996, p.70). The learning process is conceived as a sequential 4-stage cycle, involving (1) concrete experience (2) reflective observation (3) abstract conceptualisation and (4) active experimentation. In considering student learning, Kolb stressed that students will already have had a wealth of experience from which they will have learnt; some of the values and beliefs which they bring with them may conflict with the new ideas to which they are introduced, so that they will have to rearrange this new learning so it is congruent with their previous learning.

Maughan also stresses the importance of Kolb's identification of different 'learning styles'. People have different learning styles which they prefer to use; the same person may also use different learning styles at different times in the learning process. In general, people have one or two styles with which they are comfortable, but find it difficult to adapt to others. Kolb identified four learning styles: divergers, who prefer to work through concrete experiences followed by reflection and observation; convergers, who prefer to learn by working on abstract conceptualisations and testing these out by experimentation; assimilators, who are able to create convincing generalisable theories from disparate observations, and accommodators, who like to 'have a go', trying things out and carrying out plans (Maughan, 1996, p.72, Kolb, 1985). Having set out the main features of Kolb's theory, Maughan then proceeds to demonstrate how it could be applied to law teaching, incorporating the learning cycle into the actual practice of teaching. This is the type of work which, in an ideal world, all law teachers should be able to do for themselves.

The quotation with which Caroline Maughan begins her essay indicates how her work is a very good example of the integration of theory with teaching practice: 'Articulate your own theory, critically examine it, check for consistency, coherence and adequacy, compare it with alternative theories and reconceptualise it in order to increase the effectiveness of your own professional thinking' (Griffiths and Tann, 1992, p.69). Not that I am arguing that we should all be following Kolb; far from it!! But we should be familiar with Kolb's work, and be able to evaluate it in the light of our knowledge of other theories. Without knowledge of theory in the way I have been describing, this whole process just never gets off the ground, and we are left wallowing in a sea of ignorance.

Another example of practice grounded in theory is provided by Feinman and Feldman '...we have tried to present, and to embody in Contorts, a complete, theoretically grounded alternative to the dominant ideology of legal education...' (Feinman and Feldman, 1985, p.925).[7] The theory to which they refer is not confined to the theories relating to the substantive subjects of contract and tort, but includes the educational theories which inform the delivery of their teaching. Feinman and Feldman describe how in their teaching of 'contorts' they have used as the theoretical basis of their teaching a concept known as 'mastery learning', arising out of the work of Benjamin Bloom (Bloom, 1976).

> Mastery learning strategies employ many traditional methods, but require that the teacher be more explicit and systematic about what is to be learned and assert more control over how it is to be learned. In general, implementing mastery learning in a law school involves four steps: definition of objectives and formulation of learning units, formulative evaluation, development of alternative learning resources, and final evaluation and grading.
> (Feinman and Feldman, 1985, pp.897-898)

Conclusion

Clearly, the arguments put forward here about the importance of educational theory are not confined solely to law teachers. However, that fact alone does not undermine the arguments put forward. Law schools are the immediate concern of this book and it is to law teachers that these remarks are addressed. The fact that they could equally well be addressed to other members of the academy should not be allowed to distract the reader from the substantive argument.

As law teachers in a university, members of the academy, we should not only be familiar with the philosophy and theory of education, we should also be able to put them into practice, to integrate them into our teaching methods, to be confident that just as our research is based firmly in theory, and takes account of the latest developments in the field, so it is with our pedagogy. Julian Webb has argued that 'Theory matters because without it education is hit and miss: the quality of education suffers; student choice suffers; and ultimately we risk misunderstanding not only the nature of our pedagogy, but the epistemic foundation of our discipline' (Webb, 1996, p.23). In the same way, Julia Macfarlane has written:

> The role of theory, as I am concerned with it here, is to inform practice in education design and classroom delivery by enabling the formulation of

> criteria for decision-making. This includes decision-making in curriculum design, syllabus content and coverage, in methods of teaching and learning and in the development of assessment targets and standards of 'competence'.
> (Macfarlane, 1992)

Such arguments must not go unheeded if university legal education is to continue to progress and develop as it moves into the next millenium. It is also important to remember, in the present context, that educational theory and teaching practices are not divorced from the traditional strengths of university teachers i.e. as scholars, learned in their discipline. There is a growing emphasis on the central importance of discipline knowledge in effective teaching (Taylor, 1993, p.67). However, this does not mean we can all sit back with a sigh of relief and carry on as before. To do so would be to encourage a learning experience dominated by content knowledge, in which teaching promotes intellectual passivity rather than critical engagement with the subject. Acknowledging the importance of expertise in one's subject as well as in educational theory involves pursuing explicitly

> ...not only the accumulated information of a discipline, but how that information is organised into a dynamic whole; the processes by which that information can be used, elaborated and critically examined; and the conditions under which both process and content knowledge apply. These demands call for a more comprehensive utilisation of the knowledge of the scholar-teacher in the university clasrooom to facilitate the explicit teaching of a discipline's content, process and structure.
> (Taylor, 1993, p.70)

Arguments about familiarity with educational theory and teaching skills are not just empty rhetoric; they stem just as much from a concern to capture the excitement and spontaneity of teaching as from a desire to be intellectually rigorous. Talking about John Kelly, who tutored him at Oxford, Professor Peter Birks has written:

> He taught by example. He was a committed intellectual, committed to reason, to reason applied to the great moral and political issues of the day, to law as an expression and protection of the values that make life worth living. He befriended us, he made us take ourselves seriously, he made us laugh, and he caused us to work. We worked because we admired him and admired his work... .

(Birks, 1996, p.6)

Teaching informed by theory can capture the excitement, the spontaneity and the enthusiasm which go to make up the human relationships which are at the centre of the learning/ teaching relationship, and teaching informed by theory can use that enthusiasm to promote learning much more effectively than teaching which is not informed by theory.

It is understandable, but not acceptable, to say that academics are already under considerable pressure, and that to expect them to become familiar with the principles of educational philosophy and theory is just unrealistic (Taylor, 1993, p.67). There will be many, for example, who will seek to answer my arguments by pointing to the pressures of the RAE; they may argue that if I believe that the primary purpose of a university is to contribute to the advancement of knowledge then the priority for academics must be to do research, and at the moment that means contributing to the RAE. While acknowledging the pressure which the RAE exerts on those in universities, I do not accept that it provides a watertight and comprehensive answer to the argument I am making. Research is important, but it is important because it adds to the sum of human knowledge; it is also part of the essence of a university. But another part of that essence is the nature of the university as an academy, a place of learning. Learning takes place as a dialogue between teachers and taught; what I am arguing here is that that dialogue cannot be effective unless it is fully informed by theory, and if the dialogue is not effective, then the purpose of the university as an academy of learning will be undermined. To say that we do not have time to fulfil one of the primary purposes of a university is to say that academics are not committed to their vocation.

Nor should concerns about the importance of theory in legal education be sidetracked into the debate about teacher training for academics raised by the recommendations of the Dearing Report (Dearing, 1997). While I would argue that theory should form part of that training if it comes to pass, there are many debates about the existence, nature and content of such training which are outside the immediate subject of this essay. The primary responsibility for teaching in a properly academic way, as professionals who are fully conversant with, and able to utilise, educational theory and teaching skills in university teaching, rests not with those who provide or devise training courses, but with each individual academic.

However, it would be dishonest to say that I am optimistic about the prospects for change; experience elsewhere suggests that any other attitude would be unrealistic. Academics in the United States have been subject to prolonged pressure from both legislators and students to devote increased time and effort to teaching, but a recent survey conducted by the Carnegie Foundation for the Evaluation of Teaching found that research remains the path to promotion, to the detriment of teaching (Huber et al, 1997). One common assumption is that not until it becomes clear that excellence in teaching really does result in promotion in the same way as excellence in research will attitudes among large numbers of academics change. However, while this is apparently a widely-held belief, it appears that caution must be exercised in assuming that this holds the key to future improvements. Wright and O'Neil investigated the perceptions of individuals who are responsible for teaching improvement activities at 51 Canadian degree-granting instutions. Their findings reveal a widespread belief that the greatest teaching improvement potential lies in incentives in the form of employment rewards such as promotion, and they cite arguments precisely to this effect made by various researchers throughout the last twenty years (Wright and O'Neil, 1994, p.47). However, they also caution against overestimating the impact of an improved reward system on teaching quality, pointing out that there is some evidence that such a strategy could be counter-productive, and citing Ramsden's contribution in drawing attention to research which does not support the widespread belief that poor teaching and lack of incentives are linked (Ramsden,1992). Nevertheless, as Wright and O'Neil conclude, given the widespread perception of the need for incentives, it appears that this should form at least part of any strategy designed to increase teaching quality in universities. Certainly, until such strategies become common, it appears more likely that academics who take an intellectually rigorous approach to their teaching are likely to remain in a beleagured minority.

Postscript

In the course of preparing this essay, I have given conference papers on the subject and had many discussions with other legal academics about the importance of taking a rigorously academic approach to the enterprise of teaching. In many cases, I have been met with amused tolerance, with a reaction which says 'Well, in an ideal world, that might be a very nice idea, but you can't really expect us to be doing all that as well as all the other things we have to do. You're an idealist, and we'll leave you to your dreams'. In reply, I can do no better than quote Karl Llewellyn. In his article 'On What is Wrong With So-Called Legal Education', Llewellyn began by saying:

> [My] argument will base on the proposition that the health of any university, and more particularly of any law school, rests in departure from normality and deadly sanity. Freak persons and freak policies are needed; needed in very considerable measure. This is true always and everywhere. But it is peculiarly true of a discipline whose very essence is tradition; it is peculiarly true in a teaching profession at those epochs when their tradition of teaching has grown blind, and withers.
> (Llewellyn, 1935, p.651)

In this sense, contemporary law schools desperately need more 'freak persons', who not only believe in the importance of educational theory, but are prepared to put that belief into practice.

Notes

1. The author would like to thank Andrew Halpin (Southampton University), Tracey Varnava (National Centre for Legal Education), Sally Wheeler (Leeds University) and Tony Bradney (Leicester University) for their helpful comments and assistance in gathering materials which have been used in this chapter. The views expressed here remain, however, those of the author alone, as does responsibility for any errors or omissions.
2. M.F. Fox, 'Publication, performance, and reward in science and scholarship' in J.C. Smart (ed), *Higher Education, Handbook of Theory and Research,* New York, Agathon Press, quoted in M.J.Dunkin and R.P.Precians (1994), 'Award Winning Teachers' Beliefs About Teaching Versus Research', 13(1), *Higher Education Research and Development*, 85.
3. In the case of the Higher Education Funding Council for England (HEFCE) see *Further and Higher Education Act 1992*, s70.
4. It should be noted that whilst the author is the Legal Education editor of this journal, the decision to include such a section was taken by the founders of the journal, before the appointment of the author to the Editorial Board.

5. For a brief introduction to Dewey's ideas, see Husen and Poselthwaite, *The International Encyclopedia of Education*, 2nd edn.
6. Kolb's work has been used by, among others: Le Brun and Johnstone (1994), D.W. Johnson and F.P. Johnson (1991) and C. Maughan (1996).
7. 'Contorts' is a course which covers contract, tort and legal research and writing; see Feinman and Feldman (1985), p.901ff for a more detailed discussion of this course.

References

Alderman, G. (1996), 'Audit, Assessment and Academic Autonomy', 50, *Higher Education Quarterly*, 178.

Allen, M. (1993), 'Teaching Quality Assessment Exercise', Winter 1993. *SPTL Reporter*, 25.

Barnett, R. et al (1994), *Assessment of the Quality of Higher Education: A Review and an Evaluation*, Higher Education Funding Council for England, Bristol.

Becher, T. and Kogan, M. (1992), *Process and Structure in Higher Education*, Routledge, London.

Birks, P. (1996), *John Morris Kelly Memorial Lecture: Harrassment and Hubris: The Right to an Equality of Respect*, Faculty of Law, University College Dublin.

Bloom, B. (1976), *Human Characteristics and School Learning*, McGraw-Hill, New York.

Bradney, A. (1992), 'Ivory Towers or Satanic Mills: Choices for University Law Schools', 17, *Studies in Higher Education*, 5.

Bradney, A. (1996), 'The Quality of Teaching Quality Assessment in English Law Schools', 30 (2), *The Law Teacher*, 150.

Bradney, A. and Cownie, F. (1996), 'Working on the Chain Gang?', 2(2), *Contemporary Issues in Law*, 15.

Brownsword, R. (1994), 'Teaching Quality Assessment in Law Schools: A Cause for Concern?', 21, *Journal of Law and Society*, 529.

Dearing, R. (1997), *Higher Education in the Learning Society: Report of the National Committee of Inquiry into Higher Education*, HMSO, London.

Dewey, J. (1916), *Democracy and Education*, Macmillan, New York.

Dunkin, M.J. (1991), 'Determinants of Academic Career Advancement at an Australian University', *Higher Education Research and Development*, 115.

Dunkin, M.J. and Precians, R.P. (1994), 'Award Winning Teachers' Beliefs About Teaching Versus Research', 13(1), *Higher Education Research and Development*, 85.

Feinman, J. and Feldman, M. (1985), 'Pedagogy and Politics', 73, *Georgetown L.J.*, 875.

Fox, M.F. (1994), 'Publication, Performance, and Reward in Science and Scholarship', in J.C. Smart (ed), *Higher Education, Handbook of Theory and Research*, Agathon Press, New York, quoted in Dunkin, M.J. and Precians, R.P. (1994).

Freire, P. (1974), *Pedagogy of the Oppressed*, Seabury Press, New York.

Griffiths, M. and Tann, S. (1992), 'Using Reflective Practice to Link Personal and Public Theories', 18, *Journal of Education for Teaching*, 69.

Halliday, J. and Soden, R. (1998), 'Facilitating Changes in Lecturers' Understanding of Learning', 3(1), *Teaching in Higher Education*, 21.

Halsey, A.H. (1992), *Decline of Donnish Dominion*, Clarendon Press, Oxford.

HEFCE (1994), *The Quality Assessment Method From April 1995*, Higher Education Funding Council for England, Bristol.

HEFCE (1994b), *Quality Assessment of Law*, Higher Education Funding Council for England, Bristol.

Huber, M. *et al* (1997), *Scholarship Assessed: Evaluation of the Professoriate*, Carnegie Foundation for the Advancement of Teaching.

Johnston, I.C. (1991), 'Myth Conceptions of Academic Work', 221(2), *Canadian Journal of Higher Education*, 108.

Kerr, C. (1963), *The Uses of a University*, Harvard University Press, Cambridge, MA.

Kolb, D.A. (1984), *Experiential Learning: Experience as the Source of Learning and Development*, Prentice Hall, Englewood Cliffs, N.J.

Kolb, D.A. (1985), *The Learning Style Inventory* (2nd edn), Mcber, Boston, MA.

Le Brun, M. and Johnstone, R. (1994), *The Quiet Revolution - Improving Student Learning in Law*, The Law Book Company, Sydney.

Llewellyn, K. (1935), 'On What is Wrong with So-Called Legal Education', 35, *Columbia Law Review*, 651.

MacFarlane, J. (1992), 'Look Before You Leap', 19, *Journal of Law and Society*, 293.

Maughan, C. (1996), 'Learning How to Learn: the Skills Developer's Guide to Experiential Learning', in J. Webb and C. Maughan (eds), *Teaching Lawyers' Skills*, London, Butterworths, p.59.

Newman, J.H. (1987), *The Idea of a University, Defined and Illustrated*, D.O'Donnell (ed), Loyola University Press, Chicago. First published 1853.

O'Neill, G.P. (1991), 'Myths Revisited', 23(1), *Canadian Journal of Higher Education*, 108.

Ramsden, P. (1992), *Learning to Teach in Higher Education*, Routledge, New York.

Rosato, J.L. (1995), 'All I Ever Need to Know About Teaching Law School I Learned Teaching Kindergarten: Introducing Gaming Techniques into the Law School Classroom', 45,

Journal of Legal Education, 568.

Scott, P. (1995), *The Meanings of Mass Higher Education*, Open University Press, Buckingham.

Smith, A. and Webster, F. (1997) (eds), *The Postmodern University?*, Open University Press, Buckingham.

Taylor, K.L. (1993), 'The Role of Scholarship in University Teaching', 23(3), *The Canadian Journal of Higher Education*, 64.

Webb, J. (1996), 'Why theory matters', in J. Webb and C. Maughan (eds), *Teaching Lawyers' Skills*, Butterworths, London, p.23.

Weimer, M. (1997), 'Assumptions that Devalue University Teaching', 2(1), *International Journal for Academic Development*, 52.

Wright, W.A. and O'Neil, C. (1994), 'Perspectives on Improving Teaching in Canadian Universities', 24(3), *Canadian Journal of Higher Education*, 26.

4 Standing at the Crossroads: Law Schools, Universities, Markets and the Future of Legal Scholarship

ANDREW GOLDSMITH

Introduction: Power/Knowledge and the Law School

Law schools, together with other departments of the university, are caught up in what some social theorists call a power~knowledge relation (Haskell, 1996).[1] Our knowledge of the world, on this view, is tied to particular social interests and the exercise of power. The basis of academic authority is no longer so broadly accepted. Public justification of knowledge claims is increasingly called for. Distinct academic cultures and perspectives are found in our universities, which reflect differing positions on these fundamental questions (see Becher,1989). For law school, pressing issues of policy and administration presume positions on matters of institutional and intellectual politics. The "far-reaching shifts in intellectual culture have radical implications for higher education systems" (Scott, 1995). The contingency of knowledge and the politics of higher education are deeply linked.

But this politics and questions of policy have had to contend with a new economic mentality and institutional morality. The economic analysis of university policies and practices has become predominant since the 1970s. It has become the principal logic for policy making and administrative decision making. Law has not been exempted from this analysis. For example, in Australia, law schools have not only had to learn to live on reduced budgets, but have felt obliged to become explicit lobbyists in respect of the level of public funding for legal education (Centre for Legal Education, 1994). There has been disenchantment among university academics about the perceived deterioration in their conditions of work, linked to the new talk of students as consumers and the view of education as a product, rather than as a process. More and more universities seem to be losing their distinctiveness. For many now, "the university has a monopoly of nothing" (Halsey,1992). Traditional conceptions are under direct challenge. The future direction for universities has become less clear. One thing though is clear - the universities must *perform*:

> The decision makers...attempt to manage...according to input/output matrices, following a logic which implies that their elements are commensurable and the whole is determinable. They allocate our lives for the growth of power. In matters of social justice and of scientific truth alike, the legitimation of that power is based on its optimizing the system's performance efficiency. The application of this criterion to all of our games necessarily entails a certain level of terror, whether soft or hard: be operational (that is, commensurable) or disappear.
> (Lyotard, 1984, xxiv)

The transparency of this new language has been questioned by Lyotard and others. Halsey has argued that the "contemporary enthusiasm for the market disguises a politics which permits a wide range of alternatives" (Halsey, 1992 p.259).

In terms of the consequences of *new directions in law teaching* and *support for nontraditional forms of scholarship,* there are signs that those committed to innovation or diversity will be hindered, rather than unleashed, by this ideological shift. The approach I propose to take in looking at the current place of law schools in universities, but also more generally, is to undertake an explicit examination of *legal knowledge*, broadly understood.[2] This focus takes us to such crucial questions as the mission of the law school within the university (the *academic* law degree and legal scholarship), the distinction between an academic legal education and practical training (vocationalism), the compatibility of an academic education with preparation for professional practice (professionalism), and the contribution of legal scholarship to the profession (practice-related research), the wider community (law reform), and the economy (competitiveness). These important questions for law schools are more than simply institutionalist or managerial issues. They raise also intellectual issues of scholarship that should not get lost in the current economic rhetoric. Without preserving analysis of this kind, it is possible that some of the opportunities remaining will get overlooked. Preserving hopefulness in the face of these changes is crucial.

In the next section, the general implications of market ideology for higher education and practice are considered. The various performance measures used will be explored in order to better understand the context in which law schools presently and will operate. Then, I turn to the pedagogical policy debates within the law school environment in order to consider the place of law schools within the universities. Recent enthusiasm for the 'academic' or 'liberal' law degree is examined in the setting of various extemal pressures for vocational training and professional fommation, as well as pressures upon university funding from university cost-cutting and the advent of student consumerism. I also look at the law academic and legal scholarship within the university. In this section, the structural obstacles to greater recognition of legal scholarship are examined, as well as the shortcomings of dorninant conceptions of legal scholarship. These shortcomings, I suggest, are needlessly impractical and uneconomic in nature. It is crucial we do not lose sight of intellectual debates and especially the role of critical reflection in university education, among the demands for relevance, vocationalism, and efficiency in the delivery of legal education.

Bread and Circuses? Universities and Performativity

> Even if the performativity principle does not always help pinpoint the policy to follow, its general effect is to subordinate the institutions of higher learning to the existing powers. The moment knowledge ceases to be an end in itself - the realisation of the Idea or of the emancipation of men - its transmission is no longer the exclusive responsibility of scholars and students. The notion of 'university franchise' now belongs to a bygone era.[3]
> (Lyotard, 1984, p.50)

The Market Meets the University

Anyone working today in universities has come to recognise that we now live in an economist's world. A proficiency in the language of economics has transformed university administrators into managers, and academic leaders into bureaucrats. The ideological subordination of Australian higher education to this logic can be traced very strongly to a fundamental restructuring of government announced by the Federal Govemment in July 1987. Changes to higher education and other sectors have been justified in terms of the government's perceived need for "improved budgetary and corporate management processes" (Pusey, 1991, p.146).[4] This *economic rationalism* or *corporate managerialism* applied to universities reflects the fact that governments have sought to link their economic policies to the more specific processes of teaching, learning, research and management. The key features of corporate managerialism have been:

> ...strong central control associated with devolved responsibility for operations; separation of policy determination from the sphere of devolution; focus on outputs within input-output models of production; emphasis on selling the product. Other features are market-style competition, distribution and exchange; and closer management and measurement of outputs and performance. The techniques of corporate managerialism derive from economics, accounting, human resources management and marketing.
> (Marginson, 1993, p.57)

The philosophical and practical changes to Australian higher education have clearly not been unique to Australia (Miller 1995, Neave and Van Vught 1992, McDaniel 1996, Clark 1983, Kerr 1995). There are common themes, and increasingly, similar experiences. The subjection of higher education more clearly to the ends of the economy is the major example. New forms of government intervention and regulation are increasingly shared.[5] In Australia, government policy announcements to make Australia "the clever country", are heavy with irony for many inside the universities, concerned by dwindling resources, higher student numbers, and a general deterioration of working conditions. It is arguably little different in the public universities of Canada, the United Kingdom, or the United States.

Changes to the university mission, student numbers, staffing levels, curricula, expectations in terms of scholarship, and research performance evaluation, can be linked to the impact of this ideological and managerial shift. There has also been a significant change in the relationship of universities to the state, reflecting government insistence that universities expand to receive a much larger cohort of school leavers into their ranks (universities, once "elite" institutions, have become "mass" institutions), that state support for university research reflect more strongly national economic priorities (greater selectivity, priority given to "applied" over "pure" research), that universities become less dependent upon the state for funding, and therefore more responsible for fund-raising, and, somewhat contradictorily in the eyes of some, that they put in place and implement greater accountability procedures, in particular quality assurance mechanisms for teaching and curricular issues.[6]

Government policy has sought, generally, to try and articulate more closely the realms of education and employment (the erosion of the "academic"/ "vocational" distinction). In political terms, "[t]he most significant change is the shift from a fiduciary state, or the state as trustee of the national interest, to the contractual state or the state as market-maker and over-mighty contractor" (Scott, 1995, p.170).

An Appropriate Model?

The very appropriateness of the 'market' model for higher education has been criticised, drawing attention to the omissions of such a model. The proliferation of universities and university places (the 'massification' of universities) has resulted in a "crowded marketplace mentality", leaving little room for intrinsic learning objectives and professional service:

> If [the universities'] constant challenge is to attract enough fee-paying students to justify their existence, then universities will inevitably retreat from their twin ideals - encouraging the life of the mind and the life of service - and yield to the pragmatism that offers all qualifications as a passport to employment.
> (Mackay, 1997)

The role of universities in promoting vocationalism is a theme with obvious application to law, and will be examined as such later on. The applicability of the market model to human services such as education has been more broadly questioned. Marginson has suggested that given the difficulties defining and measuring outputs and productivity in education, there is the real risk of concentrating excessively on cost-cutting, thus weakening the longer-term productive capacity of education (Marginson, 1993, p.102). Short term goals of efficiency and demonstrable performance (eg being able to show 'competent' behaviour), while suggestive of employment possibilities and productivity gains, do not do justice to the complexities of the world, nor to the longer-term, intrinsic aspirations of higher education (for example, is criticism or reflection efficient? How would you ever show it to be so?). Market dependency forces universities to be highly reactive to fluctuations in student demand, which in turn reflect changes in fashion, current levels of unemployment in particular fields, and perceived job prospects. Other than short-term planning becomes difficult, if not impossible (Miller, 1995, p.34). From an academic perspective, the effect of market domination of universities is likely to be conservative, especially in those institutions more highly dependent upon student demand to survive. It is the new 'mass' universities, rather than the older 'elite' institutions, which will "entrench and legitimate social hierarchies" (Scott, 1995, p.173). Academic autonomy of a creative and independent kind is put at risk if it must be justified by an existing market, or one dominated by student demand alone. In place of the promise of academic vitality provided by "the sceptical articulation of tradition" (Donald, quoted in Marginson, 1993, p.251), we are confronted for the most part by the real probability that students (and their teachers) will confine themselves to "the reverent modification of particulars" (Riesman, quoted in Twining, 1967, p.422). Of course, progressive and radical critics of the traditional law curriculum have for some time accused legal educators of doing precisely this.

A Hierarchy by Different Means

Perhaps the most predictable outcome from the application of the market model is the emergence of clear differentiations between institutions and between different types of courses, resulting in hierarchies of resources and prestige. The expansion of university places by definition increases the number of persons with higher educational qualifications, almost certainly reducing their average value in the marketplace. In an era of high unemployment, students will enrol in those courses at those institutions offering the best employment prospects and social prestige. Burton Clark has noted the practical significance of producing a differentiated, strongly hierarchical, university sector:

> the upper part in a hierarchy of prestige become more professionalised; it is more fully based on arcane knowledge, more involved in peer judgment, more independent of clientele demands, and related market forces. The bottom half, especially the bottom quarter, becomes less professionalised: it is committed to introductory materials that many can teach, more dependent on student reaction than peer approval, and heavily driven by market demands.
> (Clark, 1987, quoted in Halsey, 1992, p.267)

Clark ventures the view that perhaps it "cannot be otherwise in a system of higher education that simultaneously seeks to function under a populist definition of equality, where all are admitted, and also tries to serve the gods of excellence in the creation and transmission of all rarefied bodies of knowledge". Scott has suggested that the mass universities are inherently likely to focus on national, even local issues, rather than participate in more global concerns. Their relative isolation in this sense is driven by their greater dependence upon part-time students, fewer prestige faculties, and dependency upon parochial research concems for research funding (Scott, 1995, p.95).

Similarly, the trend to mass university education has been linked to the increased emphasis given to vocational and professional higher education by government and the marketplace. Inevitably, the value of liberal-arts style higher education is diminished by this shift, as it does not obviously translate into market-related competencies or employment prospects. Even within the liberal arts, there is growing specialisation of courses in the attempt to preserve market share of student enrolments.[7] Student demand for professional degrees in Australia can be linked to government attempts to recoup more of the cost of educating these students through higher fees or student contributions, a measure in fact introduced in Australia in the 1996 Budget (Australia, Department of Employment, Education, Training and Youth Affairs, 1996).

A Decline of Intellectual Nurturing

The degree of intellectual nurturing of talented students in the new 'mass' universities is more limited. Edward Shils argued that substantial increases in size of the student body and the number of staff fundamentally alters the quality of relations between staff and students, between students, and between staff themselves. Inevitably staff morale declines as students and staff find it impossible to get to know each other through face-to-face contacts, and there is a growing alienation of students from their teachers and institutions.[8] An important casualty of this impersonal, large-scale education is the isolated bright student, who finds less encouragement from university staff to develop into a productive scholar or scientist:

> The academic ethic and the scientific ethic are both inculcated through face to face contact and they are maintained at a high level of intensity by such face to face contact. Mutual isolation reduces the pressure generated by the

> presence of other lively, curious and actually and potentially productive minds. The present-day university makes this process of the mutual discovery of talented and interested intellectuals more difficult and it thereby hampers - though it certainly does not prevent - the intensification of intellectual exertion.
> (Shils, 1983, pp.15-16)

Since Shils' report was published in 1983, it is probably generally true that student-staff ratios have not improved, and in many instances, will have declined substantially. In the Australian higher education sector between 1975 and 1992, ratios worsened from 11.7 to 15.3 (McInnis and Marginson, 1994, p.18). While disciplines will vary, with law usually having among the highest staff-student ratios, the overall pattern suggests a significant, probably qualitative change in the nature of higher education over the last twenty five years. One example makes the point. As McInnis and Marginson note about changes to staffing levels at Monash law school in Melbourne, "the resource situation...has deteriorated significantly since 1987", observing that '[d]espite the 39.1% growth in student numbers, the number of academic staff has been virtually constant" (McInnis and Marginson, 1994, p.129). It is at the very least *possible* that academics, while teaching more students, may be offering less in terms of teaching quality, through less face to face contact, and diminished research productivity and quality.

While these implications remain speculative in some degree, it is far from clear that corporate managerialism has been successful in promoting *meaningful* productivity and creativity among staff and students, for example, by encouraging students to go on to do graduate work, or to commit themselves, as practitioners, to public service. A narrow conception of performance threatens to measure nothing of consequence; "[h]umility about the conditions that foster creativity should give us pause before we apply any simplistic reform" (Halsey, 1992, p.265). The 'quality assurance' obligation upon universities is an example of an accountability requirement which has undoubtedly generated greater specificity in reporting obligations and self-evaluation procedures, giving rise to evidence of performance at behaviourally determined levels of competence (Higher Education Council, 1995).[9] However, these measures cannot disguise the decline of face to face contact with teachers, certainly teachers who are able to continue as effective researchers in their respective fields, deteriorating library resources, and other common sense measures of the quality of university education.

Consequences for Law

One effect has been that, consistent with other parts of the university, the number of law students and law schools has expanded considerably in Australia (Parker, 1993), and to a lesser extent, the United Kingdom. There has been no discernible drop-off in the relative attractiveness of law for students entering university. The relative prestige of law as a discipline appears to have been maintained, despite the substantial deterioration in the resource situation. In a worsening employment picture, law graduates remain highly employable by comparison with other graduates. As the grip of the market tightens, we may see even greater differentiation in student demand between different law courses, based upon employment prospects, curricula, resource positions and perceived responsiveness to student needs. Moves toward real-cost fees for university students, including law, may well not influence the attractiveness of law, but rather further skew the composition of the student body in socio-economic elite terms (Zeigert, 1992, p.155).

While vocationalism has always strongly defined law student priorities and expectations, greater student self-consciousness about employment prospects, and the various factors contributing to a more conservative student body, threaten to increase, rather than temper or substantially reduce, previous levels of vocationalism within law schools. That said, the range of employment options taken up by law students today points to vocationalism of a broader kind than simply an interest in preparing for legal practice (Roper, 1995).[10] The viability and attractiveness of a strongly academic degree in this climate is a matter discussed in the next section.

Performativity in universities has also affected the internal administration of law schools. As pressures on resources continue, budgetary responsibilities are devolved and more accountability requirements are imposed, some deans have arguably become more like chief executive officers. These changes have brought with them some of the traditional perquisites of managerial office (salary loadings, university-provided cars etc). Many law academics would echo the general complaint of the decline of collegiality brought about by a shift of management styles (Sheehan, Welch and Lacy, 1996).[11] As law schools become notionally more self-sufficient, there is a clear argument for academic managers to be able to exercise greater managerial prerogatives.[12] More vigorous attacks upon academic tenure and calls for more flexible disciplinary processes suggest a decline of collegiality. Needless to say, these strategies are functional in terms of making staff profiles more directly responsive to budgetary restrictions and student demand.

Perceptions perhaps to the contrary, corporate managerialism is yet to work its way through to the core of all university operations. McInnis and Marginson may be correct in noting that "law has been less visibly touched by the culture of corporate managerialism than have some other parts of higher education - the culture of the legal profession and of academic law are both relatively strong" (McInnis and Marginson, 1994, p31). Still, the trend is clear enough. And, as indicated, in some ways, law schools have anticipated the effects of changes in higher education policy, by already providing strongly professional and vocational programs, operating with high staff-student ratios, and being attractive in the student 'market-place'. In some senses then, they are already well-adapted and positioned to be in the vanguard of the changes sweeping through the universities. All of these changes, however, have done little or nothing to promote a more reflective model of university education in which there is room for the pursuit of fundamental understanding and criticism. This is an elusive and difficult balance in a professional setting; in a utilitarian educational environment geared to the market, the rhetoric of efficiency and its consequences threatens to render it practically invisible. This factor is one reason why the conception of legal knowledge used in law schools requires reconfiguration.

Selling the 'Liberal' Law Degree

> Practically everyone is in favour of liberal education. The enthusiasm is aided by uncertainty and confusion as to what it is.
> (Levi, 1969, p.39)

Ambivalence and Ambiguity

Despite their location within the universities, legal educators tend to be fairly explicit about the priority given within the university law degree to *professional* education. The Dean of Monash University's law faculty was reported as saying that "The Faculty's first obligation is to prepare students for the practice of law and good preparation for the practice of law is knowledge of theory" (Laird, 1996, p.7). This priority was noted among Canadian legal academics in the 1980s by Arthurs: "The primary business of the law schools for most law teachers and deans (and for most law students) is preparation for professional practice" (Arthurs, 1983). Nonetheless, law deans remain conscious of broader obligations by reason of their discipline's membership of the university.

This deep ambivalence is neither new nor surprising. The tension between vocationalism, and the responsibilities of scholarship and higher learning, associated with the university, resurfaces regularly. In a recent statement by the Council of Australian Law Deans on the general aims of legal education, six aims were listed; one only of the aims listed addressed directly the notion of *context* in any vaguely critical respect, referring to the need for law degrees to "appreciate the role of law in society". The other aims referred predictably to the importance of fundamental principles of law, fundamental procedures, fundamental practice skills, as well as the need to "understand and respect the ethical standards of the profession" (Committee of Australian Law Deans, Chapter 3). The ambiguity as well as ambivalence behind such statements tends to preserve the status quo. In the absence of a clear consensus about the goals of legal education, as Levine notes, the simple fact remains that legal doctrine continues to unite what it is that law schools do (Levine, 1993, xvi). An inability or unwillingness to operationalise effectively these alternative goals clearly contributes to this process. Nonetheless, more recent acknowledgements of the need for 'theory', 'humane professionalism', and generic skills, point to a renewed attempt to redefine the place of the law school in the university. These considerations now take place in the climate of university performativity and vocationalism. The 'liberalism' in legal education is likely to be 'market liberalism'.[13]

The fact that the 'role of law school' question arises periodically is itself revealing. In part, it surely reflects the insecurity of a discipline which has, in common law countries such as the United Kingdom, Canada, New Zealand and Australia, only assumed the predominant responsibility for professional legal training since World War Two. There are still some practitioners around who were not required to take such a course in order to practise. Support from the profession is by no means assured. Nor is the nature and contribution of their scholarship well understood.[14] Furthermore, I shall suggest there is often something banal about references to 'liberal' or 'humane' forms of education and scholarship. Many academics would have trouble conceptualising what these terms imply, with the result that there is a failure to pursue the practical, pedagogical implications of these terms. This may even reflect an attempt *at functional ambiguity,* in which law schools try to appear to be "all things to all people". Their continued commitment to *professional* preparation, in conjunction with the use of rhetoric about the virtues of the *academic* degree permits this possible interpretation to remain open.

Justifying Law in the University

Whether or not a 'liberal' law school is even realisable, let alone desirable, the plain fact of the law school's location within the university could not be more clear-cut.[15] Despite Veblen's famous dismissal of the right of law schools to form part of a university ("The law school belongs in the university no more than a school of fencing or dancing", Veblen, 1918, p.211), the reality is that professional schools, in particular law, medicine, and theology, have formed part, if not the foundation of many traditional universities for centuries. In Burton Clark's words, "After eight centuries, it seems time to accept the idea that disciplines and professional fields are inherent in academic life" (Clark, 1995, p.21). The reasons for this *now are* compellingly extrinsic *as* much *as* historical. The massive growth in law student places and numbers of law schools in Australia since 1987 is clearly linked to the fact that law schools offer universities prestigious faculties attracting relatively bright students for comparatively low investment (McInnis and Marginson, 1994, p.16). In market terms, law is a 'performer', even 'efficient'. The market, more than tradition, it seems, will ensure its place in the universities for the forseeable future.

Even so, one senses recently a concerted attempt to define the role of law schools more broadly than simply a preparation for professional (mainly private) practice. The concepts of 'liberalism', 'humane professionalism', 'interdisciplinary', 'critical', 'theoretical' and 'contextual' occur with considerable frequency in recent legal education discourse. Effort to 'liberalise' law schools has led even to the historical nexus between 'black-letter' law, legal education and employment being seriously questioned, if not entirely broken. While some students now find there is no traditional law job necessarily awaiting them after graduation others have commented upon the limits of highly specialised programs. There is much more talk now about the importance of generic skills. Much of the shift away from the notion of the law degree as purely vocational be credited to the influence of a generation of full-time law teachers, typically alienated by their black-letter law educations, pressing for more grounded, contextual forms of legal education. While England has produced William Twining, Canada has had (and continues to have) Harry Arthurs, and Australian legal education has been pushed and provoked by the likes of Jack Goldring.

Broader movements have played their part. Various kinds of interdisciplinarity and paradigm shifts in the humanities and social sciences have impacted upon law, as the influence of feminism, critical theory, and economic analysis attests. The kind of scholarship produced by legal academics is now a financial consideration. Research prestige, in important aspects, increasingly attaches to the amount of money earnt for the institution. As law schools appoint directors of research, and exhort their academics to apply for large grants, the performance of legal scholarship within law schools is increasingly under examination. Moreover, substantial numbers of academics come to law teaching with limited backgrounds in legal practice, while being exposed to theoretical movements outside law. The effect has been a more vigorous questioning of what constitutes legal scholarship, as well as the appropriate relationship between the law school and the rest of the university.[16]

In what follows, I examine three specific inquiries into legal education (one each from Australia, Canada, and the United Kingdom) in terms of what they reveal about current conceptions of a law degree as a generic university education and as a humane preparation for lifelong learning, and the balance to be struck between university aims and those of professional preparation. I want particularly to expose the limits of much of the current rhetoric about liberal law degrees, by calling into question understandings of such basic notions of 'theory' and 'practice', and by drawing attention to the lack of practical development of these notions. In considering why and how the articulations between theoretical knowledge and world of professional practice have been left underdeveloped, we encounter some of the structural factors that make 'bottom line' and consumerist thinking increasingly pervasive and influential in determining higher education policy with respect to law.

Inevitably however, beyond these constraints, are more intrinsic problems, stemming from the persistence of the classical approach to legal education. These problems entail the need for more integrative work between theory and practice, which recognises the inescapable tensions of a university-based professional education. The present absence of theoretical justifications and practical suggestions for a more integrative approach is a reflection of the very deep insecurity that continues to dog the professional identity of legal academics, leaving the traditional, doctrinal approach firmly in charge. In fashioning our 'escapes', we must find ways out that are not illusory, or at least only of limited scope or consequence. It is surely not coincidence, as Schlegel points out, that critical legal studies has more successfully penetrated law schools than the social historical critique of law: "the old is somehow better even in radical dress" (Schlegel, 1984, p.103). Methods for confronting the 'pull of the professional audience' in law require greater thought, attention, and practice (Sarat and Silbey, 1988).

The Arthurs Report: Humane Professionalism

The *Law and Learning* Report ('the Arthurs Report'), released in Canada nearly fifteen years ago, provides a thorough examination, from a Canadian perspective, of the difficulties faced by law schools since the 1960s in moving away from 'classical' or doctrinally-dominated legal education to a more academic curriculum. In many respects, things have arguably not progressed very far since the Report's release. Certainly, some of the obstacles will still seem familiar to many readers.

Despite the claims of Canadian law schools, the Arthurs Report concluded that their aspirations to offer a humane, professional legal education fell short in substance, there being real structural failings in the eclectic curriculum approach (Arthurs, 1983, p.48). Before considering the failings of this approach further, let us note what was meant by 'humane professionalism':

> learning legal rules (what we will call 'doctrine,' recognising the somewhat different common law and civil law connotations of the term) and developing the ability to use the rules; learning legal skills (such as interviewing, advocacy, and negotiation); developing a humane perspective on law, and a deeper understanding of law as a social phenomenon and an intellectual discipline.

(Arthurs, 1983, p.47)

Arthurs adopts a refreshingly candid approach to the situation of the university law school, considering a range of factors that influence the reception given to the 'academic' model of law in Canadian law schools. The point is made that much is assumed, and little is known, about the fit between what constitutes classic legal education and the needs of students. While practising lawyers concede the need to know 'the rules,' Arthurs notes the frequent dissatisfaction with legal education expressed by ex-students, partly because much of the legal knowledge transmitted is not useful in practical terms; equally, much legal work performed by lawyers does not require a broad grasp of underlying principles - it could be performed equally well by paralegals. In some ways, law schools overeducate their students for practice (Arthurs, 1983, p.51), but of course, as the argument from vocationalism asserts, law schools might do far more to integrate their students into practice immediately upon graduation.

Arthurs does not argue that law schools should abandon the objective of professional formation, but rather, that law schools should facilitate both a professional and academic stream. The Report captures well the at times muddied, if well meaning, approach of law schools to the task of defining and offering a diverse legal curriculum. Claims such as the importance of training students to "think like lawyers" are rarely defined or articulated clearly in pedagogically defensible terms (Arthurs, 1983, p.50). The varied uses of the word "theory" in Australian debates, again with little elaborated pedagogical explanation, suggests a generalised degree of discomfiture or plain incapacity among law school leaders still in connecting such claims substantively to the detail of law school practice. As Arthurs notes, "[a]lthough the intellectual issues in law ultimately do confront practitioners and are encapsulated within practical problems, law schools do relatively little to place intellectual issues in this context". An intellectual problem for students "...is seldom intertwined even with other intellectual problems - whether doctrinal or interdisciplinary - and almost always lacks any ethical, tactical, psychological, financial, evidentiary or procedural dimension" (Arthurs, 1983, p.51).

In examining the justifications for an academic model of legal education, Arthurs mixes conviction along with reasoned argument, sounding at times assertively prescriptive rather than persuasive in any detailed, empirically informed sense. Of course, given the paucity of knowledge or even discussion about what lawyers do, and what they need to know, this should not be surprising. Arthurs is very good at outlining the structural factors and temptations surrounding Canadian academics which discourage a scholarly approach to their work (consultancy work, law reform and policy projects, targeted funding for applied legal research, lack of social science research training, absence of cross-faculty appointments etc). Arthurs in fact begs his own question by posing this crucial question: "Suppose law remained almost entirely a body of professional knowledge and did not, as it were, acquire a strong scholarly limb. Who would be the poorer?" (Arthurs, 1983, p.137). He might also have asked, "And who would care?" In making the claim for academic law schools and programs, Arthurs alludes to the "insatiable claims of the world of learning" (Arthurs, 1983, p.59) and to the need for a "distinct science of law" (Arthurs, 1983, p.137). These broad assertions need much development and specification if they are to begin to bring about change at the ground level.

The Report develops its own now well-known four-fold taxonomy of legal research. In addition to doctrinal or conventional research, Arthurs identifies law reform, legal theory, and what is called "fundamental research - research designed to secure a deeper understanding of law as a social phenomenon, including research on the historical, philosophical, linguistic, economic, social or political implications of law" (Arthurs, 1983, pp.65-67). It is also marked "...by its rejection of code, case and statute as the basic and exclusive subject matter of analysis" (Arthurs, 1983, p.69). Arthurs' justification for the importance of fundamental research is ultimately reformist and oriented to the public interest, leading him to conclude: "...this country must begin to take all types of legal research - especially fundamental research 'on' law - much more seriously" (Arthurs, 1983, p.71). He exhorts, indirectly, legal scholars not to be indifferent to the impact of their work in overcoming traditional practitioner resistance to the fruits of scholarship, as "they must have credibility with lawyers" (Arthurs, 1983, p.138). This is an important point, one which I will return to later. At the same time, he well recognises the suspicion held by many practitioners with respect to legal scholarship, and the reason for such feelings. As the Report observes: "It is the job of the scholar to question old assumptions and propose new models, thus striking at one of the very bases of the law's authority, the extent to which it provides society with stability, predictability, and a process of ordered, incremental change. Moreover, innovation can devalue professional skills and habits" (Arthurs, 1983, p. 139).

This is surely also a fundamental point. Until the anti-intellectualism of the profession changes, the content and achievements of law school education is unlikely to move in the direction Arthurs would like. There is almost a forlorn air to Arthurs' recognition that scholarly teaching and research is often defended on the ground that they "...will help lawyers better discharge their professional responsibilities" (Arthurs, 1983, p.98). In the 1990s, one must surely respond to this point that this justification is hardly exceptionable, so long as the notion of professional responsibility is not approached uncritically, and that indeed, one could wish for more effort to be made to make the extrinsic merits of scholarly, 'fundamental' research more transparent and compelling to the law student 'consumers'. Where more thought is needed is in terms of developing a more self-questioning form of legal professionalism, in which "...critical understanding, not adherence or discipleship, whether uncritical or critical, is the criterion" (Pelikan, 1992, p.161). In order to persuade the professional sceptics, we must become stronger in our articulation and defence of a critical professionalism, one which points (yes, instrumentally) to the creative and lateral thinking dimensions inherent in such an approach, as well as to the contribution to be made to deepening notions of understanding and professional ethics. In other words, it is incumbent upon us to show precisely *how* professional knowledge would be poorer without a "...strong scholarly limb", and why we should care about such things.

The ACLEC Report: Independent Liberal Education

Inevitably perhaps, the latest advocates of the academic law degree in the United Kingdom reveal a distinct pragmatism. The nature of legal education is undergoing a process or redefinition (or at least, a kind of reassertion) in the face of high student demand and declining job opportunities in many areas. Recommendation 4.6 of the Lord Chancellor's Advisory Committee on Legal Education and Conduct ('ACLEC') is that "...the degree course should stand as an independent liberal education in the discipline of law, not tied to any specific vocation" (ACLEC, 1996). The pretensions for law schools to form an integral part of the university are quite evident. The Committee professes to move beyond the Ormrod Report position of the early 1970s (which argued the importance of law being taught within universities) to take account of changes in legal services and higher education. It offers what it describes modestly as a "...necessarily superficial general statement of what legal education and training should aim to achieve" (ACLEC, 1996, p.24). The five categories (which are defined by the Report in turn) are: intellectual integrity and independence of mind; core knowledge; contextual knowledge; legal values; and professional skills.

While a variety of influences upon this policy conclusion are clear, including the American Bar Association's McCrate Report (American Bar Association, 1992) and the British Academy, a book chapter by Professor Dawn Oliver of University College, London was clearly important in developing the Committee's thinking about the academic content and justification for the university law degree as a preparation for a variety of careers (Oliver, 1994). The Committee placed considerable weight upon Oliver's statement that "[a] liberal education will have as an aim that students should not merely know or know how to but to understand why things are as they are and how they might be different", and her stress (drawing from recent educational theory) upon the value of 'deep' learning, in which students "...try to relate ideas in one subject to those in others, to understand what they read, questioning material, making links, pursuing lines of inquiry out of interest" (Oliver, 1994, p.78).

As well as the need for students to develop intellectual integrity, the Committee not unexpectedly saw the continued importance of *core knowledge*, what might otherwise be referred to as legal doctrine and method, of vocationally oriented *professional skills*, which included "...learning to act like a lawyer", and of *legal values* (here, echoing McCrate) defined in terms of such commitments as to the rule of law, justice, fairness, high ethical standards, to the improvement of professional skills and to ensuring the provision of adequate legal services. *Contextual knowledge* "...involves an appreciation of the law's social, economic, political, philosophical, moral and cultural contexts" which "...may be acquired in part by the study of legal subjects in a law degree in their relevant contexts, or by taking a non-law or mixed degree which provides these perspectives" (ACLEC, 1996, p.24). The ACLEC Report, without elaborating the forms of contextual knowledge or their particular connections to an academic legal education, did indicate approval for a pluralistic approach to legal scholarship.

However, beyond this 'broad church' approach, the Report also placed considerable emphasis on the "...knowledge and transferable skills which enable them to think, in a critical way, as creative lawyers" (ACLEC, 1996, p.55). While noting the need to "...resist the temptation to provide a definitive list of abstract transferable skills and common professional values" (ACLEC, 1996, p.79), an attempt was made to list examples of intellectual skills that should be provided by the law degree. Their generic quality is highly striking, showing a clear strategic attempt to define relevant skills very differently from how previous generations of law teachers might have conceived the issue. By definition, of course, these skills might be found in other 'liberal' degrees. It might be observed that many of the skills would best be taught in small group form (eg oral communication, intelligent, critical reading of texts, and construction of logical argument), a manner of teaching delivery increasingly elusive in straightened financial times. In response to the resource implications of the kind of education she endorses, Oliver does discuss briefly a number of options, including group work, self-assessment, and the use of case studies.

One interesting aspect of ACLEC's use of Oliver's paper is the largely implicit notion of 'liberalism' underlying both positions. For Oliver, it seems to amount largely to reduce to the encouragement of questioning and independent thought, to which she adds the notion of transferable skills. Certainly, she seeks to preserve the connection between liberal education and vocational training, even in technical skills, but to stress the priority of "...understanding and intellectual skills" (Oliver, 1994, p.79). She asks whether a law degree with these priorities is a "luxury the country or the profession can ill-afford?" Few will be surprised by her answer, of course. But she adds, beyond its contribution to dealing with legal problems, a contextual liberal legal education will give students "...insights into and understandings of the processes and other disciplines associated with law - dispute resolution, politics, sociology psychology" (Oliver, 1994, p.95). Another contributor to the ACLEC Report, Professor Bob Hepple, sees the model adopted in the Report as a revival or renewal of a law degree tradition, predating the more vocationally oriented law degree. For Hepple, as indeed for Oliver and the ACLEC committee generally, it is a mistake to define a 'liberal' legal education differently from a professional or vocational one (Hepple, 1996, p.480). He invokes the authority of Blackstone, Amos, Maitland, Kahn-Freund and Gower for the proposition that a subject may be of practical value, yet still be suitable for university purposes. How matters of practical significance can be rendered in a 'liberal' or 'academic' manner, thus satisfying law's 'double constituency', is a critical consideration. Another practical hurdle lies in overcoming the resistance of many traditional 'classic' legal educators to anything that smacks of practice.

Hepple puts forward five perspectives a student should consider if she is to undertake the integration of theory and practice necessary for a liberal degree (Hepple, 1996, p.480). These are, in effect: legal reasoning, social science training, comparative law, theory or philosophy, and ethics. There is diversity and breadth, as well as some considerable ambition, in the range of approaches Hepple recommends. Leaving aside the logistical challenges presented by so much contextual material, there is the question of student demand. If we teachers and scholars are still struggling to develop methods of connecting 'theory' with 'practice', how may we presume to persuade students of the extrinsic, let alone intrinsic, virtues of a liberal education? Anticipating scepticism from the profession, he asks "...the doubters to trust the universities and to put their faith in the market" (Hepple, 1996, p.480). As a university teacher, I may be disposed to trust the university (more perhaps than many practitioner), but I do wonder whether Professor Hepple and I might be shopping at different markets. For, as he recognises himself, students are "...canny when it comes to opting for the knowledge and skills which will be most useful to them in finding jobs".

The power of student socialisation to determine the market value of different legal educational 'goods' is very real.[17] Any law student will tell you which law subjects are 'worth' more than others; sociology of law, comparative law, and jurisprudence do not perform well in what is a (perhaps intellectually stunted, but still real) student moral and financial 'economy' of legal education. While an integrated academic law degree may well, as Hepple suggests, produce better lawyers, this remains a matter of persuasion within our pedagogical practice, and indeed in our scholarship. Selling this vision of law is by no menas straightforward, given what Marginson has called the crisis in liberal education - "...education is often irrelevant either to work or to vocational selection". "Mostly", he adds, "the academic curriculum is unable to simulate (or even anticipate) work" (Marginson, 1993, p.147). If this situation persists for whatever reasons, student demand for vocational realism, and the recruitment practices of private law firms will continue to dominate conceptions of the law degree.[18]

The Pearce Report: Theoretical and Critical Perspectives

The past decade has been an unusually self-conscious time for Australian university law schools. In the mid-1980s, a committee of three law professors undertook a comprehensive discipline review of law in Australian higher education, under the auspices of the Commonwealth Tertiary Education Commission. Chaired by Professor Dennis Pearce, its tasks were to look at higher education institutions teaching law for professional admission purposes, as well as the Department of Legal Studies at La Trobe University. The issues to be examined included: the appropriate aims and objectives for the provision of legal education in contemporary Australian society, the nature and quality of courses, teaching standards, contributions of law staff to law reform and the needs of the government, community and profession, current deficiencies, and the effectiveness of resource utilization (Pearce et al, 1987, p.4). Its four volume report in 1987 included a range of recommendations and suggestions. Seven years later, the Pearce Report was followed by the publication of an evaluation of the effects of the Pearce review, *Australian Law Schools After the 1987 Pearce Report* (McInnis and Marginson, 1994). Inevitably, the relationship of the law school to the university arose in these examinations.

The first suggestion made by Pearce was that "...all law schools examine the adequacy of their attention to theoretical and critical perspectives, including the study of the relations between law and other forces" (Pearce et al, 1987, Vol. 1, p.12). By implication, this statement presumably applies as well to the range of research undertaken by law academics within the university, for the suggestions on research were largely directed to matters of time, training, research centres and research cooperation. A degree of ambivalence or uncertainty about the location of legal education and scholarship within the university is suggested by their stated position that "law schools should accept and actively pursue *to some extent* the major goals of universities in contributing to teaching research and community service" (Pearce et al, 1987, Vol. 1, p.56). Elsewhere in the report, Pearce indicates an acceptance of the role of universities in the provision of legal education, stating that as well as the organisation, transmission and advancement of knowledge, it is appropriate to be concerned with the "...cultivation of the skills of a high order which the practice of a profession requires". In addition then to the university's "critic and conscience of society" role, responsiveness to community needs warrants active involvement in professional formation (Pearce et al, 1987, Vol. 1, pp. 22-23).

The position Pearce takes in striking this balance anticipates, in many respects, the position taken by the ACLEC committee. In terms of the law school curriculum:

> Law school education should not be limited just to imparting knowledge of the law...there is room for the criticism of some law schools and some areas of their curricula that they are too rule-oriented...We agree...that law programs should be concerned with theoretical and critical dimensions, on the one hand, and also to impart understanding of the law in action, on the other. We add that law schools should seek to develop in students intellectual skills and some other skills.
> (Pearce et al, 1987, Vol.1, p.57)

Pearce later went on to provide their list of intellectual skills, including such generic skills as reasoning, analysis, critical thought and inquiry, research skills, and the application of theory, policy and information to problems (Pearce et al, 1987, Vol.1, p.58). The committee found "plenty of common ground which can form the basis of a cooperative enterprise" between universities and professional needs. It effectively endorsed sociologist David Reisman's statement that this was warranted by society's need for "...a supply of professionals who are at home in critical scholarship". This led to the conclusion that the "...university concerns discussed earlier in relation to the organisation and transmission of knowledge, critical evaluation and the development of intellectual skills can blend well with important aspects of professional education". The limits to cooperative scholarship and teaching of this kind related, for the committee, to "...coverage of detail of the law and some practical training" (Pearce et al, 1987, Vol.1, p.34). In terms of the scope of professionalism and the aptitudes and skills deemed appropriate for a university law degree, the Committee adopted the view that it is the law school role to prepare graduates for a range of careers in government and the private sector, as well as for the profession (Pearce et al, 1987, Vol.1, p.58). This acknowledgement of the uses of the law degree was to anticipate a trend in the justifications for the continued expansion of legal education in Australia after 1987.

A significant finding by Pearce was the limited degree of understanding and implementation among law schools in regard to theoretical questions. The Committee was told that many law courses, despite their claims, remained rule-oriented and haphazard in their use of theory in teaching (Pearce et al, 1987, Vol.1, p.106). They did not endorse the compulsory 'theory' course model, as it distracted from a more integrated approach to the introduction of theory to the curriculum. Without using the terminology, the Committee effectively embraced a pluralistic, 'pervasive' approach to the teaching of theory. In addition to critical considerations derived from social, political and moral theories, the Committee supported the use of social science materials for the purposes of legal understanding (Pearce et al, 1987, Vol.1, p.105).

In their review of Pearce's impact, McInnis and Marginson considered its influence on the teaching of critical perspectives as part of Australian legal education. They found that most schools now attached "considerable importance" to the critical examination of legal issues in their social context, while noting that the expression and emphasis varies (McInnis and Marginson, 1994, p.181). The pre-1987 law schools reviewed by Pearce had shown an increased interest in these perspectives, without always attributing this shift precisely to the Pearce position. Many of the newer schools acknowledged the contribution of Pearce to their thinking in developing their curricula. The authors also examined the influence of Pearce upon the degree of commitment shown by law schools to professional education and preparation for other kinds of work, and found general support for "the broader goals of a university education and lifelong learning" (McInnis and Marginson, 1994, p.156). In terms of changes in research related to law, reflecting the nature of the Pearce recommendations, McInnis and Marginson concentrated upon issues of process and support, rather than upon changes of substance per se. While adverting to the limited consideration given by the Committee to questions of epistemology and the diversity of critical approaches to law, the authors merely note that debates on such questions have "exploded beyond the bounds set by the Pearce Committee" (McInnis and Marginson, 1994, p.181).

In talking up the notion of the 'liberal law degree', it can be argued there is an attempt to simultaneously recast the 'professional' or 'vocational' component of the law degree as much as the desire to promote fundamental understanding and critique. The diminishing nexus between a law degree and professional practice is a product of student demand for law school places as well as of changes in employment patters and career aspirations. The promotion of generic skills and other broader, yet pragmatic, conceptions of the law degree is responsive to continued demand for places in law despite a more uncertain job market. It is difficult to know how meaningful the academic conception of law is for students so long as the pathway to professional legal practice remains open. Without a better understanding of how it is operationalised and valued by students and their future employers, the significance of this aspiration remains an open issue.

I shall argue in the remaining sections that the debate about the academic law degree needs to progress beyond general endorsements and bland aspirational statements, to show *how* they can be offered, ie how an education that self-consciously examines and criticises the conventions and current practices of the profession using a variety of scholarly techniques. Promoting "context" in general terms, or offering discrete courses in "theory", however conceived, within the traditional degree will not suffice. We must find ways of enabling law students to participate in their social worlds "without suspending [their] critical faculties or surrendering to the hallucinatory identification of the actual with the necessary" (Unger, 1987). Ironically, in order to achieve this, "practice" and "the world" must become more significant.

Academic Lawyers and University Research

> "He was a lawyer, not an intellectual."
> (Hill, 1965)

While Shakespeare, Dickens, and others have held practising lawyers in some contempt, it is not clear that academic lawyers have fared much better. Their scholarship and research remains little understood by others, and is accorded little public recognition or value. As Tony Becher's UK study of academic culture discovered:

> The predominant notion of academic lawyers is that they are not really academic - one critical respondent described them as "arcane, distant and alien; an appendage to the university world". Their personal qualities are

> dubious; they are variously represented as vociferous, untrustworthy, immoral, narrow, arrogant and conservative, though kinder eyes see them as impressive and intelligent. Their scholarly activities are thought to be unexciting and uncreative, comprismg a series of intellectual puzzles scattered among "large areas of description".
> (Becher, 1989, p.30)

Hardly surprisingly, self-esteem can be a problem. Becher found that "[t]his generally negative view seems to be shared by its victims, a number of whom diagnosed a common 'tendency towards self-denigration' and 'a sense of doubt about one's intellectual quality'" (Becher, 1989, p.30). Becher reports that an acknowledged insulation from other disciplines, and a narrowly conceived and isolated education were linked to this problem.

Low Regard

Why should this be? A range of factors might be suggested. There is the low regard in which academics are held by the community at large, and by their political masters. The utilitarian ideology of modern government, and a more general anti-intellectualism, expressed for example, in the common preference for "practical" over "theoretical" explanations, do not make it easy for academics. Even the esteem shown by members of the practising branch cannot be assumed. In a practitioners' world, "applied" legal research is more likely to be valued than more speculative or fundamental kinds. According to Schlegel, the fragile egos of law academics incline them to seek recognition from the appellate judiciary, whose preferred form of legal scholarship is doctrinal, or at least anything geared to assisting them (Schlegel, 1992, p.613). There would seem to be few rewards or incentives for theoretically-driven, or openended empirical, inquiry among the quotidian concerns of practising lawyers and judges.

Research Orientation

Within the academy itself, the still low number of legal academics with doctorates, or even higher degrees, presumably affects perceptions of the discipline, especially in the elitist world of universities. In many instances, humanities or social scientific academics will have spent six or seven years in graduate school, socialising them into a research culture and outlook. Their intelligence aside, there is no apparent reason to presume law graduates with postgraduate coursework qualifications or experience in legal practice will be particularly suited to academic research. In contrast to the laboratory sciences, the reticence of legal academics to collaborate in research projects means that they typically find it more difficult to be recognised by funding bodies. In turn, this lack of grants record distinguishes them, on the whole, from members of other disciplines whose research traditions more successfully incline them towards obtaining research funds. Law academics tend to face a hard time in university research committees, explaining to their colleagues in other disciplines, especially in such fields as medicine and science, the relatively paltry amounts earned for the university through legal research grants. In a world geared strongly to recognition and reward for performance, law faces an uphill challenge.

'Not Real Research'

More fundamentally, the nature of legal research itself must assume much of the blame. Academic lawyers are probably all too familiar with the frequent astonishment shown by acquaintances (including other academics) when it is explained that there is something called legal research or scholarship. Whether an outsider, suitably informed about of what legal scholarship consists (traditionally, an ability to find and explain cases and statutes, and some dabbling at law reform), would think such activities sound worthy enough pastimes, if somewhat prosaic, is difficult to know. However, they are more likely to be impressed, I think, by notions of scientific discovery or aesthetic creativity. By being grounded in particulars and ambiguities of meaning, legal knowledge is inherently 'soft' rather than 'hard', lacking the firmness of the natural world and the rigour of scientific method. Despite its claims to formalism, it is ultimately 'applied' rather than 'pure', being required to demonstrate its value in a constantly changing environment where individual differences assume practical significance. Lacking also its more transparent economic justifications, law misses out on public support for university research which tends still to favour the hard sciences. Law, like education and social work, remains stigmatised as one of the softer social sciences. As Bok observes, "In the social sciences,...there is no real public consensus on the value of research and advanced education so that such work is far more vulnerable to partisan political pressures" (Bok, 1990, p.119).

This perception is not unassailable. After all, law has proved to be an important ingredient of economic restructuring under economic rationalist government policies. The involvement of lawyers in privatisation of utilities, and generally in competition policy initiatives, stand out as two examples. However, for whatever reasons, lawyers have been slow, within the universities, to capitalise on these changes in terms of their research efforts. There is the impression, at least, that economists and persons with management degrees have taken the lead in areas like regulation, leaving lawyers well behind. A more general tendency for the corporate and government sectors to go elsewhere for much of their policy-geared research, to independently funded think tanks or to consultancy arms of multinational accountancy firms has not assisted the perceptions of academic lawyers as a knowledgeable group. Does this reflect a principled reluctance by legal academics to sully their hands in matters of government or commerce? My guess is "hardly". One must return to the dominant conception of legal scholarship, what it implies about research and teaching, and to its entrenched representation in the undergraduate law school curriculum.

Hegemonic Legal Scholarship

What law schools teach, while in part being a reflection of what it is legal academics spend their research and writing time doing, is clearly more broadly geared to the expectations of students, and to the *idea* of preparation for professional practice. The doctrinal focus of much legal research, reflects a particular conception of practice, as well as what constitutes appropriate instruction for law students intent on lives in practice. Its failure to mirror the day to day nature of legal practice of most law graduates is, in a sense, beside the point. Its dominance perpetuates a particular conception, or *tradition*, of professional formation. This means that the particular community constituted by the law school imposes limits upon the kinds of scholarship possible which is reflected in the mainstream curriculum:

> The very sense of community which law schools have... has to some extent dampened the interest in new experiments and new directions by individual faculty on their own, backed by the kind of research support which in one way or another is made available in other areas. And this indeed is strange

> with a subject as complicated and varied as law is, where the interdisciplinary work for one corner may be quite irrelevant in its lesson for work in another. (Levi, 1969, pp 120-121)

This leads Levi to suggest that "[p]erhaps we should give less attention to what law schools do and give greater encouragement to law professors to do as they please" (Levi, 1969, pp.120-121). While this idea might work for some, for law professors long inured to the demands of a judiciary and law students for 'relevant' (ie doctrinal) legal knowledge, it would require a gestalt switch of considerable proportions.

Encouraging law academics to do as they please seems an unlikely scenario in the current climate. There is still the obstacle of the curriculum, whatever legal academics may do in their research projects. Schlegel has pointed to the difficulty shown even by avowedly radical legal academics in moving away from doctrine. So long as this remains the picture, the gulf between legal scholarship and other kinds of research done in the university will persist. Schlegel's suggestion for overcoming the dominance of doctrinal scholarship amounts, in effect, to *curricular courage*:

> [D]ozens of people know that criminal law is not a matter of mens rea and criminal procedure, not a matter of constructing the Bill of Rights, yet not one of those people has killed those two courses and instead offered a course in policing an underclass. Until we, the purveyors of the new scholarship, have the courage to scrap the categories of legal instruction bequeathed to us as a result of the nineteenth century reorganization of law study that accompanied the demise of the writ system and instead organize legal study in ways suggested by our own scholarship, we will continue to be accomplices in the present marginality of that scholarship.
> (Schlegel, 1992, p.609)

The puzzle in the present economic and social climate is how such a vision might be given effect. Demands for utility and relevance in university education makes such a change unlikely. There remains, in principle, the possibility that legal educators and scholars will find ways of persuading the student 'market' that what has been perceived as 'relevant', 'essential for practice', etc, is only one very small part of what a utilitarian-minded law student requires from a university law school, and that, even more importantly, there is a realm of critically and empirically informed research *about* law that contributes to the understanding, critique and practice of law itself. The record of legal academics persuading their students of the relevance of theory for practice for extrinsic, never mind intrinsic, reasons is poor. There is little point as a teacher intoning ritualistically that 'theory is good for you' if you do not accept the proposition or understand how it might be demonstrated to students. There is a Catch-22 element to changing this scenario. Without the right kinds of scholarship available, teaching is more likely to remain the same. As a law academic, one will only engage in scholarship more reflective of traditional university ideals and expectations if one is able to show a real, albeit critical grasp, of the world of practice in one's theorising and other forms of scholarship. Fundamental legal research must be brought into closer relation to the concerns of law students. Through theorising about practice and through field-based learning, law students may be moved closer to the goals of understanding and criticism.[19]

The Pull of the Professional Audience: What Might Be Done

The pressures upon university law schools from performativity and vocational expectations do not make the mission of innovative teaching in a liberal curriculum, or the pursuit of non-doctrinal research, any easier. Conversely, the hegemony of the traditional approaches to learning and research remains unthreatened by the demands of law's "professional audience", law students intent on qualifying for practice, practising lawyers seeking graduates adequately trained for legal jobs, and the wider constellation of government, industry and the community which places a premium upon vocationalism in higher education (Bok, 1990, p.119). The tension in the law school's role is inextricably linked to its continued responsiveness to the "professional audience" I have described. Unless this can be fundamentally changed, an unlikely prospect in the present climate, the nature of professionalism, the demands for vocational education, and the current ways of doing legal scholarship need to be addressed directly. In what follows, I identify some strategies for attempting change to law schools and their environments which are both mindful of the environment, and of the importance of integrating the law school further into the broader educational and scholarly objectives of the university.

Tackling the Law School Culture

Law schools, like other professional schools, tend to have distinct cultures (Clark, 1983, p.79). This distinctiveness in part lies structurally in the separateness of law studies from the rest of the university. Law students tend to follow a common core program geared to admission requirements. Students in other subject areas have traditionally been prevented from taking law subjects. One effect is to distance the concerns of law students from other students. Even those students doing joint degrees, or who are already graduates in other disciplines, seem quickly to learn the law school way of doing things (see for example Granfield, 1992). The lack of contact with nonlaw students is compounded by the lack of bridging courses designed to help students integrate their non-law studies with their law subjects. Training in other areas goes largely unacknowledged, while learning to "think like a lawyer" is given priority. The fact that student interest in vocational preparation may reinforce this process does not obscure the fact that the law schools pay scant regard to the other areas of education or training of their students. I will say more later about specific structural changes for altering this picture.

The objective of taking on the separateness of law as a discipline or field of practice is not to pretend that the law schools will serve as a vanguard in the unseating of law's professional status. It is rather to promote a kind of constructive engagement with, or selfconsciousness about, professional formation. The substantive content of legal education (skills, values, attitudes, propositional knowledge) should not simply conform to the present priorities and practices of the profession. Here, I share Levi's view that "...the professional school which sets its course by the current practice of the profession is...a failure" (Levi, 1969). The difficult course is to steer a path between professional irrelevance and unquestioning professional reproduction.[20] This balance might be reflected in different concepts or techniques.

One way of thinking about this challenge is in terms of Lionel Trilling's distinction between *ideas* and *ideology.* An idea, for Trilling, arises when two emotions are placed in juxtaposition, establishing a dialectic which leads the mind to some sort of conclusion. By contrast, ideology is not a product of thought; "...it is the habit or the ritual of showing respect for certain formulas to which, for various reasons having to do with emotional safety, we have very strong ties of whose meaning and consequences in actuality we have no clear understanding" (Trilling, 1950, p.286). This distinction is represented by Trilling in different ways. For example, he contrasts the "traditional and aggressive rationalism" of some writers with the "humility and wisdom" of others, who "seldom make the attempt at formulated solution, they rest content with the 'negative capability"', referring to Keats' concept of "the willingness to remain in uncertainties, mysteries and doubts" (Trilling, 1950, pp.298-299). These are concepts which do not readily comport with highly rational, means-end notions of professional legal practice, nor easily with vocationally-minded traditional legal curricula. After all, 'thinking like a lawyer' ought not to lead to uncertainties or mysteries. Should it?

What Kinds of Scholarship?

Of course there is an obvious means-end implication to vocationally oriented scholarship and education. What law schools and the profession need to endorse openly and without apology is the legitimate place of *idealism* within university-based legal education. In order to *act* decisively or responsibly in the world, one needs also to *be*, in other words, to exist in a situated, existential sense. More than this, however, one needs to *understand*, which implies the capacity to empathise with others, to see different points of view, at least to some extent. This is obviously closely linked to the exercise of *tolerance*. These are personal, practical qualities as much as they are topics capable of study in an academic sense. My suggestion for how this balance might be achieved through scholarship, paradoxically perhaps for some, is to attempt to push scholars much closer to the daily concerns of lawyers in real life, to taking seriously, and theoretically, the practice of law.[21]

To achieve this, law schools must break the hold of doctrine upon teaching and research. So long as teaching and researching 'the rules' remains the essence of legal scholarship, it will continue to attract the disapprobrium of other scholars. It will also continue to fail to serve the ultimate vocational needs of the students, by neglecting aspects of the law in action which are more familiar to the practising lawyer than the cases contained in the latest appellate law reports. It may be, then, that the profession can be made to appreciate the function served by moving legal education away from such a strong dose of doctrine. One way of doing this, without abandoning the comfortable habits of law teaching altogether, is to promote the *contextualisation of doctrine*. By this, I mean that the historical emergence of particular doctrines might be shown, to establish their *contingency*; also, the *social interests* served by particular case law or statutory developments might be made explicit, in part by drawing attention to the *consequences* of legal actions.[22] In these ways, the students can be encouraged to undertake evaluations of doctrinal developments on a deeper basis than simplistic 'policy' analysis. Varieties of social, economic and political theory would clearly be useful for these purposes. Cross-faculty teaching and collaborative research on areas of doctrinal significance might assist legal academics in developing these kinds of orientation to doctrinal scholarship.

Of course, attention to consequences and interests presupposes a body of knowledge throwing light upon these issues. In addition to the kinds of excursions into, or borrowings from, other theoretical disciplines, the 'stuff of life' itself is always, and pertinently, available for empirical study and experiential learning. Moving away from doctrine leads to the consideration of legal phenomena and the law in action. A deeper understanding of the law in action might arise through systematic study of particular legal agencies or areas of social life where questions about law arise. The legal scholar thus enters the world of the practitioner, as well as the world of her client and others affected by legal actions. An outcome ought to be an evaluation of legal practices of potential value to practitioners as well as to the world at large. As for law students, an immersion in the law in action, if structured properly with appropriate mentors and guidance on what to look for and how to behave, ought to provide an opportunity to develop deeper understandings not just of the environment in which the law operates, but also of the efficacy and fairness of the law's operation. The current pattern for law students to study law with little or no exposure to legal settings does not make teaching *about* (or even *in)* law any easier. Moving law academics and their students into the field provides them both with a greater personal appreciation of what the profession of law means in practical terms. It also will equip them with materials, sources, ideas, and values which can be linked to their research and teaching interests in novel, rewarding ways. Experiences in or about law should give rise to ideas, to use Trilling's term, rather than simply the dull habits of ideology.

What Kinds of Law Schools?

The demands that the university more closely serve the needs of the community, and the current attenuation of the substantive links between those law schools serve and the practising profession, beg question about the present breadth of ends served by traditional law schools. So long as student demand is defined in terms of those seeking admission to practice, as members of an exclusionary law program, then it will be difficult as a practical matter to redefine the client community of law schools more broadly, or to modify law school aims and objectives. However, in seeking this change, there is arguably a paucity of alternative models for law schools to follow, limiting the imaginative possibilities of those working in law schools. Therefore, William Twining's championing of what he calls the International Legal Center (ILC) model merits further thought.

The essence of this idea is the establishment of law schools explicitly geared to a wider range of audiences, whilst preserving a commitment to research of different kinds. It is summarised in the following passage from the ILC's *Legal Education in a Changing World*:

> Law schools, perceived as multipurpose centres, can develop human resources and idealism needed to strengthen legal systems; they can develop research and intellectual direction; they can address problems in fields ranging from land reform to criminal justice; they can foster the development of indigenous languages as vehicles for the administration of law; they can assist institutions involved in training paraprofessionals; they can help to provide materials and encouragement for civic education about law in schools and more intelligent treatment of law in the media; they can organise, or help organise, advanced specialised legal education for professionals who must acquire particular kinds of skills and expertise.
> (Quoted in Twining, 1995, p.297)

As Twining points out, this model addresses the constituency needs of the practising profession, whilst retaining greater independence from the profession by its wider clientele base. It also has a more explicit commitment to the academic ethic than professional schools (Twining, 1995).

This is obviously an ambitious model for many law schools to contemplate, given their relative size. It is also a highly challenging one for those academics accustomed to serving elite bunches of students intent on the practice of law. However, it just might offer better 'performance' and greater 'efficiency', by offering a way of opening up law schools to a broader client base, offering the possibility of more resilient and cost-effective demand for law courses. In addition, it promises a diverse range of scholarly research in areas not confined to the doctrinal preoccupations of the appellate judiciary. As Twining suggests, "Academic lawyers are much more likely to make useful contributions to legal practice and legal development, as well as to more general understandings, if their routine professional activities are not confined to primary education and deal with all aspects of law in our interdependent world" (Twining, 1995, p.303). Within a structure of this kind, ways would still be need to be found for forging stronger connections with academics in other disciplines. Once the functions of the law school are shown to be broader than the analysis of doctrine, then the possibilities for joint teaching and research become real and numerous. The "needs of the community", as well as reconfigured notions of the "needs of practising lawyers", to include theorising about practice, both suggest ways of building a stronger constituency for legal scholarship of a more diverse, imaginative, and critical kind.

Conclusion

The future direction of legal education and scholarship is likely to remain a matter for selfexamination and public debate.[23] Within the current climate of university performativity, there are some opportunities as well as challenges and threats. It cannot be doubted that law schools stand in a position of considerable advantage in terms of student demand and enrolments. The specific challenge for re-positioning the law school more squarely within the aims of a liberal or humalle university regime lie in moving away from the expectations of the present consumers. This might best occur by supplementing, and complementing, these expectations by the addition of new, more diverse functions to the law schools. Legal knowledge, conceived as a functional necessity for highly trained employees in a variety of areas, as well as a fundamental baseline for the meaningful exercise of civil, political and economic rights, should attract broader support than the patently elitist and narrow ends of preparation of students for practice in the (predominantly private) profession. Law academics should be orienting themselves and their scholarship outwards to the world as well as to their students (they are not coterminous), and thus to tackling a narrow, often misplaced and misconceived functionalism about the nature of law and legal practice. The notion of the academic law degree, if taken seriously, should make law schools more aware that law's audience is wider than simply its vocationally minded students or the present profession.

Notes

1. This idea is usually attributed to the work of Michel Foucault. See Gordon (1980).
2. In focusing upon 'legal knowledge', I intend to construe this organizing concept broadly to embrace practical wisdom as well as abstract propositional knowledge (for some, 'theory') and applied practical knowledge, including matters of technique. For the record, I shall also quote T.S. Elliot on the topic: "Where is the wisdom we have lost in knowledge? Where is the knowledge we have lost in information?" (from The Rock). See for example Hepple (1996).
3. Lyotard uses 'performativity' to refer to the standard that has replaced 'truth' in science. He describes it as being "the best possible input/output equation" (Lyotard, 1984, p.46). In terms of the power/knowledge relation, it is associated with applied, rather than 'pure' research. On this view, "...scientists, technicians and instruments are purchased not to find truth, but to augment power" (Lyotard, 1984).
4. Specifically in the case of education, as Pusey (1991) points out in conjunction with this policy change, an economics graduate, John Dawkins, replaced the then Minister of Education, Susan Ryan, an arts graduate, as Minister of a new super-Ministry of Employment, Education and Training. Minister Dawkins' Green Paper on higher education later the same year symbolised for Pusey the mounting government pressure for a "Thatcher-like commodification of the tertiary education system" (Pusey, 1991, p.148).
5. For example, UK university policy makers have visited Australia recently, *inter alia* to examine the Higher Education Contribution Scheme, under which students effectively pay a tax covering a portion of the actual cost of their studies. Other examples could be found of such borrowings.
6. Miller (1995, p.54) notes that "...whatever the free market rhetoric, there has been an increasing tendency in the 1980s and 1990s for the state to intervene in regulating the activities of universities".

7. In my own institution, the B.A. degree, with majors in traditional disciplines such as history, politics or psychology, is being increasingly replaced by 'named' bachelors degrees, for example, Bachelor of Cultural Tourism, Bachelor of International Business, and Bachelor of Behavioural Science.
8. One can only speculate about the likely negative effects of mass higher education on the future financial returns of alumni fundraising campaigns. It hardly seems likely that former university students will dig deep into their pockets for institutions which provided them with poorly resourced, highly impersonal forms of university education. Given the apparent boom in university counselling services as a corollary of the diminishing capacity of academic departments to offer pastoral care to students, universities might be better off reminding old scholars of the sympathetic ear offered to them by the university counsellors during their three or four years at the institution.
9. For a critique of current competence-based evaluations of higher education, see Barnett, 1994. It is possible to wonder what exactly is envisioned by some who lend their endorsement to measures of this kind. What exactly does the reference to the "ever-increasing attention to quality assurance mechanisms and the re-positioning of the student as customer or client" portend? (see Hoare, 1995, p.2). Does this mean that there is no limit to the attention that can be given to quality issues? How, it might be asked, can the product ever get produced if this is the case? Is there no end to institutional reflexivity?
10. Roper found in his survey that while three quarters of final year law respondents indicated an intention to be admitted to practice within at least five years of graduation, only two in three students in this category sought to practise in the private profession. In Australia, at least, with the massive proliferation in the number of law students over the past decade, the prospects for employment in the legal profession of current students have become less clear.In response to suggestions that law schools should close or reduce their intake, one increasingly articulated argument concerns the broad applicability of the educational and vocational skills of the law graduate.
11. Chapter 7 of Sheehan, Welch and Lacy's report, which deals with academics' views of university governance and management, is especially relevant here. According to this study, 63% of respondents agreed with the statement that "The administration is often autocratic".
12. Indeed, this was explicitly claimed by Australian Minister of Education John Dawkins in his discussion paper on higher education in 1987, soon after assuming this portfolio. See McInnis and Marginson, 1994, p.30.
13. As Clark Kerr pithily expressed the point, "...an appropriate emblem for the American college might be the traditional open book, but lying on a sales counter" (Kerr, 1995,

p.128).

14. Becher's UK study of academic cultures revealed the perception among other academics that the academic activities of lawyers are thought to be "...unexciting and uncreative, comprising a series of intellectual puzzles scattered among large areas of description" (Becher, 1989, p.30).
15. Of course, there are law schools in the USA which do not form part of a university, albeit a very small minority.
16. For criticisms of the highly theoretical and interdisciplinary nature of curricula at leading US law schools, see for example Johnson, 1991 and Edwards, 1992.
17. On law school socialisation, see Granfield (1992) and Goldsmith (1995).
18. While some enlightened judges, and occasionally leaders of the profession, are prepared to speak on behalf of the value of jurisprudence and legal theory in a law degree, there is plenty of anecdotal evidence to foster the impression among law students that recruiting firms prefer particular groups of subjects to others. A high level of support for theoretical subjects has yet to emerge from the ranks of the profession.
19. Schlegel (1992 at p.110) has suggested that by building legal academic identity around theory about the practice of law, legal scholarship might improve to the point that it ceases to be an embarrassment to the rest of the university.
20. This point is well made by Pelikan (1992, p.165) who states that "...a professional school runs the danger either of affirming an ambiguous status quo in the profession and in the society or of losing touch with the profession and with the society at large by treating the concerns and structures of the profession with contempt and alienation".
21. This argument was made by John Schlegel over a decade ago (see Schlegel, 1984, p.110). Jack Goldring made a similar case (Goldring, 1987).
22. I have demonstrated elsewhere the relevance of these pedagogical objectives to the teaching of ethics (Goldsmith, 1997).
23. As the end of the century draws near, such reflexivity seems set to increase, though it is a familiar enough practice amongst academic lawyers; see, for example, Goldring (1993), Crawford (1991), Chesterman and Weisbrot (1987).

References

ACLEC (1996), *First Report on Legal Education and Training*, Lord Chancellor's Department, London.

American Bar Association (1992), *Legal Education and Professional Development* (the

'McCrate Report'), Chicago.

Arthurs, H. (1983), *Law and Learning: Report to the Social Sciences and Humanities Research Council of Canada by the Consultative Group on Research and Education in Law* (the Arthurs Report), SSHRC, Ottawa.

Australia, Department of Employment, Education, Training, and Youth Affairs (1996), *Higher Education Budget Statement 1996*, 9 August.

Barnett, R. (1994),*The Limits of Competence: Knowledge, Higher Education, and Society*, Open University Press, Milton Keynes.

Becher, T. (1989), *Academic Tribes and Territories, Intellectual Enquiry and the Cultures of Disciplines*, Open University Press, Milton Keynes.

Bok, D. (1990), *Universities and the Future of America*, Duke University Press, Durham NC.

Centre for Legal Education (in conjunction with the Committee of Australian Law Deans) (1994), *The Cost of Legal Education in Australia: The Achievement of Quality Legal Education - A Framework for Analysis*, Centre for Legal Education, Sydney.

Chesterman, M. and Weisbrot, D. (1987), 'Legal Scholarship in Australia', 50, *Modern Law Review*, 709.

Clark, B. (1983), *The Higher Education System: Academic Organization in Cross-National Perspective*, University of California Press, Berkeley.

Committee of Australian Law Deans, *Studying Law in Australia*, Committee of Australian Law Deans Home Page, via UniServe Law.

Crawford, J. (1991), 'The Future of the Public Law Schools', 9, *Journal of Professional Legal Education*, 1.

Edwards, H.T. (1992), 'The Growing Disjunction Between Legal Education and the Legal Profession', 91, *Michigan Law Review*, 34.

Goldring, J. (1987), 'Babies and Bathwater: Tradition or Progress in Legal Scholarship and Legal Education?', 17, *University of Western Australia Law Review*, 216.

Goldring, J. (1993), 'The Future of Legal Education: Why? And How? Doubtful Assumptions and Unfulfilled Expectations', 11, *Journal of Professional Legal Education*, 149.

Goldsmith, A. (1995), 'Warning: Law Schools Can Endanger Your Health!', 21, *Monash University Law Review*, 272.

Goldsmith, A. (1997), 'Heroes or Technicians? The Moral Capacities of Tomorrow's Lawyers', 14, *Journal of Professional Legal Education*, 127.

Gordon, C. (ed) (1980), *Michel Foucault: Power/Knowledge*, Harvester Press, Brighton.

Granfield, R. (1992), *Making Elite Lawyers: Visions of Law at Harvard and Beyond*, Routledge, New York.

Halsey, A.H. (1992), *Decline of Donnish Dominion: The British Academic Professions in the Twentieth Century*, Clarendon Press, Oxford.

Haskell, T.L. (1996), 'Justifying the Rights of Academic Freedom in the Era of Power/Knowledge', in A.Sarat and T. Kearns (eds), *Legal Rights: Historical and Philosophical Perspectives*, University of Michigan Press, Ann Arbor.

Hepple, B. (1996), 'The Renewal of the Liberal Law Degree', 55, *Cambridge Law Journal*, 470.

Higher Education Council (1995), *The Promotion of Quality and Innovation in Higher Education*, Australian Govt. Publishing Service, Canberra.

Hill, C. (1965), *Intellectual Origins of the Revolution*, Oxford University Press, Oxford.

Hoare, D. (Chair) (1995), *Higher Education Management Review, Summary of Report and Recommendations*, Department of Employment, Education, Training, Canberra.

Johnson, A. (1991), 'Think Like a Lawyer, Work Like a Machine: The Dissonance Between Law School and Law Practice', 64, *Southern California Law Review*, 1231.

Kerr, C. (1995), *The Uses of the University*, Harvard University Press, Cambridge.

Laird, C. (1996), 'Legal education: theory or practice?', 70, *Law Institute Journal*, 6.

Levi, E.H. (1969), *Point of View: Talks on Education*, University of Chicago Press, Chicago.

Levine, M. L. (ed) (1993), *Legal Education*, Dartmouth, Aldershot.

Lyotard, Y. (1984), *The Postmodern Condition: A Report on Knowledge*, Manchester University Press, Manchester.

Mackay, H. (1997), 'Knowledge? Ask your Dentist', *The Weekend Australian*, 25-26 January, 2.

Marginson, S. (1993), *Education and Public Policy in Australia*, Cambridge University Press, Cambridge.

McDaniel, O.C. (1996), 'Ambivalence in choice patterns on the future role of government in higher education policies', 28, *Higher Education Review*, 3.

McInnis, C. and Marginson, S. (1994), *Australian Law Schools After the 1987 Pearce Report*, Department of Employment, Education and Training, Canberra.

Miller, H.D.R. (1995), *The Management of Change in Universities: Universities, State and Economy in Australia, Canada, and the United Kingdom*, Open University Press, Milton Keynes.

Neave, G. and Van Vught, F. (eds) (1992), *Prometheus Bound: The Changing Relationship Between Government and Higher Education in Western Europe*, Pergamon Press, Oxford.

Oliver, D. (1994), 'Teaching and Learning Law: Pressures on the Liberal Law Degree', in P.B.H. Birks (ed), *Reviewing Legal Education*, Oxford University Press, Oxford.

Parker, C. (1993), 'An Oversupply of Law Graduates? Putting the Statistics in Context', 4, *Legal Education Review*, 255.

Pearce, D., Campbell, E. and Harding, D. (1987), *Australian Law Schools: A Disciplinary Assessment for the Commonwealth Tertiary Education Committee: A Summary*, Australian Government Publishing Service, Canberra.

Pelikan, J. (1992),*The Idea of the University: A Reexamination*, Yale University Press, New Haven.

Pusey, M. (1991), *Economic Rationalism in Canberra: A Nation-Building State Changes Its Mind*, Cambridge University Press, Cambridge.

Roper, C. (1995), *Career Intentions of Australian Law Students*, Department of Employment, Education and Training, Canberra.

Sarat, A. and Silbey, S. (1988), 'The Pull of the Policy Audience', 10, *Law and Policy*, 97.

Schlegel, J. H. (1984), 'Searching for Archimedes: Legal Education, Legal Scholarship, and Liberal Ideology', 34, *Journal of Legal Education*, 103.

Schlegel, J. H. (1992), 'A Certain Narcissism; A Slight Unseemliness', 63, *University of Colorado Law Review*, 595.

Scott, P. (1995), *The Meanings of Mass Higher Education*, Open University Press, Milton Keynes.

Sheehan, B., Welch, A. and Lacy, F. (1996),*The Academic Profession in Australia*, Department of Employment, Education, Training, and Youth Affairs, Canberra.

Shils, E. (1983),*The Academic Ethic: The Report of a Study Group of the International Council on the Future of the University*, University of Chicago Press, Chicago.

Stevens, R. (1983), *Law School: Legal Education in America from the 1850s to the 1980s*, University of North Carolina Press, Chapel Hill.

Trilling, L. (1950), *The Liberal Imagination: Essays on Literature and Society*, Mercury Books, London.

Twining, W. L. (1967), 'Pericles and the Plumber', 83, *Law Quarterly Review*, 396.

Twining, W.L. (1995), 'What Are Law Schools For?', 46, *Northern Ireland Legal Quarterly*, 291.

Unger, R. (1987), *False Necessity*, Cambridge University Press, Cambridge.

Veblen, T. (1918), *The Higher Learning in America*, B.W. Huebsch, New York.

Zeigert, A. (1992), 'Social Structure, Educational Attainment and Admission to Law School', 3, *Legal Education Review*, 155.

5 Professional Legal Education - A Way Forward

JOY HILLYER

Introduction

Professional legal education in England and Wales has developed in a context that owes more to 'local' i.e. national problems and opportunities than to the influences of other jurisdictions although many of the challenges it faces share similarities as well as differences.[1] Other jurisdictions have sometimes had a strong influence: on the one hand, the influence of North America and Australia, particularly in the development of 'skills' training (however loosely that may be defined), can be readily perceived, although their approaches have been adapted, rather than adopted wholesale. On the other hand, the increasing globalisation of legal work and contact with the civil systems as well, of course, as the growth of European Community legislation are having increasing impact on the work of many lawyers and on the development of the English legal system itself.[2] However, the influence of these changes on the development of legal education is more limited and, currently, tends to be most perceptible at the post-qualification level (apart from European Community law which is taught both at degree level and at the vocational stage).[3] However necessary it is to be aware of the wider context, consideration of the future of professional legal education in England and Wales cannot ignore local issues. This brief exploration cannot linger long over the historical context but there are a number of background factors which should not be overlooked.[4] Although this chapter will focus on the year of vocational legal education of intending solicitors prior to them joining solicitors' firms or other organisations for the compulsory training contract and subsequent qualification as a solicitor, it will be argued that developments in vocational education have relevance for the education and training of lawyers as a whole.

The traditional separation in English legal education between university or 'academic' legal education on the one hand and professional legal education on the other is well-known, although it can be exaggerated. It has a long history. The Select Committee on Legal Education of 1846 which was concerned about the lack of university legal education at that time commented:

> It would indeed be a total misapprehension of the purposes and character of this University Education to consider it a substitute for, or even appropriate to, the peculiar purposes of the professional student. In this, as in other departments, the special institution is absolutely essential. The province of the University is to teach the philosophy of the science, and to secure instruction in those branches for which it might be apprehended the more technical character of the special institution would inadequately provide.
> (Select Committee on Legal Education Report, 1846)

The relevance of this extract to modern debates of legal education was cited with some approval by the Committee on Legal Education one hundred and twenty five years later in the Ormrod Report (Ormrod, 1971). It noted that the results of the Select Committee of 1846 were not all beneficial:

> ...instead of producing a co-ordinated system of training for each branch [of the profession, i.e. barristers and solicitors], or for both together, two separated systems of law teaching developed, a university system, with a predominately academic approach, and a professional system dominated by its own examination requirements...
> (Ormrod, 1971)

The Ormrod Report went on to note wryly that

> ...[the] problems arising from the inter-relations and interactions of these systems [had] pre-occupied, and continue to pre-occupy, all who are concerned with education for the legal profession [and]...[t]hey have generated a great deal of dissatisfaction and discussion and a certain lack of confidence between academic and professional lawyers...
> (Ormrod, 1971)

The Report (1971) formalised the staged structure of legal education into the academic stage, the professional stage (which included both 'organised vocational training in an institutional setting, and...practical experience in a professional setting under supervision') and post-qualification or continuing education and training. This pattern of legal education persists today. The 'professional stage' for solicitors is now the one-year Legal Practice Course, followed by a two-year training contract.[5] Intending barristers take the one-year Bar Vocational Course, followed by one year in pupillage. The pattern of distinct stages of legal education may have given impetus to the development of vocational legal education and there are good reasons why some aspects or approaches may be more appropriately addressed at particular stages in the process of professional formation. However there is widespread recognition that legal education should be seen as a 'continuum'[6] and that rigid barriers can be unhelpful and misleading (Savage and Watt, 1996).

There is some 'blurring' of the dividing lines between the stages of legal education both because of institutional change within the university sector and professional legal education and also because of changes in the nature of 'academic' and 'vocational' education.[7] The Lord Chancellor's Advisory Committee on Legal Education and Conduct ('ACLEC') which was first appointed in 1991 spoke of the need for 'partnership' between the universities and the professional bodies:

> ...the rigid demarcation between the 'academic' and 'vocational' stages needs to disappear; what is required is a new partnership between the universities and the professional bodies at all stages of legal education and training. (ACLEC, 1996)

Despite the language of 'partnership' in the ACLEC Report, a recognition of the political element in debates about legal education which played such a part in the Ormrod Committee may partly underlie the move in the ACLEC Report to limit the influence of the legal profession on the initial stages of legal education at least (Twining, 1994). However, other wider factors are more important than the relationship between law teachers and the profession, even though they are often overlooked. William Twining has noted that

> Public policy discussions and reports about legal education and training and about the discipline have tended to be inward-looking and parochial, often downplaying or ignoring key factors in the wider institutional context and over-estimating the room for manoeuvre and the scope for special policies for law within the general system of higher education. The three most important reports on legal education since 1945 - Ormrod (1971), Benson (1979) and Marre (1988) - were all primarily concerned with problems of the legal profession and paid hardly any attention to trends and policies

> affecting higher education as a whole.
> (Twining, 1994)

These wider trends include the development of Quality Assurance in Higher Education. They also include issues about finance and funding and the expansion of the numbers of students in Higher Education.

Finance and Funding

The impact of financial and funding issues has been considerable in the university law school as law has frequently been viewed as a cheap subject to resource even though the reality is that there are a number of distinctive features about legal education which should be taken into account when Higher Education resources are allocated (ACLEC, 1996). It has also had a particular impact on vocational legal education because unlike many other professions, law has not attracted mandatory government funding for pre-qualification vocational training but has come within the discretionary grants system. The reduction in discretionary grants has been swift and severe.[8] Quite apart from acute personal hardship to some students, one result has been a threat to equality of access to the legal profession as students increasingly have to rely on their own resources (or their parents).[9] Student loans are not the answer. One student commented in the survey by The College of Law:

> ...students are scared of loans...if the financial situation does not improve, then less and less students from lower income brackets will try and enter the profession.
> (The College of Law, 1995)

Even though many of the students who proceed to qualification as solicitors or barristers are cushioned by accident of background or have obtained sponsorship from (usually) large City firms, they recognise the problem for the legal profession as a whole if training and sponsorship is concentrated in the commercial sector. One student commented:

> ...generally the legal profession will suffer from the absence of competent highly skilled lawyers across the spectrum of the legal profession if the money is simply not available to train students in smaller firms...
> (The College of Law, 1995)

Another result of the financial pressures is that students (and their parents), who are bearing an increasing proportion of the cost of education, are seen as increasingly important 'consumers' of education services.[10] Although insights into the importance of 'reflection'[11] and life-long learning are vital for the long-term development of modern legal practitioners, there is also a strong economic perspective to some aspects of the growth in student-centred learning.[12]

Employers and Skills

Employers generally, and within the legal profession, have begun to be more vociferous in their demands of the education process. This is not simply because of the increased realisation of the cost of training recruits. In part, it is a result of dissatisfaction with the perceived quality of graduates compared with those in the past, although this may be exaggerated.[13] It is also a realisation that the challenge of the increasing pace of change in the work place, both within and outside the legal profession, requires a work force which has skills that can be exercised in an ever-changing context. Notions of 'core' skills or 'general transferable skills' have been put forward in an attempt to regulate the standards and outcomes of what is increasingly a mass system of Higher Education. The idea of 'general transferable skills' can give students a 'language' to articulate those outcomes to reflect upon in the learning process and also to use in matching their skills to the demands of employers (Bell, 1997).[14] This is very relevant to law graduates, because as the number of those graduating is far greater than the number of training contract places available, the traditional routes to legal qualification as a solicitor or barrister are not open to many of them.[15]

Diversity and Change in the Legal Profession(s)

Changes to legal education and training are taking place against a background of even more rapid change and increasing diversity both within the legal profession and in the provision of legal services outside it (ACLEC, 1996; Shapland and Le Grys, 1994). Susskind (1996) paints a detailed picture of the actual and potential changes to the context in which the legal profession is operating and the emergence of law services as an 'information' rather than 'advisory' service, through both the inevitable impact and the potential uses of information technology. Research by the Law Society (1990; 1991) confirmed the increasing diversity of legal work in private practice. Recent campaigns for election to the presidency of the Law Society clearly illustrate the strains that the increasing diversity of types and size of practice are putting on any sense of there being *one* solicitors' profession, despite the clear political advantages of speaking with a united voice.[16]

Such diversity of legal practice and the rapid pace of change and growth both in legislation and regulation and in the size of many practices present great challenges to the profession and to legal education. One result has been a greater impetus to the development of skills-based vocational education (Sherr, 1996).

Vocational Legal Education in Transition

The Introduction of the Legal Practice Course

The vocational course for solicitors, the Law Society's Final Examination Course, which was introduced in 1979, was aimed at

> ...ensuring that students [had] a sufficient knowledge of those areas of substantive law which [were] of practical importance and to integrate substantive law with practical instruction.
> (Marre, 1988)

In terms of preparing trainees for entering the office, the course was a considerable improvement on what had gone before. For example, it should no longer have been possible for a trainee solicitor to find themselves down at the local County Court representing a client for a preliminary hearing in chambers without having the faintest idea of the purpose of any form of preliminary hearing. However, it has been noted elsewhere, in terms of content and ethos, the model of legal practice on which the course was based was that of a small and prosperous provincial firm which bore little resemblance to the growing diversity and commercial nature of much legal practice (Hillyer, 1997). The old course came to be criticised for its inflexibility, the dominance of the central examination and the imbalance between the knowledge and practical skills elements of the course (Marre, 1988; The Law Society, 1990).

Twining (1994) noted that the introduction of the Bar Vocational Course in 1989 '...represented a genuinely sharp break from the past [emphasis on knowledge] in objectives, methods and spirit' and that the Legal Practice Course introduced in 1993 '...moved in a similar direction, although it claimed to maintain more of a balance between knowledge and skills'. With such changes, it was inevitable that the new Legal Practice Course (as the Bar Vocational Course before it[17]) should be subject to scrutiny. It was also inevitable that the new courses would not get everything right first time: indeed it had come to be recognised that the such courses should be flexible enough to allow for evolutionary development. The fact that the introduction of the Legal Practice Course only just pre-dated the beginning of the first review of legal education of the Lord Chancellor's Advisory Committee on Legal Education and Conduct gave further impetus to reflection both by the Law Society and institutional providers.

Assessment

The impact of the nature of assessment on legal education should not be underestimated. Until recently, professional examinations for solicitors followed the traditional university pattern of three-hour written examinations, except that they were set by the professional body nationally rather than by the individual teaching institutions. The extent to which the central examination came to dominate the year of vocational legal education (both in terms of pedagogy and the administrative burden on the professional body) became one of the most powerful arguments for change. With the introduction of the Legal Practice Course in 1993 which gave significant emphasis to formal skills training,[18] change to the assessment regime became inevitable. Assessment was devolved from the Law Society to the institutions, although the former, as the validating and monitoring body, has retained firm control over assessment regulations.

The perceived need for assessment, including assessment of skills, to be rigorous (for example in fulfilling the statutory duty of the professional body to maintain standards, particularly in the face of some scepticism from the profession over the dilution of self-regulation) and the need to have transparent criteria, have inevitably had an impact on the way skills are taught.[19]

As in Higher Education more generally, assessment is gradually becoming better understood, and different methods of assessment are being introduced (and not merely for the formal skills element of vocational education).[20] However, assessment remains a complex issue. For example, it is inevitable that students find assessment stressful and may react to it in disparate ways: course evaluation by students can indicate these differing reactions which can affect students' attitude to the course.[21] Assessment can also make heavy demands on scarce resources. It remains to be seen how far alternative or complementary strategies for assessment become more widely acceptable, such as self-assessment and group assessment (Tribe, 1996) or formal assessment in the work place (as in the National Vocational Qualifications (NVQ) system).

Objectives for Vocational Legal Education

In the discussions about legal education which have surrounded the review by ACLEC, it has been noted that there is a need for more empirical evidence about what modern legal practice actually involves and that one aspect of the picture is the views of the profession (Cranston, 1996). The College of Law carried out a survey in 1995 into the views of the profession on the future of vocational legal education in the context of the introduction of the Legal Practice Course (Hillyer, 1996). The timing was largely determined by the ACLEC review which was then underway. In one sense the research was premature as the profession had only had its first recruits from the new course for a few months. However, it also gave an opportunity to seek the views of the profession whilst they still had recent recruits who had undergone the previous course.

Although the response rate to the questionnaire which was sent out to all firms who were registered to take trainee solicitors was disappointing, those firms and organisations that responded, had between them 2510 trainee solicitors which was about 30% of the national total. The respondents came from a wide spectrum both geographically and in the size and type of legal practice which ranged from large city commercial firms to small high street general practices and legal aid firms and some organisations outside private practice, so that the results are nevertheless of considerable interest.[22]

A central question of the research was to find out what firms felt should be the aims and objectives of the year of vocational education before trainees entered a solicitors' office.[23] No attempt was made to define 'objectives' in any narrow or technical sense, but respondents were asked to rate a wide range of objectives or potential objectives on a scale of 5-1.[24] Overall, the objectives most frequently rated as very important or important were (in order of frequency):

writing and drafting
familiarising students with legal practice and procedure
increasing students' ability to organise time and work
enabling students to identify the interests and concerns of client
legal research.

Table 1 Objectives/potential objectives for a year's Legal Practice Course most frequently rated as important or very important by different types of firm/organisation

	Percentage of respondents from different types of firm/organisation				
	ALL*	City commercial	Other commercial	High Street general	Legal aid**
Writing and drafting	84	95	87	80	83
Familiarisation with legal practice	81	71	80	82	86
Increasing ability to organise time and work	78	71	79	78	78
Increasing ability to diagnose and solve problems	77	80	82	74	74
Enabling students to identify interests and concerns of clients	74	73	74	74	80
Legal research	72	85	89	66	63
Interviewing	66	42	65	69	75
Advocacy	60	37	50	64	69
Preparing students specifically for general practice	59	19	36	75	83
Increasing knowledge and awareness of substantive law across a range of subjects	58	58	61	55	66
BASE	361*	41	62	176	35

* 'All' respondents include 47 from other types of firm/organisation

** Includes legal aid and legal aid/high street general

Source: Adapted from Hillyer (1996), 'The Future of Vocational Legal Education and the Legal Practice Course'.

Table 1 sets out those objectives or potential objectives that were most frequently rated as 'very important' or 'important' by any of the four main categories of firm. The College of Law is also following the progress of a group of its students from each of the first three years of the Legal Practice Course.[25] In the 1996 survey by questionnaire, respondents were given a similar list to that used in the survey of firms' views (Hillyer, 1996). The objectives for a year's vocational course most frequently rated as important or very important in 1996 by the 281 respondents two years after completing the 1993/4 Legal Practice Course and the 282 respondents one year after completing the 1994/5 Legal Practice Course were very similar to the findings in the firm survey. The difference was that advocacy tended to be rated highly less frequently by firms as did specific preparation for a training contract. Current students tended to value skills training slightly more than either firms or trainees.[26]

The College of Law's research reveals the most support from firms, trainees and students for a range of objectives for vocational education and training which comprise both practical skills and the application (and, by implication, the acquisition) of legal and procedural knowledge. It does not support a call for either a mainly or totally skills - based or knowledge - based course (Hillyer, 1997).

What About 'Skills'?

Overall the development of skills training in vocational legal education has been successful. This does not mean that it has been uncontroversial or without its problems. For example, the extent to which 'skills' are context-specific and not susceptible of easy transfer is a complex question for both the academic and vocational stages of legal education. Similarly, the relationship and the often exaggerated perception, of a dichotomy between 'skills' and 'knowledge' has sometimes added to the skirmishes between and within legal academia and the profession. One of the confusing factors in current discussions about legal education is the different way in which the word 'skills' is used both amongst the providers of legal education and in the interface between education and the profession. An introductory chapter by Mackie in *Learning Lawyers Skills* by Gold, Mackie and Twining (1989) gives a clear and brief account of the complexity of some of the ideas lying behind the concept 'skill'.

The book has fairly been described as a '...landmark publication [which] showed the educational establishment that legal skills were indeed to be taken seriously' (Webb and Maughan, 1996). Although it has been commented that many of the materials the book contains relate specifically to the 'DRAIN' skills[27] and the debate has now to some extent shifted its focus towards considering intellectual skills and reflective, cognitive processes particularly at degree level,[28] it would be a mistake to seem to 'write-off' the DRAIN skills taught on Legal Practice Courses as somehow concerned only with technical 'training' in a limited, behavioural sense. To do that would largely be to mistake the 'label' for the substance.

The ambiguity and confusion generated by the use of the word 'skill' or by using short-hand or 'umbrella' labels such as 'problem-solving', 'legal research', 'interviewing', 'advocacy' or 'drafting' was reflected in the responses by firms of solicitors to research into the vocational stage of legal education (Hillyer, 1996) and in the on-going research into the views of students and trainees from the Legal Practice Course referred to above. For example, a few respondents felt that either such skills cannot be learned at all, i.e. that they were innate (or not) and/or they could not be taught but can only be acquired by osmosis (Hillyer 1996). Some saw particular skills to have little cognitive or developmental value, but simply as ends in themselves. On this view skills training is only useful to the extent that trainees actually carry out advocacy or negotiation, for example, in the early months of their training contract. Other respondents wanted to carry out skills training within the firm so that trainees were taught in the 'house style' of the organisation. For others, the educational process was perceived as more complex: they appear to have valued the spectrum of skills training as part of the process of sharpening students' awareness of professional attitudes and legal knowledge, and in developing a practical approach to lawyering.

The College of Law's research (1996 and ongoing) revealed strong support for formal skills training in the DRAIN skills at the vocational stage, particularly legal research, writing and drafting, and in advocacy. However it did not reveal support for the particularly strong emphasis on practical skills to the virtual exclusion of legal subjects at the vocational stage which is found in the Marre Report (1988). That report perhaps illustrates the high watermark of the realisation that vocational education at that time did not equip young intending solicitors with the inter-personal skills to meet and deal with real clients.[29] The views illustrated in Marre and the emphasis on formal skills training in the Bar Vocational Course and Legal Practice Course provided a necessary corrective to some of the shortcomings these concerns represented. Now although the courses have demonstrated that skills can be taught outside the workplace, particularly with extensive use of case studies and realistic scenarios, there is more realism about some of the early expectations of what vocational courses can and cannot achieve at the stage the students have reached by the time they take them (Gorieley and Williams, 1996). There is a greater understanding that such courses can only make a start on the learning and practice of the practical skills that a lawyer may need in the course of his/her career (even when the foundation has been laid at the academic stage).[30] Now there is greater recognition that the teaching of practical skills should be more integrated and balanced with the enhancement of students' relevant legal knowledge and their ability to *apply* it. This recognition is not to downgrade the place of skills in vocational education nor to imply that skills training cannot be improved. But it does better recognise the cognitive aspects of skills and their contextual nature. This allows formal skills training to take a proper, not inflated, role. It does not mean that the views that the Legal Practice Course included insufficient substantive law which were expressed by some firms and trainees are a call for a return to the Law Society's Final Examination Course. One respondent to the survey of firms' views commented:

> Both knowledge and awareness of substantive law is an important attribute in those joining our practice for training contracts. However, merely to state that this is an important attribute misses the point. What we look for are trainees who are able to use their knowledge of substantive law and their general awareness of areas of substantive law so as to solve the problems they are given by their supervisors. Merely to set about increasing knowledge for its own sake...is of no use in practice where there remains a tendency for trainee solicitors not to see the wood for the trees.
> (The College of Law, 1996)

Specialisation or Focus?

One of the issues that has become more pressing in the face of increasing diversification of legal practice, is the extent and stage at which legal education should permit specialisation. It is also interesting to consider how far the increasingly important views of students have increased pressure for early specialisation. It is clear from research that law students are a vocationally orientated group from an early age and they are not necessarily happy with law courses that they perceive to be too 'theoretical' (Halpern, 1994). The ACLEC Report expressed its anxiety about premature specialisation:

> ...the Committee is concerned that what may be termed generic legal education and the teaching of core legal values are being eroded by the demands for the teaching of specialised subjects and skills both in the initial law degree and as part of the vocational stage of qualification as a solicitor or barrister.
> (ACLEC, 1996)

What the College of Law research revealed on course objectives and content was that there was comparatively little support for narrow specialisation for the year of vocational education. Rather the responses about course objectives and detailed content revealed a desire for more (but not exclusive) *focus* on the broad types of work of the kind of firm or organisation that the student intended or hoped to join as a trainee (Hillyer, 1996 and ongoing). Some students and firms expressed anxiety that students might limit their possibilities too soon. Even if the fears of premature specialisation are largely unfounded, there is clearly an issue for careful counselling and choice of options for those who do not have training contracts at the time of taking the vocational course.

The debate surrounding this issue tends to be confused, due to two main factors. One is the somewhat casual use of the word 'specialisation' itself which has overtones of expertise. Expertise and, therefore, specialisation in that sense is clearly an inappropriate and, indeed, an impossible outcome for the early stages of legal education. The other factor is the cluster of ideas, aspirations and assumptions which underlie the 'quest for a core' (Twining, 1994). Although there are practical reasons for seeking some commonality of approach, to some extent the pressure to identify a core is now being answered, not by a common list of subject areas of law, but by more abstract concepts.[31] The ACLEC Report went on to say:

> The Committee would wish to see the emphasis in the education and training of all lawyers, up to the point of initial qualification placed on providing a greater depth of learning in areas of basic legal knowledge and generic skills

> and on the development of what has been termed common professional values.
> (ACLEC, 1996)

As the profession becomes larger and more diverse and the process of professional formation of the individual and cohesion of the profession as a whole become more problematic, the pressure for other ways of promoting coherence and cohesion can be observed apart from any attempt to ensure that courses are similar. For example, the study of professional ethics and the express development of 'common professional values' becomes a more important part of the curriculum. It is not altogether clear what is meant by 'common professional values' within the English context[32] although ACLEC rightly sought to highlight the 'ethical challenge' to lawyers which goes

> ...beyond the obligations that solicitors and barristers owe to particular clients [because] [t]he legal profession also carries wider social and political obligations to society as a whole.
> (ACLEC, 1996)

A Way Forward

This chapter has touched changes in the nature of vocational education and the wider educational context and in the legal profession and *its* wider context, which can point to a way forward for vocational education.

Reflective Focus

Whilst it is imperative to avoid uncritical concentration on what the legal profession actually *does* as *the* determining factor for the theory, content or modes of delivery of legal education, particularly at the academic stage (Toddington, 1996), nevertheless legal education must take it into account as a major focus for reflection. This clearly requires closer links between academia (both in terms of research and teaching) and professional practice which will benefit the development of both. It will help to dissipate unnecessary fears. Even where there is concern about undue influence of professional concerns on academic matters, there is less difficulty in accepting that "...the *raison d'être* of professional legal education is to prepare legal professionals for professional life" (Toddington, 1996). Here the danger is not that vocational education and training should be too close to what the profession actually does. Rather, the danger is that vocational education may become divorced from reality and, instead, that it may operate on the basis of out-dated models of legal practice . *Real* attention needs to be paid to the whole spectrum of what lawyers are doing, and are likely to be doing in the future. This focus needs to be continuing, thoughtful and reflective and to include the whole range of commercial, managerial and administrative activity in addition to more traditional legal concerns.

Developments in the underlying theories of education can enhance the benefits that such focus can bring. Bines (1992) has noted that, despite the problems of competence-based approaches to assessment and course design, "...a focus on competence should considerably enhance both the rigour and the relevance of professional education". There is a realisation that competence approaches need refinement if they are to do justice to the complexity of professional education: "...it may be possible to develop a broad vision of competence involving both behavioural and interpretative approaches" (Bines, 1992). The Written Standards published by the Law Society for the Legal Practice Course are an attempt to combine a more broad approach with the specification of a considerable level of detail. They specifically refer to the need for students to be able to learn from experience of the course and in practice. Ideas of reflective practice which have their roots in the insights of Schon (1983; 1987), Eraut (1990), Barnett (1992) and others have much to contribute both in a general approach to legal education in the context of the development of life-long reflective learning and at a more detailed level of course design. The realisation of the need to develop life-long learning is not unique to legal education: for example in training medical General Practitioners:

> The aims of vocational training are to help trainees:
>
> (1) acquire the abilities that enable them to perform competently the work of a General Practitioner; and
>
> (2) to be able to continue to develop and maintain that competence and to adapt to change over a professional lifetime.

(Havelock et al, 1995)

But even though it is not unique, this realisation is providing a way to meet some of the challenges of the new context in which the legal profession is operating and a way to face the impossibility of adequately 'front-loading' legal education with all the detailed knowledge and skills required for a varied working life. However, it is important that attempts to put these ideas into practice are firmly rooted in practical realities. For example, ideas of life-long learning not only reflect an essential *attitude* but their expression in action can have practical consequences. To give an illustration at the level of detail, research amongst trainees has revealed the difficulty experienced by some trainees when the timing of their on-the-job training did not coincide with the point when particular skills and knowledge were, in fact, required. When the lack of appropriate timing is allied to a requirement for formal assessment, the strain on trainees can be severe.[33] No process of education and training can iron out all such difficulties and part of the self-reliance that an approach to life-long learning is seeking to promote is to enable students to cope with such problems. Nonetheless, the issue is a real one.

Seizing New Opportunities for Partnership

New opportunities for partnership have arisen which can enable teaching institutions and the profession to mitigate the damaging aspects of the traditional divide between them and to promote a life-long approach to learning. The profession is more aware of the need for explicit lifelong learning and the teaching institutions are more confident that they have a great deal to offer. There are other practical forces at work which have resulted in the legal profession taking a greater interest in education issues.

The introduction of the Legal Practice Course was proposed in 1989/90 before the economic recession of the early 1990's and before the very sharp downturn in discretionary funding. Whilst it was acknowledged in the consultation paper (The Law Society, 1990) that the proposed changes had cost implications, by the time the proposals were implemented, there was much greater awareness of the cost of training to the profession as well as to the students themselves. But the impetus for the closer involvement of the profession in legal education is not solely economic. The profession (as distinct from its professional body which has an active education secretariat) has begun to realise that not only does it have a large financial stake in the education and training of its recruits, but also the change to a more practical course has greatly increased the potential for genuine influence and involvement in a process of continuous development of vocational education. This interest tends to be most clearly perceived in the large (usually commercial) firms, many of which have in-house training managers and large programmes of in-house education which cover both new recruits and qualified staff. But the move away from using an out-dated model of a small provincial firm as *the* basis of a so-called 'generalist' approach to vocational education has provided an impetus for improving the education and training for those who will work in firms outside the commercial sector. It can also provide opportunities for improving the education and training for those who work outside the structures of traditional private practice altogether (regardless of whether they qualify as solicitors or barristers or not). This will be vital both for the legal profession and in the public interest as it becomes increasingly appreciated that solicitors and barristers are only one source of legal advice services amongst many.

Bines (1992), in writing about professional education generally noted that a closer integration between theory and practice requires a close partnership between tutors, institution, employers and services. At the personal level there are already many links: for example, research has shown that many law teachers in universities have professional legal qualifications.[34] There are growing institutional links both at the local level and in the approach ACLEC is seeking to promote. Partnership can be explored in different ways at the different stages of legal education. For example, in redesigning the Legal Practice Course for 1997-98, The College of Law has consulted with a large number of solicitors' firms in order to ascertain their educational needs. This process is part of an ongoing process of regular consultation. Ongoing consultation with students also plays an important role in the process. There are exciting possibilities for involvement of the profession in the development of specialist diplomas and practice-related masters degrees as part of the provision for Continuing Professional Development courses for qualified lawyers. The impact of information technology in the context of the work of the legal profession has only just begun to be realised (Susskind, 1996). Similarly its potential for legal education is only just beginning to be appreciated. Examples of developments in the use of Information Technology in legal education include the IOLIS software developed by the Law courseware Consortium based at the University of Warwick and the video education, training and updating service for Continuing Professional Development, LNTV (Dwyer, 1996).

No doubt the path ahead for legal education will have to negotiate all sorts of other opportunities and constraints as we move into the next millennium. Nevertheless, agreeing the need for clear, reflective focus and the importance of partnership, will at least provide some parameters for the way forward.

Notes

1. See, for example, the sections on France and Denmark in 'Special Issue: Legal Education and Training in Europe', *International Journal of the Legal Profession*, vol.2, no.1, pp.18-23, 60-62, and Hughes, A. K. (1994), *Developing European Professions: Delivering Continuing Professional Development in Europe*, University of Bristol, pp. 65-80.
2. See, for example, reforms of the justice system in England and Wales proposed by Lord Woolf (Woolf, 1996).
3. Although it is now somewhat out of date, research by The College of Law (1991) gave an indication of the way European Community Law had been both incorporated within the undergraduate teaching of the substantive law of England and Wales and/or treated as a separate subject. An unpublished survey of current students on the 1996-7 Legal Practice Course at The College of Law indicated that 68% of law graduates had studied the law of the European Community apart from the constitutional principles.
4. An account of the historical background can be found in Twining, W. (1994), *Blackstone's Tower: The English Law School*, Sweet & Maxwell, London.
5. Prior to qualification trainee solicitors must also undertake the Professional Skills Course comprising five modules: accounts, professional conduct, personal work management, investment business and advocacy. The PSC is constantly under review; for example, part of the accounts module was incorporated in the Legal Practice Course in 1997. Intending barristers do not have to fulfil so many requirements although continuing education is a developing area for barristers too and the Inns of Court are seeking to return to a more direct role in the provision of training, *The Times*, 10th March 1997.
6. See for instance the 'McCrate Report' (1992).
7. Some universities provide Legal Practice Courses and Continuing Professional Development: some of the CPD provision is in the form of post-graduate diplomas or degrees,

other courses are shorter or free standing. The College of Law, the professional law school and educational charity which provides vocational education for a majority of intending solicitors, is forging formal links with the Open University and is beginning to develop some of its Continuing Professional Development initiatives with university partners. In addition there are commercial providers of CPD.

8. In 1976/77, a survey of students at The College of Law revealed that 79% of students were receiving a discretionary grant for their vocational course fees (source: Benson, 1979). By 1995, funding of the total of The College of Law fees through discretionary grants by Local Education Authorities to students had fallen to 10% (The College of Law, 1995).
9. The report (The College of Law, 1995) revealed that students were taking increasing responsibilities for financing their own training, although sponsorship by the profession had also significantly increased.
10. See for instance Le Brun, M. and Johnstone, R. (1994), *The Quiet (R)evolution: Improving Student Learning in Law*, the Law Book Company Limited, Sydney for a consideration of teaching methods within the Australian context.
11. The work of Schon has been immensely influential in recent debates about legal education: very few accounts fail to mention it. See Jones (1996) for a discussion of some of the issues within the context of legal education.
12. The development of lifelong learning is not simply an imperative for the legal profession. The Chairman of Esso UK plc was reported as saying, in connection with a conference on 'What employers really want from graduates', "Industry is not homogeneous and there can be no single or simple answer to what employers really need from higher education. However, in a period of increasing globalisation and new technologies, UK plc requires flexibility and adaptability from all employees. Hence, the need for a lifelong approach to learning has never been more urgent" (Keith Taylor in *The Times Higher Education Supplement*, 7th February 1997, p. IV).
13. Some would say that the dissatisfaction is misplaced, or at the least, exaggerated. See for instance, Gareth Williams, *The Times Higher Education Supplement*, 7th February 1997.
14. The Department for Education and Employment (DFEE) is funding a number of projects for 'Discipline Networks in Higher Education'. The project in law, 'General Transferable Skills in the Law Curriculum' is intended to disseminate and promote good practice in the express development of general transferable skills in both undergraduate degree programmes and in professional training courses. A World Wide Web page will give wider access to the information being collected.
15. In the year 1st August 1995 to 31st July 1996 there were 4,063 new training contracts

registered with The Law Society. In 1994 there were 6,499 students graduating with single honours law degrees. This figure does not include students with qualifying law degrees from joint honours or modular degrees (of which there may be a further 2-3,000). In addition there were those students who qualified for the academic stage of training through taking the post-graduate Common Professional Examination or Diploma in law (after a non-law degree). There were 6,574 full-time and 918 part-time Legal Practice Course places nation-wide in 1994-5. For 1996-7, the figures are 6,844 full-time and 1,322 part-time places. Source: The Law Society (1996). The Law Society expressed its concerns over the over-supply of graduates to the Dearing Inquiry (*The Times Higher Education Supplement*, 21st February 1997). The problem with the over-supply of graduates is not unique: a report of the *Conseil superieur de l'emploi, des revenus et des couts* says that the total proportion of jobless graduates in France who have left higher education in the past five years has doubled (The Times Higher Education Supplement, 24th January 1997).

16. *The Law Society's Gazette*, 92/23, 14th June 1995, pp. 18-20 and 93/21, 5th June 1996.
17. See the series of reports by Shapland, J. et al published by The Institute for the Study of the Legal Profession at Sheffield University, particularly Shapland (1993).
18. The Legal Practice Course attempted to maintain a balance between what could be described as formal skills training and the legal and procedural subjects whilst the Bar Vocational Course is often described as a more skills-based course, although the differences between the two can be exaggerated.
19. For a brief discussion of assessment in the first year of the Legal Practice Course, see Brayne (1994).
20. For a general discussion of assessment methods in Higher Education, see for example Ramsden (1992).
21. Feedback from students frequently reflects anxiety about assessment. Students' perspectives are not always the same as those of their tutors: for example several respondents in answer to questioning about the value of 'open-book' examinations in The College of Law's research referred to in note 26 responded that they preferred 'closed-book' (traditional) examinations because they had done well at them previously.
22. According to figures supplied by the Law Society, the numbers of registered training contracts was 7390 (March 1995), 7494 (April 1995) and 7597 (May 1995) after taking cancellations into account. Questionnaires were sent out to all firms and organisations registered to be able to take trainee solicitors. There was a response rate of 19%. 16% or 361 questionnaires were completed, 3% responded by letter to say either they had no LPC trainees or too few to respond properly or that they felt it was too soon to comment.

Those who completed the questionnaire had about one third of the national total of trainees between them. There were not sufficient responses from outside private practice to be in any sense representative; although the responses were interesting and included in the survey for the insight that they did shed.

23. Respondents were also asked in what ways they felt that the structure of legal education should change. Responses were disparate and did not reveal widespread support for either the abolition of the training contract or abolition of the year of vocational education (currently the LPC) which follows the law degree or post-graduate (conversion) diploma for the non-law graduate. Concerns about the cost of legal education and a mismatch-match between the number of LPC places and the number of training contracts were expressed.
24. On a scale of 5-1, respondents were told that 5 = 'very important', 4 = 'important', 3 = 'quite important', 2 = 'not important', 1 = 'very unimportant'. The objectives/potential objectives covered a wide range including the five 'DRAIN' skills, IT, legal practice and procedure, increasing knowledge and awareness of substantive law across a range of subjects or giving major emphasis to specialist areas relevant to intended area(s) of practice. The list included both specific objectives such as accounts, and more general ones such as developing general intellectual skills.
25. The research, which is not yet published, is following a group of students from the LPC 1993/4 and 1994/5 at The College of Law. The findings referred to relate to 282 questionnaires completed in 1996 by respondents from the LPC 1993/94 (i.e. two years later) and 281 questionnaires completed by respondents from the LPC 1994/5 (i.e. one year later). All 282 respondents from 1993/4 were either in training contracts or had completed them (except 6 who were exempt). 205 of the respondents from 1994/5 had a training contract (except 10 of these who were exempt).
26. Research in progress into the views of just under 500 students on the LPC 1995/6 at The College of Law.
27. The 'DRAIN' skills are drafting, legal research, advocacy, interviewing and negotiation.
28. See, for instance, Webb, J. and Maughan, C. (1996).
29. The Law Society's Final Examination Course, which was introduced in 1979, did not purport to concentrate on practical skills in the way Marre later proposed.
30. Students from the over 70 university law schools bring a wide diversity of educational experience both in terms of legal subjects studied and practical skills. In addition, a significant number of students are older and/or are non-law graduates.
31. In order to try and circumvent previous difficulties over prescription of the content of law degrees by the legal profession, the university law schools were requested by the

former to provide a first draft of the successor to the Joint Announcement (1995) by the Law Society and the Council of Legal Education on full-time qualifying law degrees (set out in ACLEC 1996).

32. See the McCrate Report and the subsequent Report of the Professionalism Committee (1996), *Teaching and Learning Professionalism* (American Bar Association) which defines 'lawyer professionalism' within the American context, p.5.
33. Ongoing and currently unpublished research by The College of Law referred to above.
34. Research by Leighton, Mortimer and Whatley (1995) revealed that about 60% of law teachers held professional legal qualifications although the report noted that less than half had practised as a legal professional for a significant period of time. In addition, the figures will have been significantly affected by responses from law teachers specifically involved in vocational legal education.

References

ACLEC (1996), *The Lord Chancellor's Advisory Committee on Legal Education and Conduct First Report on Legal Education and Training* (the 'ACLEC Report'), Lord Chancellor's Department, London.

Bell, J. (1997), 'General Transferable Skills In the Law Curriculum', paper presented to Law Discipline Network workshops, Institute of Advanced Legal Studies, London and Leeds Metropolitan University, Leeds.

Bines, H. (1992), 'Issues in Course Design' in Bines, H. and Watson, D. (eds), *Developing Professional Education*, The Society for Research into Higher Education and the Open University Press, Buckingham.

Brayne, H. (1994), 'LPC Skills Assessment - a Year's Experience', 28, *The Law Teacher*, p.227.

Cranston, R. (1996), 'The Bad Reviewer: Three Gaps in the First ACLEC Report', 13, *SPTL Reporter*, 7.

De Witte, B. (1994), 'The European Dimension of Legal Education', in P.B.H. Birks (ed), *Reviewing Legal Education*, Oxford University Press, Oxford, p. 68.

Dwyer, G. (1996), Never Mind the Quality-feel the Width?: The Use of Video as a Medium for Continuing Skills Training, in *Skills Development for Tomorrow's Lawyers: Needs and Strategies*, The Australasian Professional Legal Education Council (APLEC), pp. 333-354.

Eraut, M. (1990), 'Indentifying Knowledge which Underpins Performance', in Black, H. and Woolf, A. (eds), *Knowledge and Competence: Current Issues in Training and Education*,

Department for Employment, Sheffield.

Gold, N., Mackie, K. and Twining, W. (eds) (1989), *Learning Lawyers' Skills*, Butterworths, in conjunction with the Commonwealth Legal Education Association, London.

Goriely, T. and Williams, T. (1996), *The Impact of the New Training Scheme: Report on a Qualitative Study*, The Law Society, London.

Halpern, D. (1994), *Entry Into the Legal Professions, The Law Student Cohort Study Years 1 and 2*, The Law Society, London.

Havelock, P., Hasler, J., Flew, R., McIntyre, D., Schofield, T. and Toby, J. (1995), *Professional Education for General Practice*, Oxford University Press, Oxford.

Hillyer, J.V. (1996), *The Future of Vocational Legal Education and the Legal Practice Course: A Survey of the Views of Solicitors and Other Organisations which are Registered to take Trainee Solicitors*, The College of Law, London.

Hillyer, J.V. (1997), 'From Theory of Practice, into Practice', paper presented to a conference on Theory in Legal Education at the Institute of Advanced Legal Studies, University of London.

Hughes, A.K. (1994), *Developing European Professions: Delivering Continuing Professional Development in Europe*, University of Bristol.

Jones, P.A. (1996), 'We're All Reflective Practitioners Now: Reflections on Professional Education', in Webb, J. and Maughan, C. (eds), *Teaching Lawyers' Skills*, Butterworths, London.

Latrup-Pedersen, T. (1995), 'Legal Education and Training in Europe: Denmark', 2, *International Journal of the Legal Profession*, pp. 89-94.

Le Brun, M. and Johnstone, R. (1994), *The Quiet (R)evolution: Improving Student Learning in Law*, The Law Book Company Limited, Sydney.

Leighton, P., Mortimer,T. and Whatley, N. (1995), *Today's Law Teachers: Lawyers or Academics?*, Cavendish, London.

Masclet, J-C., Ludet, D. and Delcros, X. (1995), 'Legal Education and Training in Europe: France', 2, *International Journal of the Legal Profession*, pp.18-22.

Ormrod (1971), *Report of the Committee on Legal Education*, Cmnd 4595 (the 'Ormrod Report').

Ramsden, P. (1992), *Learning to Teach in Higher Education*, Routledge, London.

Report of the Committee on the Future of the Legal Profession (1988), *A Time for Change* (the 'Marre Report'), General Council of the Bar and the Law Society, p.130.

Report of the Professionalism Committee (1996), *Teaching and Learning Professionalism*, American Bar Association, Chicago.

Report of the Task Force on Law Schools and the Profession (1992), *Legal Education and*

Professional Development - an Educational Continuum: Narrowing the Gap, American Bar Association, Chicago (the 'McCrate Report').

Savage, N. and Watt, G. (1996), 'A House of Intellect for the Profession', in P.B.H. Birks (ed), *What are Law Schools for? Pressing Problems in the Law, vol. 2*, Oxford University Press, Oxford, pp. 45-57.

Schon, D. (1987), *Educating the Reflective Practitioner*, Jossey-Bass Inc, San Francisco.

Select Committee on Legal Education Report 25th August 1846, H. of C. 686.

Shapland, J., Johnston, V. and Wild, R. (1993), *Studying for the Bar*, Institute for the Study of the Legal Profession, University of Sheffield.

Shapland, J. and Le Grys, R. (eds) (1994), *The Changing Shape of the Legal Profession*, Institute for the Study of the Legal Profession, University of Sheffield.

Sherr, A. (1996), Foreword to Webb, J. and Maughan, C. (eds), *Teaching Lawyers' Skills*, Butterworths, London.

Susskind, R. (1996), *The Future of Law: Facing the Challenges of Information Technology*, Clarendon Press, Oxford.

The College of Law (1991), *European Community Law Research Project 1991: What European Community Law have Trainee Solicitors Studied in their Law Degree?*, The College of Law, Guildford.

The College of Law (1995), *Survey of Students' Funding on the Legal Practice Course 1994/5 at The College of Law*, The College of Law, Guildford.

The Law Society (1990), *Training Tomorrow's Solicitors: Proposals for Changes to the Education of Trainee Solicitors*, The Law Society, London, a consultation paper by the Training Committee.

The Law Society (1996), *Annual Statistical Report 1996*, The Law Society, London.

The Royal Commission on Legal Services (1979), Cmnd 7648-1, vol. 2, Part B (the 'Benson Report').

Toddington, S. (1996), 'The Emperor's New Skills: The Academy, The Profession and the Idea of Legal Education', in P.B.H. Birks (ed), *What are Law Schools For? Pressing Problems in The Law, Vol. 2*, Oxford University Press, Oxford.

Tribe, D. (1996), 'DIY Learning- Self and Peer Assessment', in Webb, J. and Maughan, C. (eds), *Teaching Lawyers' Skills*, Butterworths, London, pp.353-368.

Twining, W. (1994), *Blackstone's Tower: The English Law School*, Sweet & Maxwell, London.

Webb, J. and Maughan, C. (eds) (1996), *Teaching Lawyers' Skills*, Butterworths, London.

Woolf, Rt. Hon. Lord (1996), *Access to Justice: Final Report to the Lord Chancellor on the Civil Justice System in England and Wales*, HMSO, London.

6 Legal Education, Globalization, and the New Imperialism[1]

JOHN FLOOD

Introduction

Law and legal education are being exposed to tough developments as globalization alters the configuration of world society. This chapter speculates on a number of themes. What, if any, is the role of legal education in globalization? If elements of globalization are imposed by the international governmental organizations (IGOs), and NGOs, such as the World Bank, European Bank of Reconstruction and Development, and the IMF, how will their constituencies respond to the demand for the "rule of law" within their societies? As more economies and societies are brought under the rubric of global trade, what means will be adopted to co-ordinate them? Perhaps an important point is that legal education has only just begun to respond to these pressures and is ill equipped to deal with them. In fact, it is uncertain if there is anything in legal education (or the discipline of the law) itself that will furnish a creative response. Legal education is rather compelled to find other means of joining in the game. I explore this aspect by ascribing a role of engendering trust to law schools. They do it in conjunction with law firms that are often the conduits to employment in IGOs and NGOs and related governmental institutions. The principal idea for the creation of trust is taken from Luhmann, who views it as a means of reducing complexity in the modern era. There is one particular problem with my approach: it is too partial. The story of globalization is not really one that involves law and lawyers very much. Other players have a more significant role; among them are bankers, financiers, traders, and accountants. Lawyers are not in the vanguard of this movement. This might be the result of the conservatism of lawyers and the domestic orientation of most jurisdictions. In a few cases we can locate a juridical field that is not bound in these ways, e.g., *lex mercatoria.* My approach may be summarized as institutional in that I emphasize the roles of organizations and categories of professionals rather than concentrate on issues of substantive law or the contents of particular law courses and training programmes. I believe that law and lawyers have roles to play in globalization —whatever that may be— but they are unsure as to what they are and they have been, and continue to be, slow in developing them.[2]

The remaining sections of the chapter include an outline of some of the potential players in globalization and legal education; a mapping out of the economic context; a discussion of elite law schools and the potential for globalization, loosely construed, in their curriculum, and the ways law firms enhance this process; and finally I attempt to bring together these themes. 'You cannot trust chaos. If nothing connects with anything else, or everything with everything else, it becomes impossible to build generalizations. In other words, a single system cannot, by itself, generate higher generalization or trust' (Luhmann 1979: 39).

Globalization, as a set of processes, economic, cultural and economic, has the potential to engender chaos.[3] Trust is a necessary condition for global business to work because much business takes place outwith the law. And it is outside because there is hardly any global law for global business to operate within. Until law and regulation catch up with the practices of global business, trust is one of the few means of reducing chaos and complexity and promoting order. One way of creating trust, then, is through engendering and sharing common cultural values with others that accrue from common institutional bases, e.g., college, law school, profession, by creating moral and epistemic communities that transcend national categories. Trust, therefore, has to be learned (Luhmann 1979: 27), even though it is irrational. Trust is always contingent: its proofis in the absence of breach. Tradition and modernity coexist; the process of economic rationalization never totally disempowers tradition and cultural differentiation because the habits of religion and ethics that help generate trust are deeply rooted within many societies (Fukuyama 1995: 352-53).

Global business is prospering, as is the business of attempting to regulate restructure its activities.[4] The surge in globalization has entailed significant modifications in the ways communities and nations function, the dramatic changes in eastern Europe and the former Soviet Union are cases in point. While business has flourished, social and economic life for many has become impoverished as the mainstays of socialist or state systems of welfare have collapsed or been destroyed (cf. Rhodes and Nabi 1992). Western ideals of economic development reign supreme, but are they prevailing at the expense of the ideals of justice and community?

Potential Players

In 1996, the Bank for International Settlements (BIS) was able to report that:

> The international financial system continues to grow steadily in size, complexity and geographical scope. Cross-border transactions in bonds and equities among the Group of Seven countries (excluding the United Kingdom) rose from 35% of GDP in 1985 to around 140% last year. The survey of derivatives markets carried out by central banks in April 1995 indicated that the outstanding notional value of derivative contracts amounted to over $40 trillion in over-the-counter markets alone. Moreover, restrictions on cross-border rights of establishment for financial institutions have been virtually eliminated in industrial countries and are being sharply scaled back elsewhere. These developments are to be welcomed. They allow a more efficient allocation of capital both domestically and internationally, lead to lower-cost financial services, and offer new means for hedging risks of all sorts. (BIS 1996: 166)

The ideas promoted by the BIS in this paragraph are saturated in law. To take Llewellyn's conception of law jobs, an international financial system requires appropriate sets of technologies, processes, and ideas to enable the participants to function in rational ways (Twining 1973; 1993). There are issues of regulation, deregulation, comity, supra-national legislation, supervision, and dispute resolution. Halliday (1995: 742-43) argues that, 'We live in a world of growing global structures, or of transnational, but not state-related, structures that escape orthodox control'. Even so, for economic development and the extension of markets the role of law—whatever form it may take and under whose authority it is exercised—is crucial. People need rules to sanction their plays in the marketplace. Now that the marketplace for many is global, there has been a resurgence in the idea of *lex mercatoria* (Teubner 1997). Many of these developments have occurred among the elite players in the field of law (e.g., Flood and Caiger 1993; McBarnet 1994; Dezalay and Garth 1996, Arthurs and Kreklewich 1996; cf. Epp 1992; Santos 1995). The relationship between globalization and the field of law is reflexive: as the economy expands and integrates, its need for regulation also grows; the economy demands particular kinds of law and law thereby shapes the economy. A number of questions are posed and there are also resonances in this relationship. Is globalization a new name for modernization with its imperialist connotations? Are we seeing domination through a particularly western mode of law discourse, a deterritorialization of law? Does globalization mean that the global and local coexist or are the tensions too great? Can ideas of economy and justice coexist or are they antagonistic to each other? Are the great international organizations promoting economic discourse at the expense of discourses on community, ethics and justice?

The relatively small numbers of players in the global law field, i.e., transnational law practice, means there is a paucity of formal educational skills at large, and so the result is that much of the craft of lawyering for the global order is learned through apprenticeship with elites rather than through academic routes, following Samuel Butler who wrote, 'An art can only be learned in the workshop of those who are winning their bread by it'. Formal educational institutions subsequently came late to these challenges. The first to do so were the major business schools in Europe and the US. Legal education has, however, been slow and inadequate in its response (cf. Flood 1996).

Elite status is reinforced by the open recognition of many consumers of law and lawyers that of all the legal regimes in the world only two are of significant consequence in transnational work, namely, English law and New York state law (Flood 1996, Economist 1996a).[5] The number of potential law schools able to supply graduates capable of doing legal work at this level is small. Other jurisdictions are significant, of course, but they are dominated by this western duopoly. I have shown elsewhere that international business lawyers often define themselves by three attributes: A mastery of the English language, which is the common language of international business and finance, an ability to draft contracts, more in the prolix Anglo-Saxon style rather than in the concise continental way, and an understanding of private dispute resolution systems, such as arbitration. On occasion a fourth requisite is claimed, namely, admission to another jurisdiction, notably the New York Bar (Flood 1996: 190).

The key here is that the prototypical international business lawyer can operate in any system of law provided the conditions above are met. This is reinforced by advertisements for lawyers in the major financial institutions. The European Bank for Reconstruction and Development, for example, advertised for counsel with the following characteristics:

> Education: graduate law degree from a leading university required; post-graduate degree from a leading university in another country desirable; Work Experience: at least four years international lending, investment or project/asset finance experience in a leading international law firm or the legal department of a leading international bank or other financial institution required; Skills: excellent legal drafting in English required; evidence of good negotiating skills desirable; Languages: excellent spoken communication in English required; fluency in a language other than English, preferably a central or eastern European language, desirable.
> (Econlis, 25 January 1997, 129)

Although legal education is parochial and prescriptive, it has a residual power. Most of the major institutions—governmental, NGOs, supranational—in the western world (and many elsewhere) are partly staffed by people with legal training (but not necessarily legal education) (cf. Miller 1995). It is one of the ultimate portable skills. There is a paradox, however, in the skills required and those supplied by the academy. Finance and capital are more or less the same anywhere; a unit of labour is a person, and so on, but legal rules are inextricably embedded in jurisdictions that operate largely within national boundaries (EBRD 1995). Despite this inherent parochialism, there has been an explosion in the development of global law firms and some would say global law (e.g., lex mercatoria), and in the global roles of professionals who work alongside law. What is happening here? Does it have any impact on legal education or vice versa (cf. Bradney 1995)? Have certain dominant educational institutions become gatekeepers for a global corps of leaders? How do all these developments affect lawyers in developing and emerging countries? How have a few law schools become the major credentialling institutions in the race towards globalization?

A different set of issues is to ask do law schools add value? This question is allied to another, which is what value do lawyers add to transactions? Gilson (1984) argued that lawyers reduced transaction costs by reducing information asymmetries and therefore were not a net cost and necessary liability to business, but rather enhanced the value of transactions.[6] It is possible to contend that as law becomes increasingly specialized and that mastery of that specialization must occur at an earlier stage in lawyers' careers, the craft mode of learning skills becomes expensive (i.e., through loss of billable time) relative to the tyro developing the skills in graduate school.[7] This presupposes that the undergraduate curriculum remains the same in order to establish the infrastructure of skills—but we could ask why it should—which can then be built on by specific graduate programmes. Law schools can also add value in other ways, by instilling and emphasizing notions of the good and the ethical.[8] This is the idea of the lawyer as good citizen. But law schools have a number of roles (Twining 1995), among which is a growing training element for organizations.[9] And globalization is a spur to this end.

Not all of these questions can be answered here but some are best examined within the context for the operation of international business law as a function of foreign investment. This framework takes into account the regulatory and normative infrastructures of markets and finance. The condition of international business is predicated on the concept of trust. As Giddens bluntly puts it, "Modernity is inherently prone to crisis, on many levels...Crises in this sense become a 'normal' part of life, but by definition they cannot be routinized" (Giddens 1991: 184). Globalization, a key feature of modernity, encapsulates this sense of crisis by inflaming uncertainty: the idea that business ignores borders does not negate the cultural and moral dangers that inhere in dealing with strangers. Another way of putting this has been framed by Luhmann (1979: 8) who postulated that 'Where there is trust there are increased possibilities for experience and action, there is an increase in the complexity of the social system and also in the number of possibilities which can reconciled with its structure, because trust constitutes a more effective form of complexity reduction'. And, although globalization appears faceless and technology driven, it nevertheless requires some face-to-face interaction and means of formulating relationships of trust (cf. Boden and Molotch 1994). Among elites this is facilitated by membership of a relatively small number of institutions, such as leading law and business schools and professional service firms. Some of these institutions are examined to explain how they contribute to the cadres of international business.

Four vignettes signify the themes in this chapter. In the first an Eastern European government agency tried to purchase wheat on the world futures market to reduce shortages of bread. The head of the agency was inexperienced in the ways of capitalist markets, so he relied on a well-tried technique for dealing with these things: he asked an expatriate friend living in the west to buy it for him. The wheat was bought and delivered but was useless for making bread as it would not rise more than two centimetres. Moreover, the prices paid had varied widely. The agency head was at a loss to account for these variations because as he noted the wheat was mostly purchased in Geneva and Vienna and climatological maps clearly showed that there was little difference between the two cities. In fact, he had bought wheat imported from other areas. A UK white-collar crime lawyer was later called into explain how futures markets worked and how fraud was practised.

The second vignette involves the World Bank, which advertised a $30 million programme for modernizing the Venezualan judiciary only in the US and UK. Only western expertise was capable of bringing the Latin American judiciary up to the standards necessary to reassure global business. And if this project was successful, the World Bank would fund the modernization of more state judiciaries elsewhere.

The third is a letter to the Economist in 1996 from an Asian correspondent: 'Your article on Asian business empires acknowledges that many successors to family businesses are educated at western business schools. But you fail to point out that many also spent much of their childhood in a western country. The cultural make-up of these successors is therefore quite different from that of their parents. The new generation is more westernised; delegation is more acceptable to them, hence a willingness to restructure the family business.'

Finally, at the 1995 International Bar Conference in Paris during a session on the globalization of the legal profession, an East African delegate remonstrated with the UK and US members who were talking of the dominance of their respective laws and professions in the global marketplace as synonymous with globalization. The delegate made it clear that he resented bodies such as the International Monetary Fund coming to third world countries and issuing edicts on the appropriate measures to modernize their economies. What galled him particularly was the way in which the IMF ignored local professionals, preferring instead to work with UK and US law firms. The delegate warned that if such bodies refused to acknowledge the contributions that local professionals could make, then foreign advisers would find themselves excluded from practising in these countries. They had to learn to work in partnership with locals. This intervention was met with silence.

Inherent in these vignettes is a poignancy that laissez-faire capitalism has ignored: the expansion of 'free markets' does not necessarily enable local communities to participate fully in the world market and polity. Indeed, the new imperialism of the supranational bodies is deficient in the benign paternalism of the old-style colonialism which at least pretended to have the welfare of communities at heart. The present emphasis of bodies such as the IMF and the World Bank is, at a basic level, on technical restructuring leading to a hope that markets will, as a spillover effect, generate new social structures. If these fail to come about, the restructuring cannot be blamed because technical restructuring is value-neutral, non-repressive and therefore not the cause. The cause will most likely lie in some cultural and social peculiarities of the particular societies.

Economic Context

In order to understand lawyers and legal education in the processes of globalization, the following context is adumbrated. Economic reasons have driven the expansion of finance and commerce throughout the world, but it is worth examining where the bulk of the investment takes place. The major form of investment in global business is foreign direct investment (FDI) (Thomsen and Nicolaides 1990), which has been defined by the International Monetary Fund (IMF) as

> ...investment that is made to acquire a lasting interest in an enterprise operating in an economy other than that of the investor, the purpose being to have an effective voice in the management of the enterprise.
> (IMF 1977a)[10]

The development of FDI therefore gives a proxy for the growth in and scale of global business. Since the 1970s there has been a high rate of growth in FDI as Table 1 below illustrates (see also Economics Focus 1996).

Table 1 Stock of foreign direct investment in selected countries

Country	**Assets**				**Liabilities**			
	1975	1980	1985	1989	1975	1980	1985	1989
USA	124	215	230	373	28	83	185	401
Japan	17	20	44	154	3	3	5	9
Germany	15	31	43	104	19	25	23	40
France	14	28	73		17	37	61	

Italy	3	7	18	47	9	9	19	51
UK	38	79	107	224	24	63	63	138
Canada	10	23	39	64	40	60	62	103
Netherlands	20	42	50	63	20	11	15	30
Australia	1	5	7	27	9	25	27	57
Total	**228**	**436**	**566**	**1129**	**152**	**296**	**436**	**890**

Note: Figures in billion US dollars. *Source*: Allison, 1993, p.115.

The USA has the largest rate of FDI, but Japan, Germany and the UK have grown considerably over the period shown in Table 1.[11] Although Bank for International Settlements' figures show FDI still increasing overall (BIS 1995: Table III.8), indicators provided by UNCTAD demonstrate that the rate of growth of FDI is not directed uniformly upwards (UNCTAD 1994: Table 1).

The direction of FDI also indicates how economies are opening up in the global marketplace. Primarily FDI flows among "Triad" members, i.e., the United States, the European Union, and Japan (Ohmae 1991). Figure 1 shows the flows in billions of dollars.

The largest FDI flows are within the European Union and between the US and the EU. Developing countries receive relatively little, with one exception, namely, China, which received inflows of $34 billion (BIS 1995: 67). Latin America's inflows of FDI, however, are less than those of Asia, and generally there is a greater reliance on portfolio investment rather than direct investment flows (BIS 1995: 68).

In addition to FDI the evolution of capital markets may well reduce the options available to governments (Eichengreen 1994). The Mexican financial crisis "...highlighted the volatility of many forms of capital movement, drawing attention in particular to the risks that can arise when capital inflows cause exchange rate overvaluation and unsustainably large current account deficits" (BIS 1995: 141). Both sound financial and regulatory systems have to be in place to encourage, enable and empower development while preventing the kinds of crises of which Mexico was one. The general manager of the BIS, Andrew Crockett, outlined what might be happening and what needed to be done:

> The deepening of global integration at all levels of economic activity implies a continuing need for policy-makers to exchange views regularly and to

seek a consensus where possible on issues that bear on their countries' joint well-being. Such cooperation works in the main through country representatives agreeing on what needs to be done, relying on the moral force of such agreements to encourage any needed changes to national policies, legislation and regulation. Such a cooperative approach may at times seem slow and laborious but experience has shown that it can succeed and that the benefits warrant the effort invested.
(BIS 1995: 212)

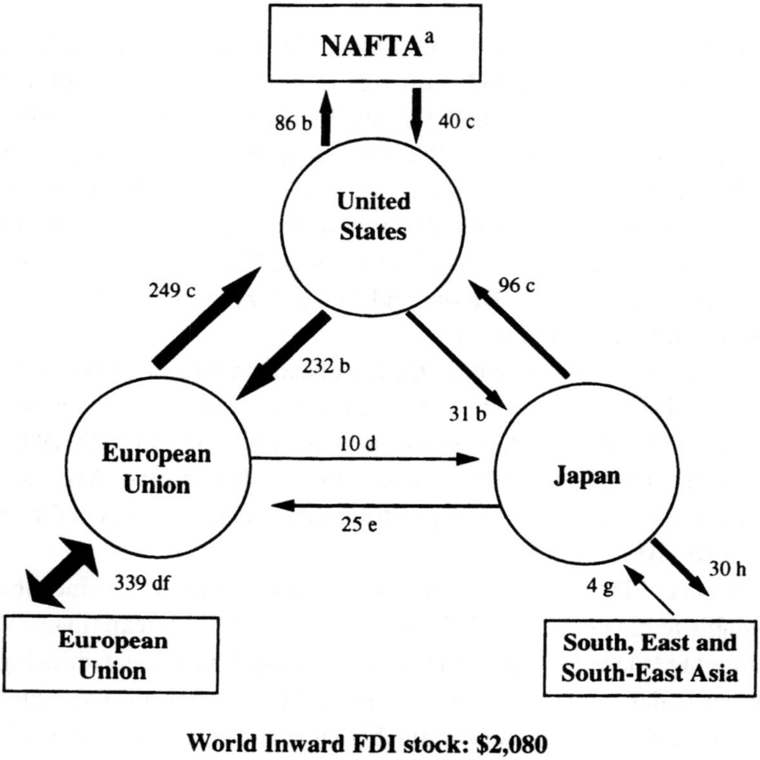

Figure 1 FDI Stock among Triad members and their clusters, 1993 (billions of US dollars)

Source: UNCTAD, Division on Transnational Corporations and Investment, *World Investment Report 1995: Transnational Corporations and Competitiveness* (United Nations publications, Sales No. E.95.II.A.9).

a. Canada and Mexico.
b. United States outward FDI stock.

c. United States inward FDI stock.
d. Data from inward FDI stock of Austria, Finland, France, Germany, Italy, Netherlands, Sweden and the United Kingdom. Data for Austria are for 1991 and data for France and the Netherlands are for 1992.
e. Outward FDI stock of Austria, Finland, France, Germany, Italy, Netherlands and the United Kingdom. Data for Austria and France are for 1991 and data for Italy and the Netherlands are for 1992.
f. For Sweden, the data reflect FDI to and from all European countries, Intra-European Union FDI, based on inward stocks, is $225 billion.
g. Data are based on approvals/notifications and represent those from countries other than those in North America and Europe.
h. Estimated by multiplying the values of cumulative flows to the region according to FDI approvals by the ratio of disbursed to approved/notified FDI in developing countries.

The integration of developed and developing economies necessitates a levelling of institutional understanding and operation. For example, central bankers must be able to cooperate with each other or risk disrupting the fragile international financial system,[12] but achieving a level field is difficult.[13] In countries which have just begun to emerge from centrally planned economies or authoritarian regimes, banks may not appear to have the expertise and autonomy to act within international rules. This is especially so in Eastern Europe. Indeed, the general counsel for the European Bank of Reconstruction and Development (EBRD) said

> The EBRD's mandate is to foster the transition towards market economies in the countries of the Former Soviet Union and Central and Eastern Europe, and to promote private and entrepreneurial initiative...Recognising fully the importance to sustainable economic development of stable "rules of the game" and the establishment and continued strengthening of law administration and enforcement institutions, the EBRD has embarked on the provision of legal technical assistance to its countries of operation that will foster the transition process.
> (Taylor 1996: 98)

The EBRD has carried out two surveys on progress in legal reform in its constituency countries, both of which show reform is directly proportional to inward investment flows (Law in Transition 1996: 4). As investment increases, reform speeds up to accommodate it; where investment is slow, reform remains low on the political agenda. The EBRD's Transition Report 1995 (EBRD 1995), shows how various countries are dealing with the implementation of investment. The figures demonstrate that development throughout regions is uneven and irregular, that western modes of doing business will not suffice in other cultures, and that the residual effects of previous social and economic systems linger long after they have been usurped. But whereas markets can flourish, the state is often inadequate to the task of providing regulatory and legal frameworks for their successful and uncorrupted functioning. The figures contained in the Report illustrate the different levels of development in respect of investment regulation and support. Differences occur in the ability of foreigners to own businesses and land, whether investment laws are drafted by legally trained personnel or not, how easy or difficult it is to gain access to laws, what kinds of administration exist to protect interests, and the expertise and status of the judiciary involved in investment disputes. Implicit in this survey is a goal of certain targets that each constituent country should meet. Failure to do so is deemed a matter of inadequacy more than a taste for local norms and customs that are at odds with western ways. The terms 'emerging', 'transitional', and 'developing' carry within them a connotation of the primitive, the precursor to the maturity of the modern.

Even though legislative change may occur, and it is clearly necessary for economic development, it is not sufficient unless there is institutional change to match it. Taylor argued that:

> The EBRD has also recognised that there is very little point in having well drafted laws on the statute books of its countries of operations unless such laws are properly enforced by trained lawyers and judiciary in a consistent, effective and non-discriminatory manner. The area of institutional development and legal training, there, is another important element of the EBRD's legal transition efforts.
> (Taylor 1996: 99)

Part of the task of world institutions as demonstrated by the activities of the World Bank and the EBRD is to enable a diverse group of nations to participate in global markets and enhance the skills of the local professionals in that endeavour. Some commentators see institution-building as the third wave of development economics, after the initial phase of subsidizing economies followed by market-based development (Economist 1997a: 93). In addition to building credible legal systems and freeing central banks, political reform is necessary.

Sustaining and implementing reforms is not simply a matter of ticking off a checklist, but a question of strategy and priorities. Governments not only need to do the right reforms in the right order; they also need to make them stick. This means building a consensus for reform. It sometimes means compensating losers, even government elites themselves. The difficulty is how to create the kinds of incentives that will ensure these elites want to continue reform (Economist 1997: 94).

Since the Mexican crisis the IMF has suggested that:

> ...investors have become more sensitive to economic fundamentals in host countries- -the size of current account deficits in relation to foreign exchange reserves, external debt, and domestic saving; growth potential; and the soundness of the banking system. Furthermore, those segments of the international investment community—mostly institutional investors—that invested heavily in the emerging markets appear to have become more knowledgeable... .
> (IMF Research Dept Staff 1996a: 5)

The results of these moves are illustrated, for example, by comparing the levels of FDI into the Baltics, CIS and Eastern Europe, with a population of 400 million, with that of Malaysia with a population of 19 million: they are the same (World Bank 1995).

From one perspective, then, the emerging integration and restructuring of the world economy calls for a reshaping of the normative frameworks that have customarily been used, at both macro and micro levels. The major institutions operate at the macro-economic level dealing with bank regulation, investment laws, and budget laws, for example. While at the micro level we see organizations, such as the Association of Chartered Certified Accountants, training accountants in developing countries in how to interpret the UK 'true and fair view', with the aid of the British Government's 'Know How' fund.

Most FDI then is still directed at the developed world rather than emerging markets, which are still eyed with suspicion. Moreover, some emerging markets lack the moral, social and cultural infrastructure that encourages reciprocity of behaviour. The reactions of users to courts' actions when such a state is a party are telling (e.g., Armenia, Kazakstan, and Turkmenistan; see EBRD 1995). Although, to an extent, action is predictable—albeit the wrong way—the ability to rely on common values in business is absent. This absence is a strong barrier to investment. And this is where education and training can assist, because they begin to create those shareable values, values which are worth sharing in the eyes of western, developed countries. If western values are to prevail, then many problems that now exist will grow over time as orientalism (Said 1995) or the 'Confucian challenge' (Fukuyama 1995), broadly defined, emerges as a powerful force in the global economy.[14]

Law Schools and Globalization

In an attempt to discern law schools' responses to globalization I analyzed the prospectuses of a set of the top law schools in the US and the UK. I was interested in the kind and quantity of international courses offered and, more importantly, whether there was an explicit embrace of globalization within courses or elsewhere. As long ago as 1991 one American commentator was arguing that law schools should not just introduce courses with international dimensions, but should in fact internationalize the entire curriculum because internationalization/globalization had begun to infuse all aspects of life (Khan 1991).[15] I adopted these indices as proxies for the law school response to a perceived need for legal development in the way that the EBRD general counsel was mentioning above. In comparing legal education in the US and UK it is essential to bear in mind that in the former law is a graduate degree whereas in the latter first degrees are part of the undergraduate curriculum. To compensate for that I have mainly examined graduate prospectuses in the UK and ordinary American law school catalogues.[16] Both American and British universities actively market their degrees to overseas students who bring in lucrative amounts of tuition fees.

One important point must be made here. What follows is largely speculative and needs considerable amounts of further research.[17] I have not delved into the history of these courses, nor have I computed student numbers, so I cannot say what the student demand is for these courses. I have glossed over the distinction between international, transnational and global. They are distinct terms, but to some degree I have made them fungible.

In the UK the top law schools are clustered in the 'golden triangle' of Oxford, Cambridge and London.[18] Each offers a taught one- year, self-contained, graduate degree, usually the LL.M. Of the three London is unusual in that six separate law schools combine their efforts to produce a London-wide programme of graduate study with many more courses than either Oxford or Cambridge.[19] Table 2 shows the proportions of international (i.e., non-domestic) course.

Table 2 International graduate courses at top UK law schools

Name and Degree	Total Graduate Courses	International Courses
Cambridge LL.M.	28	8 (28%)
London LL.M.	142	60 (42%)
Oxford B.C.L.	24	6 (25%)

Source: Derived from law school prospectuses.

Oxford and Cambridge have not capitalized on the international/global market in a substantive way, although their names are recognized everywhere.[20] International courses comprise about one quarter of their law courses. London, however, has close to a half of its LL.M. courses focussed on international themes.[21]

The American situation is quite different. For purposes of comparison I selected the four top national law schools, namely, Harvard, Yale, Columbia, and Chicago, which offer the J.D. degree and separated out the proportions of their international courses. See Table 3.

Table 3 International courses at top US law schools

Name and Degree	Total Courses	International Courses
Harvard J.D.	249	48 (19%)
Yale J.D.	10	11 (10%)
Columbia J.D.	265	37 (14%)
Chicago J.D.	155	22 (14%)

Source: Derived from law school prospectuses.

In absolute terms the numbers of courses provided are greater than in the UK, with the exception of London. Despite the greater numbers, in percentage terms American schools offer fewer courses than their British counterparts. The real difference lies in the approach of the schools. Oxford and Cambridge offer a traditional array of courses along the lines of private and public international law, with perhaps alternative courses on international dispute resolution. London has internationalized a bigger range of courses, e.g., labour law, environmental law, energy law, investment law. The addition of SOAS to the London law schools also provides courses on topics such as

Chinese and Japanese law, African and Islamic law. While it is possible to concentrate on particular areas of study in the London LL.M., the courses are distributed quite widely through the London law schools. In this respect the delivery of international courses in the US law schools is probably more highly developed, especially at Harvard and Columbia. For example, Columbia organizes its courses under various rubrics e.g., corporate and securities law, human rights, international, foreign and comparative law. Within the latter group there are courses on international economic law (GATT and WTO), Russia and the CIS, cross-border legal transactions, and specialist courses on aspects of Japanese, Korean, Latin-American and East European law. This is bolstered by centres that specialize in some of these areas, such as the Parker School of Foreign and Comparative Law, the Center for Japanese Legal Studies, and the Center for Chinese Legal Studies. Finally, the intellectual stature of these schools is underpinned by journals that produce and disseminate knowledge. Columbia, for example, has at least four journals concerned with non-domestic matters, namely, the American Journal of International Arbitration, the Columbia Journal of Transnational Law, the Journal of Chinese Law, and the Journal of East European Law.[22]

Reasons for the differences are not difficult to find. UK universities usually have highly bureaucratized systems of course delivery. Introducing a new course is a long-term project, often involving validation by others than the instructor. American law schools are largely autonomous units within the university structure and have a much more flexible response to the organization of law courses. There is considerable room for experiment. For example, at Harvard the ongoing O.J. Simpson criminal trial became the basis for a criminal evidence course.[23]

American law schools are primary institutions, although their J.D. degrees are considered terminal. That is the award of the J.D. degree permits the holder to sit the bar examination and begin practice.[24] In the UK a law degree enables one to apply for a vocational law course, not to practise. Furthermore, American law professors are generally paid more than other professors in the university, which has the effect of enhancing their status.[25] They also retain stronger links with key practitioners, often giving them adjunct faculty status. For example, in the international, foreign and comparative law curriculum at Columbia four courses are taught by adjunct faculty: three by attorneys with major New York law firms; one is jointly taught between a law firm partner and a senior counsel to the Chase Manhattan Bank; and one by the chief counsel to the World Bank.

If law schools tackle the problems of globalization, they make a pass at it by running courses or graduate degrees specializing in the area. Only one law school has attempted to mark itself as a global law school. New York University Law School has created a 'global law school program' which has been supported by $75 million in donations (Deal 1994: 1; Myers 1994: 2). It has three main aims: to create a global faculty of 20 law professors from around the world who will teach in conjunction with NYU faculty; to endow 20 full scholarships for overseas graduate students; and to support research through a centre on property and innovation in a global economy (NYU: The Law School Magazine 1995: 5-6). The visiting faculty are predominantly UK, German, and Japanese, representing the more powerful interests in the world. There is one from Egypt, representing both the Arab and African interests, although he teaches in Switzerland. This is the most explicit form of merchandising yet by a law school, and one with imperial ambitions, when it says,

> As the processes of transformation and globalization unfold, law is playing and increasingly will play a critical role; indeed, the success of the emerging global community will depend in large part upon the integration and accommodation of disparate traditions through law. American law and its lawyers are playing a pivotal role: the United States has developed the world's most elaborate legal system; our Constitution is an obvious model for compacts governing the relationship of governments to their citizens; and American commercial law is providing the reference point as others develop their own legal regimes.
> (NYU: The Law School Magazine 1995: 5)

Although this single instance cannot be taken as a general trend in legal education, it is, I believe, indicative of a burgeoning commercialization of legal education. NYU has developed a 'super-niche' through co-opting globalization as its motif (in contrast to its well-known niche tax LL.M. programme). Most others, whether British or American, have relied on the adjective international rather than global. It is a transition that business schools have already undergone.

The role of the global law school as presented here is one that will export American legal ideas and concepts throughout the world, especially among the emerging markets. In some ways it is a backward step from what is already being done by law firms and other international institutions. For example, Gordon et al. (1996) argue that a significant role of international institutions like the IMF is to offer 'technical assistance' by transplanting basic, so-called 'neutral' laws, e.g., tax and budget laws, to countries that either do not have them or possess inferior versions of them. These are evidently not value-neutral exercises in legal technical assistance. Amongst other things, tax and budget laws exercise a considerable impact on social welfare programmes, which might have far-reaching consequences for a developing country. This is evident in the IMF's own words when it writes:

> Much [technical legal] assistance was to members with economies in transition from central planning that are seeking advice to establish an appropriate legal framework for a sound fiscal structure, modern financial sector institutions, and market-oriented financial transactions. Often the assistance to these countries involved revision of legislation passed early in the transition period that has since proved inadequate...The department helped to build capacity among local officials both through the discussions involved in giving advice and by conducting courses and seminars... .
> (IMF 1997b: 150)[26]

This kind of development is being taken further as the United Nations attempts to establish a global accounting qualification through the intergovernmental working group on International Standards of Accounting and Reporting (ISAR); 'ISAR hopes a global qualification will provide a "benchmark" which will be used by developing countries to reduce the "education gap" with the developed world'.

> The stated purpose is to enhance local professionals and place them in fair competition with western accountants. It is also a means of imposing a western view on the manner in which accounts should be done.
> (The Accountant 1996)

Perhaps the last point to be made here, although not insignificant, is that the elite law schools are key credentialling institutions that feed candidates to the major law firms, international NGOs and big corporations.

The Role of Law Firms

Law firms are becoming central players in globalization, in both interpreting norms and creating them for states and individuals.[27] But what is their role in training lawyers for globalization? The top 20 law firms in the US and the UK were asked whether they had an internship programme for foreign lawyers.[28] Most have no formal scheme, but many run informal internships. In the US a typical example of the ad hoc approach is Weil Gotshal and Manges which takes on interns through contacts made by partners: for 1996 the firm had two interns from Japan and one from Hungary. An example of the formal programme is Shearman and Stirling which runs a Foreign Associate Program out of its New York office for 10 to 12 non-US lawyers a year, who are hired for one year. The countries represented by the programme include Argentina, Australia, Brazil, Chile, Colombia, England, France, Germany, Greece, Hungary, Japan, Korea, Mexico, Peru, Philippines, Russia, Switzerland and Venezuela. In the UK the situation is highly variable, with some firms running internship programmes and others not. For example, Slaughter and May runs a programme that takes about 12 lawyers per year for six months from firms that it has associations with. The most developed programme is that of Simmons and Simmons. It runs eight schemes. See Figure 2 below.

Figure 2 Internship schemes run by Simmons and Simmons

1. *Overseas Associated Offices*: lawyers come from associated offices in other jurisdictions.
2. *Blanche Lucas Scheme*: in connection with the British Hungarian Law Association one Hungarian lawyer visits the firm for one month.
3. *BELLA Scheme*: in connection with the British Estonian, Lithuanian and Latvian Association one lawyer visits the firm for one month.
4. *Chinese lawyers*: in association with the British Council one Chinese lawyer per year visits the firm for a two-month period.
5. *Pilot Scheme*: in association with the British Council and the College of Law Indian lawyers follow a six-week course at the College and a six-week internship with the firm.
6. *EFB Scheme*: in association with the Ecole de Formation des Barreaux, Paris, two students spend between two and three months at the London office.
7. *Practice Development Scheme*: involves taking on foreign lawyers for substantial periods of time to facilitate practice development. Interns have come from *inter alia* China, Germany, Luxembourg, Mongolia, Spain and Sweden.
8. *Other Schemes*: The firm has established links with a number of law firms overseas whereby lawyers are exchanged, e.g.:
*with a Japanese firm; interns may be in post for up to three years

*with an association of lawyers in South America, Club d'Abogados
*in a joint practice in Italy with Grippo & Associati
*in a joint venture with other law firms in Lisbon: the participants are called Groupe O'Legal Portugese, with firms from Spain, Brazil and Portugal.

The law firms outside the top ten usually run informal internships, e.g., Cameron McKennas takes in a variable number each year from usually Poland or Russia.

If globalization is taken seriously then, like the law schools above, law firms have to calculate how they can deliver uniformly high-quality services from lawyers who come from and practise in a range of cultures. The question is: can organizations impose uniform standards throughout their domestic and offshore offices? Most likely not. Horner (1997) argues that large, multi-regional law firms must train on a regional basis, taking into account the peculiar characteristics of local jurisdictions. Yet this type of training can be cross-cut by holding 'practice group-based' training that takes lawyers from different jurisdictions and immersing them in topics, such as international securities.

Law firms are important because they supply the key officers of the international NGOs, major domestic financial institutions, and central government offices. For example, both chief counsel of the Asian Development Bank and the EBRD were partners in large law firms. Also within the US they are becoming ad hoc educators in the elite law schools, as illustrated above.

Discussion

One way of interpreting globalization is to see it as a means for international elites to congregate in larger and denser patterns than hitherto. The processes of regulation are becoming more formalized and less 'mesocorporatist' (Moran 1991). These moves have been necessary as a greater number of 'strangers' interact with each other in the global markets. It is increasingly difficult, yet still necessary, to rely on the old system of ties that bind them - e.g., 'my word is my bond' - even though some cultural values might be shared across borders. To develop trust in these circumstances indicates that the institutions that contain the potential to create systems of trust must be seen to function globally and enhance the possibility of global understanding among elites. Trust in these systems is necessary because arm's-length relationships mediated through private governance schemes, i.e., contract or franchising, are not self-sustaining. They depend on external means of enforcement and regulation. As the figures in the Transition Report show (EBRD 1995), enforcement might not always be available, especially in situations of uncertainty where the opposing party is the state which expects to triumph regardless of the merits. Trust acts as a broker between rationality and tradition - neither subjective or objective; it assists in dividing up complexity into manageable bits and raising one's tolerance of ambiguity and uncertainty (Luhmann 1979).

In law some institutions already satisfy this condition, namely, the large law firms. They provide systems of patronage that transcend the professional boundaries since all commercial, non- governmental and international organizations require legal counsel, and they also export lawyers into mainstream management positions. The sources of such counsel are often the law firms who provide personnel and knowledge.[29] Although large law firms are havens of expertise (e.g., Powell 1993), they rely on traditions of apprenticeship and craft to instil skills in novices. They do not possess the theoretical knowledge and its means of dissemination found in the academy.[30] In order to improve the means by which globalization could progress, the academy was be co-opted into the globalization game. The example of New York University's Global Law School programme is one such recent instance. Nevertheless, other law schools have made efforts in these directions, with an increasing number of courses aimed at transnational topics, e.g., London, Harvard, Columbia. Others now try to build niche markets, whether geographically (e.g., Pacific Rim) or substantively (e.g., international human rights). There is now intense competition for students from overseas among law schools in the UK and US, much of which, although not all, is based on offering international business courses.

Still, the export of expert knowledge to 'developing or transitional' countries is not a clear, unilinear course. In a way it demands a paradigm shift in conceptualizing society and economy (cf. Kuhn 1970). The clearest example of this move has been the guiding philosophy behind George Soros' thinking in establishing the Central European University (CEU). Soros, a committed Popperian, believes that the former Communist countries of Eastern Europe can benefit from the ideas of Popper's *The Open Society and Its Enemies* after 40 years of totalitarian rule. The intellectual agenda is a grand one: it contains more than merely grafting laissez-faire market philosophies on top of proto-democratic modes of authority. It entails the creation of a new politics, which is not easy or quick. But following the honeymoon of the revolutionary late 1980s and early 1990s, there has been a backlash against the domination of Western expertise. The Times Higher Education Supplement (Opinion 1996) reported a Polish speaker at a CEU seminar saying of Western experts, 'They treat us as if we were ignorant, as if these were third-world countries. They know nothing about the history and make-up of the countries they are advising'. The article goes on to say that the CEU is 'much less interested in providing what emerging companies in the region are eager to buy - training in law, business studies, information technology' (Opinion 1996).[31] And by this is meant low-level technical training rather than the exalted educational philosophies of the CEU. Indeed, the private educational sector in the Czech Republic has begun to adapt itself to meeting these immediate practical needs.

Perhaps the epitome of this move is the rise of the 'corporate university'. The Association of Business Schools in evidence to the Dearing inquiry into higher education said, '...the Corporate University poses an outside threat to higher education and brings attendant risks and large unknowns...The ingress of major world corporations into the education sector is already under way with Disney 'edutainment' centres...'(Baty 1997: 2). All training takes place in 'mono-functional' ways in 'mono-cultural' institutions. It is an explicit rejection of the values of education in favour of short- term mechanical skills that enhance pragmatics at the expense of ideals. The nearest analogue in law is the move by some large law firms in the City of London to establish their own Legal Practice Courses.

A similar theme is emerging in other countries as governments and local professionals tackle the invasion of foreign experts. A growing number of countries have restrictive provisions on the establishment of foreign lawyers, e.g. Poland, India and Vietnam. In India the Lawyer's Collective is suing Ashurst Morris Crisp, a UK City law firm (and two US firms), for illegally practising law, as it failed to obtain recognition from the Indian Bar Council (Watching Brief 1995; Page 1997). Vietnam regulates the activities of foreign lawyers by licensing branches and compelling them to pay tax (Inside 1996). The effect of the regulation was expressed by a Western lawyer this way, 'The problem is not that we can't practise Vietnamese law but that we cannot hire Vietnamese lawyers. This means that Vietnamese lawyers aren't going to get trained. They need it and want it and so do we' (Inside 1996: 3).

The export of expertise and knowledge from the West to emerging countries is contentious. It is based on a perception by Western institutions - whether law schools, international organisations or law firms - that Western skills are needed and that their lack will be deleterious to the economies (and polities?) of developing countries. Caufield (1997) argues that the World Bank, for example, has basically responded to its own failures to effect economic change among its constituency countries. Its programmes have induced environmental damage, especially its promotion of hydroelectric dams,[32] or its loans have resulted in the creation of huge debts to the Bank. Moreover, Wade (1996) describes Japan's efforts to alter the World Bank's negative approach to the role of the state in development. Ultimately, Japan failed to shift the development paradigm from a predominantly American one to another that would incorporate Asian values.

Can we accept the notion of disinterested need-fulfilment at face value? I doubt it. Some years ago, the West itself faced the question of needs in relation to social welfare law. It was believed by policy makers and lawyers that needs had an objective reality and therefore could be fulfilled. Scholars who deconstructed this theory showed that needs referred more to lawyers' own ideas of needs and satisfaction of those needs rather than to the needs perceived by potential clients (Morris et al. 1973; Hosticka 1979, cf. Auerbach 1978). We are facing similar problems now, only this time it is on the global scale: entire populations are perceived to have problems in common with each other that diminish their own cultural values. If this dimunition continues, there is bound to be a backlash. We see it emerging in the arguments for an Asian conception of morality and community, which emphasizes the group over the individual thereby reproving the west for its constant, if muted, criticisms of human rights abuse. Referring back to the programmes being offered by Western law schools, however, the stress there is on trade and it is kept distinct from issues of human rights. Even the international organizations, such as the IMF, reduce changes in legal systems to one of 'technical assistance' which assist economic change without particularly paying heed to the social effects of these policies. Indeed, one argument asserts that

> In order to justify, or discount, the divisive consequences of restructuring—notably the social concentration of resources and the fragmentation of

> previously coherent social systems (e.g., economic arrangements, social protections, communities)— globalization advocates appeal to a higher good, namely, efficiency, and stress the importance of discipline in the global economy....In short, as the rationale for recent restructuring of states and economies, "globalization" is an historically specific project of global economic (financial) management. Prosecuted by a powerful global elite of financiers, international and national bureaucrats, and corporate leaders, the globalist project grows out of the dissolution of the development project. (McMichael 1996: 28)

Globalization transforms states into corporate enterprises to which the same rules apply: they can be restructured or go bankrupt; technologies can be transferred; labour forces can be downsized, all being done independently of the cultural milieux of the 'exporters' and 'importers' (cf. Bob 1996).[33] The globalization project supplies a *modus operandi* that isolates the processes of change from the larger questions about society. It is not too remote from the types of analysis used in law: the ability to think of two things, ineluctably connected, as separate. Law and legal education are in a struggle where they may become the handmaidens (Santos 1995), or maybe the consiglieri, of economic efficiency and the juridification of daily life,[34] in the pursuit of global hegemony and as a result are devoid of a sense of justice and community (Gordon 1988: 52; cf. Epp 1992 and Magee 1992).

Notes

1. Earlier versions of this paper were presented at the Socio-Legal Studies Conference, Southampton, 1996 and the Working Group on the Legal Profession of the Research Committee on the Sociology of Law, International Sociology Association, Peyresq, 1996. I am grateful to Harry Arthurs, Andy Boon, Yves Dezalay, Gerard Hanlon, Philip Lewis and Eleni Skordaki for comments. One person especially deserves my thanks: William Twining commented in detail and gave me a number of his reprints which galvanised a series of rethinks. Avis White and Alicia Ash provided valuable research assistance.
2. It would be misleading if the reader were to be left with the impression that lawyers were newcomers to the international stage; they are not. The City of London Solicitors' Company's evidence to the Royal Commission on Legal Services in 1977 stresses how English solicitors conceived of themselves as in competition with other jurisdictions because they were marketing a commodity called law.

3. For some recent interesting texts on globalisation see Robertson (1992), Santos (1995), Appadurai (1996) and Latouche (1996).
4. In this chapter I focus on business rather than on other aspects of globalisation, such as the media and the arts.
5. One example of the power of these systems is the question of what happens to ecu bonds if they are converted into euro bonds with the inception of the single currency. If their value declines, then there could be litigation. Ince (1997) reports that "the City of London euro working party has...taken fright. It wants the state of New York to pass laws to prevent such action being taken...".
6. Ramsay (1993: 359-363) adumbrates further roles for lawyers, namely efficient resource allocators, property rights' enforcers, lawyers as gatekeepers, lawyers as relationship orderers, and lawyers as producers of social goods.
7. In this respect the income foregone is that of the novice lawyer, not the law firm's, assuming that tyros are not complete profit centres.
8. For an extensive analysis of the various aspects of legal ethics see Kupfer (1996). For a treatment of the law schools' role in "adding value" see Boon (1996).
9. In the UK when the solicitors' and barristers' professions introduced vocational courses, there was a race among higher educational institutions to provide these courses. That they required expensive facilities and expensive faculty to run them was no deterrent, convinced as the institutions were that full-cost vocational courses would be 'cash cows'. They haven't. In the academic year, 1996-97, some institutions found their enrolments down by 50%, so that they are losing money. These courses are fundamentally skills-based, borrowing their pedagogical models from North America, and they have virtually no theoretical input, however see the trenchant comments of Webb (1996) and Boon (1996). A more cynical view might be that these are expensive, winnowing credentialling institutions.

   Compare, for example, the operation of the London Approach, a non-statutory form of corporate rescue where the Bank of England acts as a peacemaker, sometimes in conjunction with foreign bank regulators (Flood et al. 1995).
10. Allison notes that all other forms of investment are classed as portfolio investment (Allison 1993: 109).
11. Note that variation in accounting practices means that the US and UK figures are overstated (BIS 1995: 66).
12. Compare, for example, the operation of the London Approach, a non-statutory form of corporate rescue where the Bank of England acts as a peacemaker, sometimes in con-

junction with foreign bank regulators (Flood et al. 1995).

13. For instance, India, while wanting to increase its share of FDI from 2 billion US dollars a year to 10 billion, still puts obstacles in the way of joint ventures, e.g. Tata Industries and Singapore Airlines had many problems, and other investment projects, e.g. the Enron Dabhol power plant was scrapped when Maharastra state elected a right-wing government (Page 1997: 47).
14. Two examples will illustrate: the Islamic bar on usury and its effect on banking practice; and the Asian ambivalence, if not detestation, of rugged individualism versus group values, exemplified by their repugnance of Nick Leeson and Yosuo Hamanaka, the rogue traders in Baring's Singapore office and the Tokyo offices of Sumitomo Corporation respectively (cf. Tickell, 1996; Economist, 1996b). Nick Leeson engaged in misjudged, and sometimes fraudulent, derivatives trading without the knowledge of the bank's management which resulted in losses exceeding £900 million (Tickell, 1996, 9-10; Fay, 1996). Yosuo Hamanaka was head of copper trading at Sumitomo Corporation and traded fraudulently for 10 years resulting in losses of £1.6 billion (Parry, Rogers and Treanor, 1997: 17).
15. Business schools have already faced this. For example, Duke University's Fuqua School of Business offers an MBA via the internet and short residential classes in places as far apart as Salzburg, Shanghai and Sao Paulo.
16. I believe this can be justified by the fact that most international institutions, e.g., World Bank and EBRD, demand a graduate degree as the minimum qualification for entry. Many American law schools also offer the LL.M. degree, partly as a way of upgrading J.D. degrees from lower-rank schools for US students, and partly as a way of inducting foreign students into US law.
17. William Twining has pointed out the gaps here, and I hope at a later stage to study them more closely.
18. Many other law schools in the UK offer taught graduate programmes - e.g., Warwick, Leicester, Manchester - and they market themselves vigorously to overseas markets, but I would argue they do not have the same 'brand' recognition as these three schools.
19. The six law schools in London University are University College London, King's College London, the School of Oriental and African Studies, Birkbeck College, London School of Economics, and Queen Mary and Westfield College.
20. There are possible reasons for this state of affairs. American lawyers who came to Oxford and Cambridge, e.g., Bill Clinton, came as undergraduates before returning to law school in the US. They rarely read law in the UK. Others who came from Common-

wealth countries came to acquire expertise in law that closely approximated their own.

21. In the UK there is the Legal Practice Course which is designed to prepare students for actual practice, and while they contain business-related courses, the international content is virtually zero. Most City law firms fill the lacuna themselves. Notably, Queen Mary and Westfield College contains the Centre for Commercial Studies which provides many of the business-related courses on the London LL.M.
22. In total, Columbia Law School has 11 in-house law journals, including the Columbia Law Review.
23. Perhaps this was encouraged by Harvard Law Professor Alan Dershowitz being part of the defence 'dream' team (see Schiller and Willwerth 1996).
24. In some instances diploma privilege exists, e.g., Wisconsin, where merely holding the J.D. from a law school in that state allows a person to practise without passing a bar examination.
25. Many college and university presidents are former law school professors. And law professors can be appointed as judges. For example, the University of Chicago Law School has at least three former faculty on the bench of the United States Court of Appeals for the Seventh Circuit - Frank Easterbrook, Richard Posner and Diane Wood.
26. See also Vries (1986) and Armstrong (1982) for further details on the IMF and international organisations.
27. However, see Chapter 5, "US Litigators, Continental Academics, Petrodollar Construction Projects, and the *Lex Mercatoria*: A Case Study" in Dezalay and Garth (1996: 100-113) for an example of the minimalist role law firms can play.
28. The lists were derived from American Lawyer and Legal Business Magazine, both of which publish lists of the top 100 law firms in the US and UK. Moreover, I excluded normal training programmes for domestic lawyers, even though some of these include rotations through foreign offices.
29. To work as legal counsel in some organizations, such as the United Nations, it is almost a prerequisite to have worked in a Wall Street law firm (personal communication, Dr Luke Harris, Vassar College).
30. In some respects this is a static picture. Large law firms have hired directors of education from the legal academy to remedy these deficiencies and they may become repositories of theoretical knowledge. Such moves will be influenced by the introduction of multidisciplinary practice and other organizational innovations.
31. In some respects the CEU has realised this. The acting rector of the CEU said in an interview, "Until now, the university was a kind of cathedral in the desert which did not

really have any connection with other higher educational institutions in the region. We would like to achieve more active cooperation with other universities, to invite scholars, to implement different scholarship programs. We would like to send out our professors to give lectures at other institutions. CEU will be unique in the sense that it will be the first regional university in the world participating in the transformation of higher education in the countries from which the majority of CEU students come" (CEU Gazette 1996/97).

32. "The Sardar Sarovar dam on the Narmada river, in India, is a stark example of how the World Bank's conditions on resettlement and environmental damage - which were attached to its loan in 1985 - could fail. An independent report found that, among other things, the benefits were over-estimated, environmental impact assessments were not carried out and resettlement conditions were not met. The Bank's own India department altered a study criticising the resettlement, to hide the problems from the Bank's directors. The loan was cancelled in 1993 and India's Supreme Court suspended construction in 1995. The angry protests against Sardar Sarovar became a model for others and focused attention on how bad dams could be" (Economist 1997b: 114).
33. There are, of course, limits to this. When governments decide to sell off sensitive state assets, they sometimes prefer not to sell to foreigners. France wanted a French buyer for its defence group, Thomson; Germany wants a defence contractor, STN Atlas, also to remain in German hands; and Austria wants to keep the Creditanstalt Austrian (Economist 1996c: 97).
34. Weber (1978: 669) saw the proliferation of legal transactions, contracts, as characteristic of modernity.

References

Allison, R. (1993), 'The Multinational Enterprise: Some Theoretical Issues', in J. Preston (ed), *International Business: Text and Cases*, Pitman, London, pp.107-118.

Armstrong, D. (1982), *The Rise of the International Organisation: A Short History*, Macmillan, Basingstoke.

Arthurs, H. and Kreklewich, R. (1996), 'Law, Legal Institutions and the Legal Profession in the New Economy', paper presented at the Working Group on Legal Professions meeting, Peyresq, France.

Auerbach, J. (1978), *Unequal Justice: Lawyers and Social Change in Modern America*, Oxford University Press, New York.

BIS (1995), *65th Annual Report*, Bank for International Settlements, Basle.

BIS (1996), *66th Annual Report*, Bank for International Settlements, Basle.

Bob, C. (1996), 'Transferring Legal Institutions: Governance Theory and the Role of Law in Developing Societies', paper presented at the Law and Society Association Meeting, Glasgow, Scotland.

Boden, D. and Molotch, H. (1994), 'The Compulsion of Proximity', in R. Friedland and D. Boden (eds), *NowHere Space, Time and Modernity*, University of California Press, Berkeley, pp.257-86.

Boon, A. (1996), 'Skills in the Initial Stage of Legal Education: Theory and Practice for Transformation', in J. Webb and C. Maughan (eds), *Teaching Lawyers' Skills*, Butterworths, London, pp.99-136.

Bradney, A. (1995), 'Raising the Drawbridge: Defending University Law Schools', 1, Web Journal of Current Legal Issues. http: //www.ncl.ac.uk/articles1/bradney.html.

Caufield, C. (1997), *Masters of Illusion: The World Bank and the Poverty of Nations*, Henry Holt, New York.

CEU Gazette (1996/97), 'An Interview with Laszlo Bruszt, Acting Rector of CEU', 6, *CEU Gazette*, p.2.

Deal, C. (1994), 'NYU Unveils New Law Programs', *New York Law Journal*, 26 July, 1.

Dezalay, Y. and Garth, B. (1996), *Dealing in Virtue: International Commercial Arbitration and the Construction of an International Legal Order*, University of Chicago Press, Chicago.

EBRD (1995), *Transition Report 1995: Investment and Enterprise Development: Economic Transition in Eastern Europe and the Former Soviet Union*, EBRD, London.

Economics Focus (1996), 'Free Trade, Fettered Investment', *Economist*, 14 September, p.108.

Economist (1996a), 'The Globalisation of Corporate Law: Red Tape Around the World', *Economist*, 23 November, pp.109-112.

Economist (1996b), 'Cultural Explanations: The Man in the Baghdad Cafe', *Economist*, 9 November, pp.25-30.

Economist (1996c), 'Business in Europe: Games with Frontiers', *Economist*, 21 September, p.97.

Economist (1997), 'Time to Roll Out a New Model: The World Bank Wants To Be the Best in the Development Business. Does That Business Still Exist?', *Economist*, 1 March, pp.93-94.

Eichengreen, B. (1994), *International Monetary arrangements for the 21st Century*, The Brookings Institute, Washington DC.

Epp, C. (1992), 'Do Lawyers Impair Economic Growth?', *Law and Social Inquiry*, 17, pp.585-

623.

Fay, S. (1996), *The Collapse of Barings*, Richard Cohen Books, London.

Flood, J. (1996), 'Megalawyering in the Global Order: The Cultural, Social and Economic Transformation of Global Legal Practice', *International Journal of the Legal Profession*, 3, pp.169-214.

Flood, J., Abbey, R., Skordaki, E. and Aber, P. (1995), *The Professional Restructuring of Corporate Rescue: Company Voluntary Arrangements and the London Approach*, Certified Accountants Educational Trust, London.

Flood, J. and Caiger, A. (1993), 'Lawyers and Arbitration: The Juridification of Construction Disputes', *Modern Law Review*, 56, pp.412-440.

Fukuyama, F. (1995), *Trust: The Social Virtues and the Creation of Prosperity*, Hamish Hamilton, London.

Giddens, A. (1991), *Modernity and Self-Identity: Self and Society in the Late Modern Age*, Polity Press, Cambridge.

Gilson, R. (1984), 'Value Creation by Business Lawyers: Legal Skills and Asset Pricing', *Yale Law Journal*, 94, pp.239-313.

Gordon, R. (1988), 'The Independence of Lawyers', *Boston University Law Review*, 68, pp.1-83.

Gordon, R., Lindsay, J. and Hager, M. (1996), '"Technical Assistance" and the Globalisation of Black Letter Law: the good, the bad and the ugly', paper presented at the Law and Society Association Meeting, Glasgow, Scotland.

Halliday, F. (1995), 'International Relations and Its Discontents', *International Affairs*, 71, pp.733-746.

Horner, F. (1997), 'Training Lawyers in the 1990s', *New Law Journal*, January 17, pp.66-67.

Hosticka, C. (1979), 'We Don't Care About What Happened, We Only Care About What Is Going To Happen: Lawyer-Client Negotiations of Reality', *Social Problems*, 26, p.599.

IMF (1977), *The Balance of Payments Manual*, International Monetary Fund, Washington DC.

IMF (1997), *Annual Report 1996*, International Monetary Fund, Washington DC.

IMF Research Dept. Staff (1996), 'Global Financial Markets: Moving up the Learning Curve', *Finance and Development*, 33.
http: //www. worldbank.org/fandd/english/1296/articles/0131296.htm,1-5.

Inside (1996), 'Vietnam Awards Licences', *International Financial Law Review*, March, p.3.

Khan, L. (1991), 'Internationalising the Law School Curriculum', *Syllabus*, 22, p.8.

Kuhn, T. (1970), *The Structure of Scientific Revolutions*, University of Chicago Press, Chicago.

Kupfer, S. (1996), 'Authentic Legal Practices', *Georgetown Journal of Legal Ethics*, 10, pp.33-113.

Law in Transition (1996), 'The Contribution of Law to Fostering Investment', *Law in Transition*, Autumn/Winter, pp.1-4.

Luhmann, N. (1979), *Trust and Power*, John Wiley, Chichester.

Magee, S. (1992), 'The Optimum Number of Lawyers', *Law and Social Inquiry*, 17, pp.667-693.

McBarnet, D. (1994), 'Legal Creativity: Law, Capital and Legal Avoidance', in M. Cain and C. Harrington (eds), *Lawyers in a Postmodern World: Translation and Transgression*, Open University Press, Buckingham, pp.73-84.

McMichael, P. (1996), 'Globalisation: Myths and Realities', *Rural Sociology*, 61, pp.25-55.

Miller, M. (1995), *The High Priests of American Politics: The Role of Lawyers in American Political Institutions*, University of Tennessee Press, Knoxville.

Moran, M. (1991), *The Politics of the Financial Services Revolution*, Macmillan, Basingstoke.

Morris, P., White, R. and Lewis, P. (1973), *Social Needs and Legal Action*, Robertson, London.

Myers, K. (1994), 'NYU's International Approach is Education on a Global Scale', *National Law Journal*, 22 August, p.2.

NYU: The Law School Magazine (1995), 'The Global Law School Program', *NYU: The Law School Magazine (Special Issue)*.

Ohmae, K. (1991), *The Borderless World*, Fontana, London.

Opinion (1996), 'Fly Away Patrons', *Times Higher*, 26 January, p.9.

Page, N. (1997), 'Indian Reservations', *Legal Business*, March, pp.47-54.

Parry, R., Rodgers, P. and Treanor, J. (1997), 'Winchester "Paid £75,000 Gratuity" to Hamanaka', *The Independent*, 18 February, p.17.

Powell, M. (1993), 'Professional Innovation: Corporate Lawyers and Private Law Making', *Law and Social Inquiry*, 18, pp.423-452.

Ramsay, I. (1993), 'What Do Lawyers Do? Reflections on the Market for Lawyers', *International Journal of the Sociology of Law*, 21, pp.355-389.

Said, E. (1995), *Orientalism*, Penguin, London.

Schiller, L. and Willwerth, J. (1996), *American Tragedy: The Uncensored Story of the Simpson Defense*, Random House, New York.

Taylor, J. (1996), 'New Laws, New Lawyers and the EBRD', *International Business Lawyer*, 24, pp.98-99.

Teubner, G. (1997), '"Global Bukowina": Legal Pluralism in the World Society', in G. Teubner (ed), *Global Law Without A State*, Dartmouth, Aldershot.

The Accountant (1996), 'UN to Develop International Qualifications', *The Accountant*, No. 5912, September.

Thomsen, S. and Nicolaides, P. (1990), *Foreign Direct Investment: 1992 and Global Markets*, The Royal Institute of International Affairs, London.

Tickell, A. (1996), 'Making A Melodrama Out of A Crisis: Reinterpreting the Collapse of Barings Bank', *Environment and Planning D: Society and Space*, 14, pp.5-33.

Twining, W.L. (1973), *Karl Llewellyn and the Realist Movement*, Weidenfeld and Nicolson, London.

Twining, W.L. (1995), *Blackstone's Tower*, Sweet and Maxwell, London.

UNCTAD (1994), *World Investment Report 1995: Transnational Corporations and Competitiveness*, United Nations, New York.

Vries, M. (1986), *The IMF in a Changing World 1945-85*, International Monetary Fund, Washington DC.

Wade, R. (1996), 'Japan, the World Bank and the Art of Paradigm Maintenance: *The East Asian Miracle* in Political Perspective', *New Left Review*, May-June, pp.3-36.

Watching Brief (1995), 'Lawsuit Attempts to Block Foreign Firms in India', *Asia Law*, September, pp.4-5.

Webb, J. (1996), 'Why Theory Matters', in Webb, J. and Maughan, C. (eds), *Teaching Lawyers' Skills*, Butterworths, London, pp.23-51.

Weber, M. (1978), *Economy and Society: An Outline of Interpretative Sociology*, University of California Press, Berkeley.

World Bank (1995), *The World Bank Annual Report 1995*, World Bank, Washington DC.

7 The Policy of Legal Higher Education in Europe

VITTORIO OLGIATI

Introduction

The aim of this paper is to discuss the policy of higher legal education in the European Community from a socio-legal perspective and with particular reference to legal professionalization. The study is conceived as a contribution to the understanding of the wider process of EU socio-political governmentality via formal-official mutual recognition of chartered professional bodies and academic institutions credentialling systems.

This subject can be approached on a number of different levels, the most important of which is political, the extraordinary implications of which have been too often hidden or ignored by contemporary literature on law-and-society. This arises from the fact that a deep-rooted need for security at a constitutional level (not mere pressure for economic change) has been and still is at the core of the institutional action of EU State-members towards the European unification programme. So much so that law, as a specific constructionist 'sociotechnique' has been and still is the pivotal synergizing regulatory propeller of this programme.

As is well known, this issue is now gaining a new momentum. It is likely to increase in importance in the future, since with the signature of the Single European Act (1986) the political/constitutional nature of the EU process has also been fully recognized at a formal level. An official change of such historical and normative importance is a ready catalyst for enquiry into the problem of the local assets and strategic positioning of European legal professions, since they, by virtue of their active status-role as boundary agents between public and private spheres, are ascribed a special political 'citizenship', a *status activae civitatis*, within the EU province of State law, as well as a specific expertise with regard to the technicalities of European institutional *strukturbildung*.

The problem of the local assets and the strategic positioning of European legal professions vis-à-vis the dynamic of the EU legal setting is intriguing indeed, for it concerns both structural and cultural mainstreams related, in the last instance, to the many facets of 'the consequences of Modernity' (Giddens, 1990).

When dealing with such a problem, and therefore with the definition of general aims of EU legal education, styles of conduct, standards of excellence, etc, it is important to realize that official law (in Europe) is not a science at all, but a highly refined 'symbolic token', instrumentally fit for practical (politically relevant) 'embedding' and/or 'disembedding' social action. In other words, one has to be aware that, since the birth of modern State (Schmitt, 1938), law-making and legal education, as Locke would say, are a function of government(Locke, 1968; 1989), for, as Hobbes would put it, *auctoritas, non veritas, facit legem* (authority, not truth, makes law) (Hobbes, 1890; 1968).

As this self-evident truth particularly concerns positive paper-law (EU paper-law included) and, in turn, legal reasoning, legal training, legal expertise, etc. (which are not related to everlasting Cartesian doubts or Socratic ignorance, but rather to political struggles for authoritative allocations of values and goods) it should come as no surprise to note that what is at stake, since the political/constitutional nature of EU process has been formally declared, is nothing less than the construction of a 'New Order' of continental dimensions. A process that, in turn, necessarily implies the definition of a new cultural, technical and political identity, and of models of legal education and professional status-roles as intertwined *organic* devices, in order to assess and promote an EU (continent specific) geo-political governmentality.

The Instability of the EU Legal Setting

The subject is complicated, however, by the fact that while EU policy on higher education is defined by now ex art. 126, 127 of Maastricht Treaty, the same Maastricht Treaty is certainly one of the most singular treaties in the whole of European political history, for it recalls its own revision, even before its actual enforcement. Thus, it is not by chance that the whole bureaucratic machinery of the EU Community is already planning to set up new structures and tasks. In turn, the quest for inclusion/adhesion on the part of new European countries challenges a number of previously settled professional arrangements. Last, but not least, various items seem to lead not to a mutual integration proper but to a sort of gradualistic 'approach' to some given EU pillars (based on Kern Europe, opting out, easing out, etc. principles). Altogether, therefore, basic issues such as those concerned with social mobility, public order and cultural diversity (the core items of the Maastricht Treaty) seem certain to be re-thematized.

On the other hand, it is equally apparent that the limited support of European public opinion as regards the Treaty's common parameters, as shown by the results of a number of national referendums, will also force European elites to couple such a re-thematization with a further refinement of EU governmentality strategy, possibly throughout the repertoires of the *arcana imperii* (hidden power structures) of ancient European legal tradition.

The growing interest in EU legal education and the patterns of legal professions in academic circles is precisely a sign of such constitutional instability as well as a condition for dealing with it, for the 'thickness' of European legal pluralism appears as one of the most general, powerful and problematic tools for dealing with current and prospective EU social dynamics. Given the overall context briefly described above, it is not a matter of mere subjective preference that this study does not concern law students' behaviour, aptitude tests, curricula, teaching methods, etc., but focuses on major issues of current EU policy on higher legal education and professionalism. The problem is not that of mastering data collections, or narrating more or less theoretically sophisticated stories, but to try to rationally decipher, as far as possible, the way in which European legal culture, once again trapped into a Vicoean return at the turn of the II Millennium, is politically involved in the framing of a new normative continental setting to face the environmental changes that *Homo Europaeus - levis, argutus, inventor* (versatile, shrewd, inventive), as Linnaeus said (Lepenies, 1994) - is implementing for Europe and the whole World-society.

For analytical and discoursive purposes, this chapter will be divided into two parts: the first, about the boundaries of EU legal fieldwork; the second, about access to EU legal education. Also this methodological choice is not arbitrary. As we will see, with regards to these items EU policy strictly follows the canonic principles according to which Western culture defines dominant knowledge and know-how as a means of institutional hegemony: by exclusion and coordination. Exclusion of whatever is (or could be) 'external' (the principle of identity), and coordination of whatever is (or could be) 'internal' (the principle of integrity) to a pre-constituted political aim.

The Boundaries of EU Legal Fieldwork

EU Legal Experience as an 'Independent Variable'?

In a joint contribution to a large EUI research project on European Integration, published in 1986, Friedman and Teubner wrote:

> Law is dependent on politics, and thus legal unification in the strict sense is tied up with the progress of political unification. This point seems obvious, even trivial, but the consequences are not trivial at all. In Europe today the ideal of political unification is dim, and progress has slowed down to a crawl... The so-called functional approach to political integration, which assumes a European polity as more or less necessary spill-over from economic and technological integration, has been, alas, refuted by harsh reality. If legal integration really does depend on political integration, then the chances for legal unification are slender. But does legal unification depend so utterly on politics? Is there another way? Some jurists feel that there is. They look to the legal profession and legal science as a way to promote legal unity, independent of political integration.
> (Friedman and Teubner, 1986)

Moving on from this premise, and taking seriously what 'some jurists' have said, Friedman and Teubner try to sort out workable paths that could allow European legal professions 'to promote legal unity' without waiting for the impulse of political action. After a detailed analysis, they maintain that the solution which should be envisaged is the development of increasingly internationally oriented legal practice, in accordance with the processess of socio-economic internationalization. This solution, however, implies congruent cultural and attitudinal models and, consequently, a corresponding legal education. The two authors then devote their attention to the form and substance of dominant educational patterns and finally reach a drastic conclusion: in order to create a new typology of jurists 'trained in methods and theories which transcend national diversities', 'reworking the curricula of law schools of Member States' is necessary but not sufficient. Although it is clear that 'to find some sort of common denominator would require a level of abstraction way up in the stratosphere', they argue that what is needed is that 'traditional norms and doctrines have to be discarded in the seach of tools for European Unification' (Friedman and Teubner, 1986).

As one can see, although Friedman and Teubner seem to be aware of the complexity of European normative realms and of the fact that cultural processes require longer periods of time and much more favourable conditions than those fit for political decision-making, they do not hesitate to claim that, by rejecting traditional legal doctrines and educational models, new generations of European jurists will be able to self-orientate towards a radical professional reconversion, thus creating the conditions for a legal integration independent from politics.

Unfortunately for the two reknowned socio-legal scholars, both the premise and the whole argumentation proved to be totally wrong. The Single European Act, signed in 1985 (i.e. a year *before* the publication of Friedman and Teubners' paper), explicitly states that cultural, social, institutional, etc. *diversity*, not unity, is the leading principle of the EU process, for diversity is politically considered a resource and an enrichment, not a limitation or a disfunction. In turn, EU General Directive 1989/48 on the Mutual Recognition of Professional Qualifications explicitly mantains and even reinforces, by virtue of formal-official mutual recognition, traditional professional and educational credentialling systems, the majority of which were and are structurally and functionally orientated not to international sources of power, but to national and/or local constituencies. Finally, arts. 126, 127 of the Maastricht Treaty, signed in 1992, explicitly ascribe to the Community the task of encouraging cultural cooperation among EU Member States in order to improve the quality of educational systems, but without interfering with their own organization and content, which are and will remain under the competence of autonomous local (national) bodies.

Given the above, it is undeniable that at least since the second half of the Eighties, EU policy has rationally pursued the de-construction from above of a potentially one-dimensional professional trend. Equally, it is undeniable that Friedman and Teubners' suggestion of conceiving law as an independent variable as regards the space-time conditions of political action proved to be nothing more than a mere 'doctrinary' hypothesis, typical of certain idealistic legal models which both authors seemed to criticize. So much so that just before the enforcement of the Maastricht Treaty, during an international conference of European jurists held in Oxford in 1992, the President of the Society of Public Teachers of Law, Roy Goode, was able to state - quietly using Friedman and Teubners' words - that 'National law schools would continue to focus on their own legal systems...for...a common core curriculum in European Law was neither feasible nor desirable. To find a common denominator will require a level of abstraction way up in the stratosphere' (The Times Higher, 1992).

This statement should not be surprising, since in terms of legal/ costitutinal structures, the EU includes so far fifteen different types of government, seven monarchical and eight republican regimes, seven different types of constitutional control procedures, two century-old legal systems (one based on parliamentary legislation, another on consuetudinary jurisprudence), and an amazing variety of age-old judicial and bureaucratic settings and functionally differentiated legal professions, all run under an equally amazing number of legal theories, practices, concepts, etc., related to different historical contexts and constructed through different languages. How can one ignore that legal pluralism, not legal uniformity, is a core dimension of European history, as well as the main epochal mainstream in contemporary law-and-society dynamics? And one should not underestimate the fact that even the EU Community is producing a plurality of legal systems, as the dicothomy beween 'EU uniform legislation' (mainly based on the 'harmonization' criteria) and 'EU common law' (based on the 'subsidiary' principle) demonstrates.

Indeed, a proper analytical and operational entry point is required to deal with the matter: what sort of real conditions, not abstact expectations or idealistic perspectives, link European legal professionalization and legal culture to the EU political project, and vice versa?

The Plurality of EU Professional Projects

To fully appreciate current EU policy about higher legal education and legal professionalization, one should focus on the rationale of the everlasting redefinition of EU general principles: unification, integration, harmonization, approximation to unity, reciprocity, mutuality, subsidiarity, etc. However, for the purpose of this study, it is sufficient to synthetize the issue with a rapid socio-legal *tour d'horizon*.

As I have argued elsewhere, looking at creationist EU law-policy, one discovers that no less than three different 'professional projects' are contemporaneusly assessed (Olgiati, 1996). First, the overall EU legal constructionism is, indeed, a veritable macro-trans/professional project of continental dimension, as is demonstrated by the coupling of Maastricht Treaty provisions and General Directive 1989/48 with other pieces of EU law - e.g. that about EEIG (European Economic Interest Group) (1985), the Right of Establishment (1989), etc. Such a large project not only concerns all types of European professions (legal professions included) but is orientated to frame them *as* EU professions. Therefore it aims at setting up two major professional cleavages. On the one hand, these legal materials define the standards by which to distinguish professional patterns and action systems that are 'internal' to the overall issues of the Single European Space, thus excluding those that, by contrast, are 'external' to such governmentality area (i.e. excluding any chance about a 'global' transplantation of certain foreign professional models). On the other hand, they define the standards by which those practitioners that, being recognized as 'internal' to EU Space, will be able or not to move around EU Member States, thus creating the framework for an 'organic' (elitist) professional stratification and mobility.

Next, within this macro-trans/professional project, a variety of meso-inter/professional projects run also. These projects concern any fieldwork of a whole service-area and are officially oriented to strengthen mutual cooperation among all the professional groups involved in it. Ad hoc EU Directives are now enforced in areas such as architecture, health, economy, science, etc. As far as law is concerned, one might recall a number of Court of Justice decisions since the Reynes case (1974) onwards, various Directives, as well as the activity of the CCBE. As this meso-inter-professional project does not deal with one single legal profession, but deals with the entire action system of law as a disciplinary discourse, quite paradoxically it sustains a process of professional integration that internally undermines traditional professional formal bodies. Consequently a cleavage is created within each professional organization-set, expecially in relation to horizontal and vertical 'core' and 'periphery' professional patterns.

Thirdly, like Pandora's box, all the above holds out the possibility of enhancing a number of micro-intra/professional projects on the part of local factions within and/or outside each professional group. With specific reference to the legal domain, one could mention the Professional Law of 1971 in France, which cancelled the internal professional division between *avocats* and *conseils juridiques*, the professional change envisaged in the Courts and Legal Services Act (1990) in England, the abolition of the old Code of Ethics (1987) in

Germany, and so on. Indeed, the EU process is a good opportunity for those local elites who wish to secure secondary adjustments.

As one might have already realized, the dicothomy between EU uniform legislation and EU common law vis-à-vis national legal contexts is not foreign to such a complex dynamic. This could explain why, in spite of a EU Parliament Resolution (A3-365/90, par.8) EU law is not yet included as a compulsory matter in many European law faculties. The more the three professional projects go on, the more EU policy will be forced deal to with their multidimensional social impact, for a typical technical characteristic of EU law-making, among others, is that it is socially responsive, i.e. it has to take into account its own social consequences.

The Boundaries of Professional Action

A proper understanding of EU policy also requires a detailed analysis of basic legal texts. However, it is sufficient here just to consider those legal sources which directly deal with our topic.

As is well-known, since the Treaty of Rome, professional status/roles involving direct or indirect participation in the exercise of powers conferred by public law or functions whose purpose is to safeguard the general interest of the State and which therefore require a special relationship of allegiance to the State have been explicitly excluded from the so-called 'free mobility'. Equally a number of mobility restrictions enhanced by State Members in the operation of business matters such as banking, insurance, credit, etc., have been 'justified' at EU level by 'imperative reasons to public interest' (i.e., consumer and/or investor protection, public order, etc.). The Single European Act and, in turn, the General Directive on Mutual Recognition of Professional Qualifications follow precisely the same criteria (Speeding, 1987; Tyrrel and Yaqqyb, 1992; Adamson 1992).

General Directive 1989/48, in particular, embodies two fundamental provisions. It applies only to 'regulated' professions, that is those professions which, especially in Continental Europe, are protected by State law as 'civil' (public) services. It also states that a 'legal profession' within the EU Community is only '...one which requires a precise knowledge of national law and involves providing consultation and/or assistance on national law as a constant and essential aspect of professional activity'.

The implications of such formal-official statements are of great importance for the conceptual definition and material structuration of EU legal education and practice. Firstly, as has been already noticed, the Directive reassess and somewhat further protects, by mutual recognition, traditional arrangements of official national/local professional guilds and academic disciplinary jurisdictions, for it defines as 'certificates' not only a university degree, but also professional qualifications (enrollment, title, etc.) granted by the State. By enforcing a mutual recognition of these certificates, therefore, not only all (existing and future) official national professional rites de passage, standards of excellence, curricula, etc., but also the institutional procedural means of their production, already recognized by State law, often as a monopolistic prerogative, have also been formally confirmed at EU level (Olgiati, 1995). In turn, by recognizing mutual rights and duties to define the nature of professions and the character of their expertise on the part of officially recognized institutions according to their own criteria, the same Directive also aims at legally neutralizing certain problematic professional issues.

Even at a superficial level, it is apparent that the Directive aims at distinguishing professional multidisciplinary areas, such as business legal consultants, which still lack an officially recognized autonomous jurisdiction (at least, insofar as these areas will not be included within formal-official national credentialling systems). Additionally, by confirming that *national* (official State Member) legal systems and *national* legal culture are the basic reference-points for legal practice in Europe, and ensuring that these elements are the basic criteria that qualify European legal professionalism, the Directive aims at sharply distinguishing European from non-European legal culture and practice. Last, but not least, it aims to trace a neat distinction among the self-same European legal professions, for those legal practitioners educated and trained in national law, but dealing with other sources of law or other legal systems (e.g. a local discretionary legal system such as *lex mercatoria*) as a prevailing aspect of their activity, will not formally be considered as members of a European legal profession at all.

The overall strategy embedded in the Directive is therefore absolutely clear: on the one hand, to foster the '...production of distinctive producers', as Sarfatti Larson would put it (Larson, 1977), in the field of legal professionalism, and, on the other hand, to distinguish, in the last instance, those using law as a mere delocalized medium, i.e. as an instrumental technicality, from those who are still politically committed and culturally linked to official law as a veritable institution. It goes without saying that this highly refined EU policy can hardly be ignored by those who deal with higher education standards.

The 'Unitas Multiplex' of the EU Professional Model

Since the Treaty of Rome a substantial exclusion of EU general mobility principles has been enforced when a profession is related to a national State's political sovereignty. From a legal technical point of view such an exclusion is based on a traditional legal doctrine, dating back to old Roman jurists and still embedded in European professional models, about the notions of 'public service' and 'status-roles' (see art. 48, 51, 59, 60 of the Treaty of Rome). In fact, according to this doctrine a public, official service/function differs from a mere socio-econonic service/product, for there is a gap between public and private action systems, so that a 'true' intellectual profession, legally protected and qualified as a status/role performing public functions, cannot be confused with any other private professionalized occupation. The true profession realises a unique *facere* (to do, to act) performance, rather than a *dare* (to give) performance; and as a result, it implies an individualized interaction based on a personal *intuitu personae* (perception), and avoids the risks and interests of merely entrepreneurial profit-making tasks (Martin Bernard, 1990).

A systematic legal coupling of these legal tools with the Maastricht Treaty arts. 126, 127, now permits the EU Community to kill no less than three birds with one stone: firstly - as has been already mentioned - to put beyond the pale extra-European legal professions and their issues; secondly to avoid professional intrusion by the so-called para-legal professionals; and thirdly, to distinguish non EU national-law orientated European practitioners. In an important ruling handed down by the European Court of Justice in 1995, EU lawyers were judged to be governed by the Treaty rules on establishment, not services. In particular, in relation to art. 60 of the Rome Treaty, the Court distinguished the legal practice of a resident foreign national whose professional activity has been stable and continual from that of a mere service provider.

Yet the EU legal framework goes even further than this, for the interpretation of the phrase 'who will be able to move around Europe and under what conditions' is based on a *duplication*, not a reduction, of a number of traditional professional cultural, structural and institutional constraints. In fact, if one reads carefully EU Court of Justice decisions and ordonances from the Reynes case (1974) onwards in a systematic way, one discovers that EU law/policy doubles, rather than excludes, already existing national monopoly mechanisms. This is due to the enactment of the principle of 'reciprocal acknowledgement' in relation to formal qualifications, 'proportional equivalence' in relation to cultural standards, the 'double rule' in deontological behaviour, 'double residence' in relation to performing in Court, 'double enrolment' in Bar associations, etc. Equally, if one reads certain EU Directives, one discovers discriminatory criteria - such as that of 'limited duration and frequency' of practice in host Courts (EU Directive 77/249), or the requirement of 'national membership' of elective professional governing bodies, even among those professionals who embody all the above principles. Altogether, therefore, it is apparent that, by reinforcing, rather than liberalizing, national control of EU mutually recognized credentials, EU policy confirms that legal professions in Europe not only are and will continue to be anchored to both national bodies and official (national) law, but are also involved in a refined 'transpositioning' strategy based on an undeclared selective competition of an elitist character (Olgiati, 1995).

If one now considers all the above in relation to the preservation of the extraordinary variety of legal professional models, practices, discourses, techniques, etc. currently in force within each European national context (in Spain, for instance, one can count five different legal professions), one can easily imagine to what extent the cultural identity, technical specificity and political loyality of each European legal professions is protected and nurtured in order to foster the *effect utile* (positive aim/result) of the self-same EU policy. Indeed, the complexity of such a *unitas multiplex* will be even more marked in the future, a real source of experience and experiment for all EU legal education programmes.

Access to EU Higher Legal Education

The Task of EU Higher Legal Education

What has been said so far could not be omitted. It is not a mere scholarly digression from the issues at stake at educational level. On the contrary, it is the necessary 'understanding net', to use Habermas' concept, (Habermas, 1981), for approaching the issue of EU policy on higher legal education from a realistic socio-legal perspective. Indeed, these insights bring to the fore a general legal framework that is of extraordinary importance for such a policy, for they qualify EU legal professions' status-roles in accordance with EU continent-specific geo-political needs and trends. Given this general framework, what sort of educational standards fit in? How far can legal culture and training reinforce it? How can this be done in actual practice? To deal with these questions, two main issues deserve immediately a special mention here.

Firstly, it is apparent that EU legal arrangements offer a workable grid for a structurally determined sociographic account of the 'cultural capital-in-action' of EU legal systems vis-à-vis EU society at large. As we will see, these arrangements should be considered as a strategic response to the disquieting state of affairs of the European professional realm vis-à-vis epochal mainstreams of socio-cultural change.

Additionally, and consequently, they also make clear that widespread claims about the occurrence of so-called 'professional Big-Bangs' (i.e the radical collapse of traditional assets), 'marketization' (i.e. the changing of legal jurisdictions into mere market systems), and 'globalization' (i.e. the spreading of a relatively uniform professional model worldwide), are, in terms of European legal professionalization, both misleading and false.

In particular, the hypothesis of an incoming 'globalization' is totally meaningless for both the legal profession and EU legal education policy. On the one hand, because it is self-evident that, in Europe as elsewhere, socio-legal pluralism is at the one time irrepressible and a vital resource. On the other hand, because a *Universale Monopolium*, as Pufendorf would say, is '...a policy of purely imaginary interests' (Meineke, 1924).

In any case, since the metaphorical hypothesis of an alleged 'globalization' has become a sort of *leit-motif* in current academic debates, it is worth stressing that this trend is precisely the opposite of what EU policy officially aims at: the promotion of a continent-specific European cultural identity as a unity of differences. The access to higher legal education in Europe is based on this apparently straightforward policy. Proof of this can be drawn from art. 16 of the Single European Act (now included as the second paragraph of art. 57 of the Treaty of Rome). Contrary to the enforcement of the new general majority principle, art. 16 states that *unanimity* among EU State-members is still necessary for Directives whose executions imply a change in current national legislation on professions. Consequently, as unanimity requires extraordinary political conditions, overall EU policy-making is pursued by means of organizational coordination through cooperation and mutual recognition, not by virtue of alleged self-fulfilling globalization trends.

The political implications of this EU policy are of the greatest importance for legal education and cannot be ignored If one looks at current EU arrangements, one immediately realises that the methods and content of legal teaching and research, on the one hand, and of legal training and know-how, on the other hand, are not legally defined at all, not only because (by definition) cultural patterns cannot be legally constrained, but also because mutual recognition and cooperation imply autonomy, not standardization. Consequently, it is not by chance that EU policy on access to higher education is not based on specific statutory rules, but on general principles, directives and memorandums. It is not based on 'hard' laws and decrees, not even on the so-called 'soft' law or quasi-legislation, but on recommendations and suggestions. So much so, that general organizational programmes, not detailed norms, embody the guidelines for the advancement of EU higher education policy.

To offer a detailed account of this outstanding framework, a cluster of official EU sources will be analysed hereinafter, including recommendations suggested by various EU Council units, such as the Commission's Task Force on Human Resources, Education, Formation and Youth; the Permanent Conference on University Problems; the Committee on Education; the Commission on Cultural Cooperation; etc. A reference will also be made to suggestions made in the course of special EU Conferences, such as that held in Parma (1992) under the aegis of European Council, and in Pisa (1994), under the aegis of European Commissions; conferences in which the emphasis on cultural relativism, as a method, was constantly coupled with the claim for substantial recognition of the variety of memories, identities, biographies and communities of European society.

EU Higher Education Strategic Planning: Open Education and Open University

According to the EU Treaties, the EU Memorandum on Higher Education (1991) and the Parma Conference Recommendations on Access to Higher Education (1992), as well as the EU Commission's White Book on Growth, Competitiveness and Employment (1994), EU policy is orientated towards enlarging, strengthening and developing European culture as a binding condition for strengthening and protecting the intangible capital of European society i.e. its human resouces.

Three intertwined challenges compel the EU towards this policy: (1) the rising negative demographic trend in all European countries vis-à-vis the countries of other continents; (2) the increasing importance of local culture in the evolution of worldwide economic systems; and (3) the absolute need for a cultural assessment of EU political-institutional and internal/external legitimation. On this basis, two pivotal strategies have been developed: (a) to open up, enlarge and facilitate access to higher education; and (b) to set up structural devices to foster active interactions between the variety of carriersor agents of European 'formal' cultures.

According to official sources, in 1992 one could count in the European Community 3,500 higher education institutions containing about 6,750,000 students (Demichel, 1992). Each national education system not only differs in terms of many different variables: type of language, culture, methods, enrolment, administration, location, financial assets, etc, but has also been conceived and set up historically according to specific national (social, political, economic, etc.) purposes. These differences have resulted in a number of problems that require local (i.e. country specific) arrangements.

Altogether, the problems at stake can be summarized as follows: (1) the number and type of agents; (b) the amount and location of resources; (c) the methods and content of cultural discourses. In turn, these problems are related to three main questions: (a) who decides what? (b) What sort of operational criteria? (c) What sort of (socio-institutional) consequences? It goes without saying that the action-oriented thematization of each item is conditioned by the fact that educational systems are, by definition, loosely coupled systems, either internally as organizational units, or externally as organizational networks. (For both culture and its use are not fixed mechanisms/products at all, and therefore, as Weick put it, the structure is disconnected from activity, and activity is disconnected from its effects (Weick, 1976).)

However, it is also worth stressing that what European Community has developed to deal with the whole matter so far has to be valued in terms of *longue durée*, i.e. by using not statistical data or narratives only, but prospectivist and intuitionist view-points. Additionally, it is important to emphasize that any achievement is a mere stepping-point, the political meaning of which has to be valued in relation to the everlasting process of refinement of the idea of Europe (Ginkel, 1994).These remarks are even more relevant here, as we are specifically concerned with higher legal education, i.e. with social re-production, institutional credentialling and the cognitive framing of those agents who are entitled to define it in formal-official terms. In this respect, one thing has to be stressed: to the extent that EU policy not only follows a geo-political ideal as a basic guideline, but also tries to enforce such an ideal by means of a epochal creationist strategy, the structural gap and functional differentiation of European legal professions as regards any other non-European legal professions will increase at both theoretical and practical levels. In other words, as the construction of European legal professions in Europe is not, and will not be, concerned with a mere economicist competition based on mere market logic (e.g., as among US legal professions), but on a political strategy based on a political idea of Europe, its macro-meso-micro differential assets and identity will be strongly emphasized and will turn out not to be used as a limitation, but as a *sui generis* continent-specific resource.

The Dual System of EU Higher Legal Education

Leafing through current literature on legal education it seems that student issues form one of the main concerns. Certainly the student population is the basic source of legitimation of any educational system. Yet, to understand what EU higher education policy is about, it is important to keep in mind its historical roots and also to look at the future of universities and professional guilds, since they are the institutional agents of European formal knowledge and know-how, the vocational calling of whom typically has been and still is the official and legitimate re-production of teachers, researchers and practitioners.

With reference to the province of law, since the twelth century higher legal education has been two-fold in Europe: as Petrus Blesensis put it: *Juris theoria docetur in scholis, practica exercetur in curiis* (legal theory is lectured at school, legal practice is trained in court) (Blesensis, 1180). Repeated claims have been made at various times that such a dual system is neither plausible nor socially adequate, for what is socially and culturally needed is rather a contextual combination of theory and practice. Yet the dual system has never been abolished and it is rather unlikely that the rationale that it embodies will ever be abandoned. In fact, contrary to common opinion, the political-institutional rationale of this system is still valid and active, for law is always under the everlasting pressure of political power, and political power needs law to gain a stable degree of legitimation. So much so that the most plausible and socially adequate way to deal with these problems is precisely a degree of diversification between the teaching of legal theory and legal practice.This statement should not be shocking: it neither contradicts claims for new or better educational patterns, nor, as we will see, contrasts with EU policy, nor does it confute critical legal studies. In fact, it takes seriously a thousand-years old cautionary legal experience, and what Marxist-Leninist thought teaches, i.e. that the unity of theory and practice always has revolutionary effects.

Legal education based on mere practical know-how only, presupposes that the functioning of the corresponding legal system is, or could be, unproblematic, so that what is needed is just a 'tuning' operational performance. In turn, legal education based on a mere doctrinal knowledge presupposes that the functioning of the corresponding legal system is, or could be, internally coherent, so that what is needed is just a 'tuning' conceptual refinement. Unfortunately, however, these pure models never fit with harsh reality and a degree of coupling between formal knowledge and practical know-how is always necessary. What is important and what historically changes, therefore, is precisely the type of arrangement necessary to set up such a operational degree: an arrangement, however, that not only has to prevent the danger of a total hypostatization and/or subsumption of one item by the other, but also and above all has to cover the harsh reality of a legal system which is somewhat politically weak, technically unrefined, socially moulded and/or culturally unsettled (in brief: not 'pure' at all).

The necessary distinction between learning legal theory and legal practice apprenticeship has always been re-produced by means of a dual system set up within the given institutional unit under consideration, or put outside it, by devolution to other (semi-autonomous) units. Significantly, EU higher legal education policy, following a continuously reformist legal experience, enhances the same distinction within and across all European law faculties while sustaining it within professional guilds as well.

The fact that the EU Directive on mutual recognition of higher education diplomas is about both university degrees and guilds certificates, not only gives evidence of what has been said so far, for it confirms the persistent need for such a dual system. It also confirms the cultural and political *rationale* of a long-lasting tradition of the functional division of legal work between European academic jurists, lawyers, notaries, judges and public functionaries. As the controversial experimentation and rapid abandonment of the so-called *Einstufige Juristenausbildung* (one-stage legal education) in several northern German Universities in the late 1960s and early 1970s demonstrates, evidence shows that the more legal theory and practice are linked, expecially at legal educational level, the more it is likely that settled political-institutional constituencies might be put into serious question (Plett, 1986). EU policy does not follow this one-stage path.

The Functions of the EU Higher Legal Education Credentialling System

According to Bourdieu, the function *du système de production des biens symboliques* is correlated to the structural conditions of cultural development and change (Bourdieu, 1971). Accordingly, in the last decades, in Europe, one can count three main sub-systems: the academic (university) system; the professional (guild) system; and the corporate (private, often profit-making) system. In fact, in one way or another, each of them is concerned with the three main areas of higher education: teaching, research and professional training.

However, EU higher education policy still basically deals only with official public-oriented institutions (universities and guilds), as the lacking of any formal recognition of private agencies and their credentials indicates. Such a discriminatory choice does not imply that EU policy-makers are not aware of the actual structural conditions of cultural re-production in Europe. On the contrary, it reveals that a selective support strategy is enforced to balance current and prospective power/knowledge gaps at a political/institutional level.

The need for a support strategy is clearly apparent in the case of EU higher legal education, for an increasing number of powerful semi-autonomous trans-continental socio-legal orders are systematically challenging, by means of in-house teaching and training courses, as well as in-house courts performances and law-making, the social control mechanisms and cultural hegemony of the traditional agents of EU law. Thus, as the struggle for organizational dominance is always about symbolic, not merely economic, rewards (Olson, 1986), the functions which EU policy assigns to European law faculties and guilds are self-evident: to strengthen the political legitimacy, cultural identity and technical diversity of the overall European normative domain (Olgiati, 1995).

These functions are of particular relevance for the university system. In fact, once it has been fully recognized, as in the University Charter (1988), signed in Bologna on the occasion of the ninth centenary of the *Alma Mater Studiorum*, that the university system has lost its monopoly over scientific research and higher education because of the above structural conditions, European universities are compelled to re-vitalize their traditional universal mission as specialized institutions of *learning*, and not just as institutes of technical and vocational calling, by re-assessing an *ad hoc* interaction between formal knowledge and know-how (Ginkel, 1994). To fully appreciate the point as regards law faculties, it is thus necessary to relate the issues of current and prospective EU theory learning and practice training to a broader socio-institutional educational context in which powerful business corporations act as competing agents, but without ever forgetting that the dominant EU university model still is, as far as its core meaning is concerned, to a large extent that defined, since the times of Von Humboldt and Hegel, in civil law continental Europe (Bonvecchio, 1980).

University legal education in Europe is not primarily concerned with teaching students how to become good practitioners. Its basic mission has always been to institutionally re-produce legal scholars, researchers *in primis*, in order to be able to confer legitimacy upon, and promote the validity of, a given socio-legal order. The fact that educated students could gain a professional occupation within the legal setting was, and still is, a mere consequence of the offer of a general legal culture to a relatively undetermined universe of applicants. To put it another way: the functional differentiation of the University as a cultural/institutional agent is not, and cannot be, based on situational and ephimeral job conditions. The current generalized dismay of law students as regards the alleged emptiness of University formal credentials as far as the access to the market for legal services is concerned, is a typical case in point, for it demonstrates how misleading an ideological conception and instrumental use of higher education as learning is. In any case as the above is also true at EU level, it shows that EU policy is following a longlasting tradition.

In turn, legal training in professional guilds has been, and still is neither primarily devised, nor orientated, to teach students how to use the technicalities of law. Its basic mission was, and still is, to select through a highly refined socialization processes a social group fit for conferring validity on a given socio-legal order. So much so, that the inner normative core of professional guilds, i.e. their professional ethical standards, does not refer directly to legal technicalities, but to all the possible variables of specific social behaviour (prestige, autonomy, correctness, etc.). As we will see, the rejection of the so-called 'technicist, specializing obsession', and the appreciation for any effort aimed at creating a renewed sense of vocationalism in professional practice on the part of the EU Council, is an unquestionable sign that in this area as well EU policy is following a longlasting tradition.

To sum up, the evidence shows that both those claiming for the abolition of the legal value of law-degrees and the guilds' professional monopoly, and, by contrast, those expecting a market-oriented liberalization of EU credentialling system, are totally misreading the EU policy context, for both of them ignore and/or undervalue the institutional nature of the 'learning' mission of the EU university system and the social dimension of training in EU professional guilds.

EU Higher Legal Education Organizational Modelling

The fact that EU policy is directly concerned with the assessment of a continent-specific ideal function of official higher legal education in Europe does not contradict, but rather confirms, the importance of its organizational interventionalism from above. Here, in fact, one can see major innovations and what sort of change is occurring.

In this area it is important to distinguish the social mobility of EU students, teachers, researchers and practitioners across Europe, on the one hand, and the structural harmonization of territorially settled EU higher education institutions, on the other hand, i.e. universites and guilds. As an extraordinary amount of study has been devoted to these items, there is no point here in focussing on them in detail. More useful and perhaps more interesting is just to recall, in synthesis, the organizational principles that have been developed to deal with the matter.

As far as social mobility is concened, up to now law students', teachers' and researchers' mobility has been performed, as for any other discipline, within general EU free mobility programmes such as Erasmus, Lingua, Tempus. More recently, however, the need for an improved (top-down) coordination among university units and an improved (mutual) control of quality standards and credit systems, is leading, as shown by the Socrates and Leonardo programmes, to a system of institutional co-design and co-decision, based on contractual cooperation agreements between official academic governing boards. This will drastically reduce the freedom of individual mobility planning, while improving research group joint institutional coordination. More precisely, from now on, social mobility will be channelled by and subsumed under official centralistic cooperation strategies, as mutually defined by each academic institution. Consequently teachers and researchers, as institutional status-roles, will be favoured, while students will gain a mere virtual mobility, the rate of which will be determined by the degree of open access to higher legal education.

As far as the social mobility of legal practitioners is concerned, there is little to add to what has been previously said about the variety of legal constraints and limitations enforced since the Treaty of Rome. So far the coupling of a relative (mainly symbolic) liberalization of the right of establishment and the above mentioned duplication of professional standards has fostered a process of professional socialization at elite level only. This is occurring basically for a temporay length of time and among young practitioners already employed as legal clerks in law firms dealing with international law. Contrary to those claiming that professional 'Big-Bangs' have taken place, the same constraints have also forced these law firms to create networking systems, rather than reproduce American-style multipractice corporate models. In any case, as recent empirical studies demonstrate, cross-border legal disputes in foreign State courts are currently domesticated by local legal constraints, and issues such as language, trust, etc. cannot easily be by-passed (Gessner, 1996).

A completely different and much more complex matter is the structural harmonization of territorially settled, often age-old, academic institutions. Here the main issue (the opening of access to higher education) is pursued by means of a general reform of (a) enrolment and services, and (b) education proper. According to official sources, both enrolment and services have to be: (1) flexible, (2) transparent and (3) permeable. In turn, education has to be: (1) general, i.e. not specialized and/or specializing, and (2) diversified, i.e. not uniform and/or one-dimensional. This does not imply that EU policy aims at a sort of 'access vs excellence' model (Twining, 1989). On the contrary, it aims at multiplying institutional excellence through a broader social recruitment, for a great cultural mobilization of all possible human resources is what is needed to politically face the challenges of contemporary society.

Interestingly, both the extension of access and the general character of education are based on two organizational pillars, the extraordinary importance of which is self-evident. First, a generalized shifting and overlapping (not a selective reductionism) of traditional boundaries relating to professional jurisdictions, disciplinary discourses, teaching methods, crediting systems, etc. Second, a generalized modular (not single-minded, unilateral) structuration of educational patterns.

At first glance, one could say that the shifting and overlapping of traditional power/knowledge 'mandates' and the modular structuration of educational patterns is a binding outcome, i.e. a necessity, derived by the complexity of matching altogether economic, human and cultural resources. This explanation is certainly true. Yet, as the same organizational pillars are consciously set up as operational devices to reduce the so-called 'technicist, specializing obsession' and foster a 'renewed sense of vocationalism', both of them undermine the idea that cultural excellence is synonymous with a never-ending socio-cultural fragmentation. Thus, looking more closely, one can also perceive that, within this framework, an unavoidable issue has finally been put on the EU agenda: how to solve another everlasting problem, i.e. the cleavage between education for true (political) command i.e. learning and education for mere (technical) management i.e. training (Miglio, 1969) in a historical context in which extraordinary socio-technical and socio-political changes make high-tech specialization rapidly out-dated, while a diversified, multidimensional, continuing general acculturation provides any actor with a variety of meanings, choices and opportunities.

The De-Coupling Criteria of EU Higher Education: the Academic System

As has been mentioned, official EU recommendations now suggest concentrating educational programmes on institutional excellence via the appointment of visiting (i.e. part-time) professors and reseachers in accordance with pre-defined networking projects based on institutional contracts between Universities. Consequently they also suggest a more efficent centralized coordination of the same programmes via the empowerment of academic administration structures.

These arrangements specify, from an organizational point of view, the way in which the European University system tries to govern, through a shifting of co-design and out-sourcing devices, the political need to keep under control both 'schools for trade' (mere know-how) and 'schools for command' (formal knowledge) in a context characterized by strong and increasing cultural competition with private profit-making corporations.

To give evidence of these issues in relation to legal education as an academic asset, it is useful briefly to focus on each one of the four institutional tools that shape it in actual practice: (1) the law faculty, (2) the law course, (3) law teaching, and (4) the law degree.The law faculty is the organization-set concerned with the number of students, economic resources and the type of culture. To deal with it, EU policy recommends improving competition at national and continental level by de-coupling two criteria: (a) a common (national-oriented) standard, and (b) a individual (autonomy-oriented) standard.

The law course is the structure concerned with education patterns. As these patterns should reflect the legitimacy and validity of a given order, EU policy recommends confirming traditional methodology based on a single course (with a fixed number of exams, teaching matters, etc.), divided according to two criteria: (a) a 'propedeutic' (first 2 years) period, and (b) a 'orientative' (last 2 years) period. Law teaching is the method concerned with educational discourses. As it should favour vocationalism while at the same time attracting both human and economic resources, EU policy recommends that teaching methods and subject matters should be divided according to two criteria: (a) common and compulsory, and (b) experimental and elective.

Lastly, the law degree is the formal credentialling device. As the legal value of this device has been reinforced by mutual recognition, while at the same time its substantial function as a class mobility tool has been eroded by other types of social stratification grids, EU policy recommends grading its formal value according to two criteria: (a) short degree or diploma (first 2/3 years), (b) degree proper (full course).

As one can see, what EU policy is really promoting is a multidimensional modular system within an institutionally integrated European University area. The effort, it is worth stressing once again, is a conscious response to external challenges, namely the rise of powerful semi-autonomous socio-legal orders now competing for a worldwide organizational dominance and the weakening of official nation-States legal and cultural constituencies. In turn, it is also a highly refined attempt to develop criteria of institutional correspondence between legal theory and legal practice in a general socio-legal context characterized by constitutional instability and socio-economic insecurity, in order to re-assess the universal mission of the University system as a proper, functionally differentiated, institution of *learning*.

What is striking, therefore, is that by de-coupling the 'internal' asset of law faculties, courses, teaching methods and degrees, on the one hand, and by centralizing the 'external' function of social and cultural mobility by means of institutional contractual arrangements, on the other hand, EU policy is turning European academic legal education into a veritable post-modern corporate networking system of continental dimensions, i.e. a transnational, continent specific 'organizational texture' (Gherardi and Strati, 1990), constructed by the 'community of engaged learners' (Eckert, 1993) or, if one prefers, by the so-called 'community of practice' of the same EU law school system as a 'learning context/agent' (Lave and Wenger, 1991; Jordan, 1992; Pontecorvo et al., 1995), typically oriented towards learning re-production.

The De-Coupling Criteria of EU Higher Legal Education: the Guild System

Within the above mentioned structural-functional framework, the fact that proposals have been made (as suggested in the organization papers for the forthcoming 5th EU Framework Programme for Research) to stress, from now on, not high-tech specialism, but the development of the Humanities and

Social Sciences (Ginkel, 1994) is an indicator that can hardly be underestimated. In fact, it not only explicitly highlights the political locus of cultural competition among any sort of corporate systems at worldwide level at the entry of II Millennium. It also implicitly puts to the fore a major weakeness of EU political *struckturbildung* at present: the decline of the normative social function of professional guilds (Durkheim, 1978), and the changing of learned professions, legal professions included, into rising anomic social strata, lacking normatively-oriented principles (Sarfatti Larson, 1997; Olgiati, 1996).

Unfortunately, the issue is related to broader epochal mainstreams that cannot be discussed here. Yet, it is undeniable that much of it is due to the impact of EU transpositioning policy. At any rate the overall result is clear: professional guilds, as current debates on professional ethics demonstrate, hardly play a real pedagogic/regulatory role any more. Equally, as debates on professional intrusion, stratification and specialization also indicate, professional guilds are far from enforcing a real socializing/integrating function any more (Olgiati, 1997). In fact, the very existence of the guild system, as a legally protected monopoly, challenged by extraordinary external pressures, has recently been questioned (Krause, 1996).

Given such a disquieting state of affairs, it comes as no surprise to note that the same professional guilds, individually and/or collectively, are now increasingly reacting. As the symbolic cases of French and Italian latin-type notaries (Olgiati, 1994) and English lawyers (The Lord Chancellor's Advisory Committee, 1996) show, the critical point of the problem (and its prospective solution) has been envisaged in the already mentioned degree of diversification between practice-oriented knowledge and know-how: thus, as the two variables are extremely unsettled, the institutionalization of their own, higher education system has been recognized and taken on by the same guilds as an essential organizational task.

Interestingly, as the status-roles, social functions and technical perfomances of both individual practitioners and professional groups are strictly defined by official formal law, the aim of the guilds' internal education system is not to by-pass or exclude university learning, but to offer a plausible and socially adequate '...degree of confidence and control' about professional credentials and career patterns (Shapland, 1996). Yet, as professional credentials and career patterns are not the same thing, guilds' courses have to deal with these professional issues accordingly, i.e. by means of context-specific modular devices. Evidence shows that this will be done by means of two items: (1) access courses, to relate formal academic education to the substantial entry conditions to given professional arenas (enrollment and apprenticeship), and (2) conversion courses, to relate old and new skills and expertise to the changing cultural career patterns and workarea assets under consideration. Significantly such a binary tool is also a way of re-assessing the unity and identity of the profession without jeopardizing the traditional principle of professional autonomy.

At first sight, the coupling of formal education and practical training within professional guilds does not seem to have anything to do with the modular structuration of the university system. On closer inspection, however, it is apparent that the so-called 'rush to formal continuing professional development' on the part of professional guilds is a totally coherent strategy towards the overall EU higher education guidelines discussed above. In fact, not only does the professional education model reflect the rationale of the corresponding dual criteria that characterize the university system. It is also conceived as a veritable post-qualification rite-de-passage, i.e. as a further reinforcement of official institutional credentials, particularly as regards competence vs motivation of mid/senior-career performances, as the current controversy about how to define the requirements for the accreditation of career conversion indicates. Last, but not least, it confirms the socio-institutional legitimation of the functional differentiation beween the university, as a proper institution of learning, and the professional guild, as a proper *socio-technic* agency.

Indeed, one might say that all the above is just the way in which EU policy of mutual recognition between academic and professional certificates might be fully realized, i.e. that an operational coupling-by-differentiation between guilds' and universities' educational systems is precisely what is recommended by overall policy of EU governmentality. After all, what really sustains the intangible human capital of European society is just a plausible and socially adequate relational texture for cultural advancements throughout past social experience, not the achievement of high-tech specialism at any cost.

Concluding Remarks

If one considers what has been said so far from an historically determined perspective of *longue durée,* one can hardly doubt that EU higher education policy is based not on globalizing trends, but on the universal principle of laws of form (Spencer Brown, 1969) i.e. *divide et rule* by the exclusion of what is, or could be, 'disorganic' (a principle of identity) and coordination of what is, or could be, 'organic' (a principle of integrity), applied to the overall dynamics of the EU geo-political process.

The principle concerns, first of all, the means used for its implementation. As we have noticed, the EU university system is governed by virtue of general directives, recommendations and organizational arrangements, rather than binding legal provisions. By contrast, the EU professional system is governed by a number of highly refined sets of norms concerning practictioners' status-roles. Both systems however are provided with a degree of autonomy as regards the definition of the frameworks of their performances and reputation, expecially in relation to their socio-institutional backgrounds. Thus, mutual intertwiment of the two governing criteria not only marks the identity of the EU higher education credentialling system as a *sui generis* context/model, but also offers an important guideline for a reflexive introspection about any sort of mutual cultural and professional project and trend.

The same principle also applies to the two areas under consideration: academic institutions concerned with learning, and professional guilds as a socio-technical agencies. With regard to the former, the study makes apparent that EU policy tries to face the consequences of the loss of the monopoly of higher cultural production on the part of the overall university system. To counterbalance the challenges of transnational economic corporations in the field of symbolic production, research, etc., an operational tool (institutional network contracting) has been developed, which is able to link each European academic unit within a highly selective lean (not herarchical) 'relational texture' of continental dimensions. Within this frame of reference, European cultural imprintings and developments are defined as a continent-specific resource, as 'cultural capital' (Bourdieu, 1971), while the historical mission of the university as a proper (functionally differentiated) learning institution is strongly reassessed. Thus, the peculiar complexity of the thousand-years old traditions and experiences of European legal, cultural, social pluralism, far from being subsumed under the cover of contingent and situational mainstreams, is emphasized as a strategic source of identity, as well as a basic epistemic condition for enhancing further EU harmonisation issues.

In turn, with regard to professional guilds, the study shows how many variables have been taken into account by EU law-makers in order to set up a professional legal framework coherent with a geo-political ideal of Europe, and how selective are the conditions concerned. Albeit implicitly, it is also apparent that EU policy tries to face the challenges that transnational corporate orders have launched to the official legal system and officially protected legal jurisdictions. Indeed, the efforts which have been made in order to reinforce the technical specificity, cultural identity and political loyalty of European legal professions towards EU governmentality projects are also a consequence of such challenges. Altogether, however, both tasks appear extremely difficult, for, as in the story of the Damned of the Tartarus told by Homer, EU policy continuously changes its own reference enviroment (Arnaud, 1975). Thus, just the setting up of continuing re-education courses seem to become a primary workable remedy to reduce professional *anomie,* while providing an operational coupling between internal and external professional constraints.

Last, but not least, the divide and rule principle is at the core of the structural/functional distinction between academic education for political command and professional education for socio-technic management. As has been mentioned, the social/institutional rationale of such distinction is grounded in a deep-rooted continent-specific cultural tradition, but it is also related to prospective scenarios about the interplay between law, economy and society at a worldwide level, and therefore to the pivotal role of European cultural pluralism as a local resource as well as common social capital.

This last point leads directly to another challenge to EU *strukturbildung* that has not been mentioned so far: the irreversible decline of the classic political economic and Enlightenment constitutional principles upon which EU policy has been basically constructed up to now. It goes without saying that it is impossible to discuss this complex topic here. But no one can be so politically naive as to miss the fact that this is the major cultural, political and institutional challenge for any sort of EU higher education policy.

The fact that European legal professions and the academic system are intimately concerned with such an irreversible decline is not a new idea (given the amount of availabe literature on Post-modernism). Yet, it is highly symbolic that EU policy-makers do not even mention the possibility that it could imply nothing less that '...the lack of a legal reason able to rule contemporary law' (Arnaud, 1975; 1991) i.e. the spreading of social conflict and political disorder at continental and even at worldwide level, unless a new legal culture is created.

References

Adamson, H. (1992), *Free Movement of Lawyers*, The Law Society, London.

Arnaud, J.A. (1975), *Les Juristes Face à la Société du XIX Siècle à Nos Jours*, PUF, Paris.

Arnaud, J.A. (1991), *Pour une Pensée Juridique Européenne*, PUF, Paris.

Blesensis, P. (1180), *Speculum Juris* quoted in Burmeister, K.H. (1974), *Das Studium der Rechte im Zeitalter des Humanismus im Deutschen Rechtsbereich*, G. Pressler Verlag, Wiesbaden.

Bonvecchio, C. (1980) (a cura di), *Il mito dell'Università*, Zanichelli, Bologna.

Bourdieu, P. (1971), 'Le marchè des biens symboliques', *L'Anneè Sociologique*, vol. 29, pp. 49-126.

Burns, T. R. and De Man, R. (1987), 'Science and practical action: Studies in Competing Logics', in T. Burns and H. Flam, *The Shaping of Social Organization*, Sage, London, pp. 348-365.

Collins, R. (1972), 'Sistemi educativi e tipi di stratificazione', in M. Barbagli (a cura di), *Istruzione, Legittimazione e Conflitto*, Il Mulino, Bologna, pp. 143-178.

Consiglio d'Europa (1992), *L'accesso all'istruzione superiore in Europa, Atti della Conferenza, Parma 13-16 ottobre 1992*, Centro grafico Università di Parma, Parma.

Demichel, F. (1992), 'Demografia e istruzione superiore', in Consiglio d'Europa, *L'accesso all'istruzione superiore in Europa, in Atti della Conferenza, Parma 13-16 ottobre 1992*, Centro grafico Università di Parma, Parma, p. 79.

Durkheim, E. (1978), *Lezioni di Sociologia*, Etas Libri, Milano.

Eckert, P. (1993), 'The School as a Community of Engaged Learners', unpublished paper quoted by Strati, A. (1996), *Sociologia dell'organizzazione*, NIS, Roma.

Friedman, L.M. and Teubner, G. (1986), 'Legal Education and Legal Integration: European Hopes and American Experience', in M. Cappelletti, M. Seccombe, J. Weiler (gen. eds.), *Integration Through Law: Europe and the American Federal Experience: Methods, Tools and Institutions*, vol.1: *Forces and Potential for a European Identity*, Book 3, De Gruyter, Berlin.

Gessner, V. (1996), *Foreign Courts. Civil Litigation in Foreign Legal Cultures*, Dartmouth, Aldershot.

Gessner, V., Hoeland, A. and Varga, C. (1996), *European Legal Cultures*, Dartmouth, Aldershot.

Gherardi, S. and Strati, A. (1990), 'The "Texture" of Organizing in an Italian University Department', *Journal of Management Studies*, 27 (6), pp. 605-618.

Ginkel van, H. (1994), 'Conclusioni, Commissione Europea, Ministero dell'Università e della Ricerca Scientifica e Tecnologica, Università di Pisa', in *Atti del Convegno 'La responsabilità Europea delle Università'*, 23-26 Novembre 1994, p. 186.

Habermas, J. (1981), *Theorie des Kommunikativen Handelns*, Suhrkamp, Frankfurt am Main.

Hobbes, T. (1890), 'A Dialogue Between a Philosopher and a Student of Common Laws of England', in *The English Works*, London.

Hobbes, T. (1968), *Leviathan* (C.B. Macpherson ed.), Harmondsworth, London.

Jordan, B. (1992), 'Artifacts and Social interaction in High Technology Work Settings', paper presented at a conference on organizational learning and technological change, Siena.

Karabel, J. and Halsey, A.H. (1977), *Power and Ideology in Education*, Oxford University Press, Oxford.

Krause, E. (1988), 'Les Guildes, l'Etat et la Progression du Capitalisme: les Professions Savantes de 1930 a Nos Jours', *Sociologie et Société*, vol. XX, n. 2.

Lawe, J. and Wenger, E. (1991), *Situated Learning: Legitimate Peripheral Participation*, Cambridge University Press, Cambridge, Mass.

Lepenies, W. (1994), 'Intellectual Responsibilities. Institution Building in Central and Eastern Europe: Some Consequences for the West', in *La responsabilità Europea delle Università*, Commissione Europea, Ministero dell'Università e della Ricerca Scientifica e Tecnologica, Università di Pisa, Atti del Convegno, Pisa, 23-26 November.

Locke, J. (1968), *The Educational Writings* (J. Axtell ed.), Cambridge University Press, Cambridge.

Locke, J. (1989), *Some Thought Concerning Education*, Clarendon Press, Oxford.

Lonbay, J. (1990), *Training Lawyers in the European Community*, The Law Society, London.

Martin Bernard, J.M. (1990), *Abogados y Jueces ante la Comunitad Europea*, COLEX, Madrid.

Meineke, F. (1924), *Die Idee der Staatsrason in der Neueren Geschicte*, Oldenbourg, Munchen-Berlin.

Meyer, J. W. and Rowan, B. (1978), 'The Structure of Educational Organizations', in M. W. Meyewr et al. (eds.), *Environments and Organizations*, Jossey-Bass, New York, pp. 71-

97.

Miglio, G. (1988), 'La trasformazione delle università e l'iniziativa privata', in *Le Regolarità della Politica*, Giuffré, Milano.

Olgiati, V. (1990), *Saggi sull'avvocatura. L'avvocato italiano tra diritto, potere e società*, Giuffrè, Milano.

Olgiati, V. (1994), 'The Latin-type Notary and the Process of European Unification', *International Journal of the Legal Profession*, 1, no. 3, pp.253-268.

Olgiati, V. (1995), 'Process and Policy of Legal Professionalization in Europe', in Y. Dezalay and D. Sugarman (eds), *Professional Competition and Professional Power*, Routledge, London, pp. 170-204.

Olgiati, V. (1996), 'Le professioni giuridiche in Europa. Politiche del diritto e dinamica sociale', Quattroventi, Urbino.

Olgiati, V. (1996), 'Risk, Professions and the Claim for Human Rights', paper presented at a conference on de-constructing professions, entitled 'Professional Identity and Professional Order in Comparative Perspective', IISL-Onati.

Olgiati, V. (1997), Professional Self-regulation of Private Lawyers in Italy, *International Journal of the Legal Profession*.

Olson, M. (1986), *The Logic of Collective Action*, Harvard University Press, Chicago.

Padoa Schioppa, A. (1985), 'Le facoltà di giurisprudenza: problemi e proposte', *Foro Italiano*, V, 325, pp. 1-22.

Padoa Schioppa, A. (1996), 'Il diritto comune in Europa: riflessioni sul declino e sulla rinascita di un modello', *Foro Italiano*, V, 14, pp. 1-16.

Plett, K. (1986), 'The Rise and Fall of the Reform in West German Legal Education', paper presented in the Interdisciplinary Legal Studies Colloquium, Institute for Legal Studies, University of Wisconsin Law School.

Pontecorvo, C., Aiello, A.M. and Zucchermaglio, C. (1995) (a cura di), *I contesti sociali dell'apprendimento*, Edizioni Universitarie di Lettere, Economia e Diritto, Milano.

Sarfatti Larson, M. (1977), *The Rise of Professionalism. A Sociological Analysis*, University of California Press, Berkeley-Los Angeles.

Sarfatti Larson, M. (1997), 'Professions' Nomic Functions and the End of Modernity', *European Yearbook of the Sociology of Law*, Giuffrè, Milano.

Schmitt, C. (1938), *Der Leviathan in der Staatslehre des Thomas Hobbes. Sinn und Fehlschlag eines politischen Symbol*, Hanseatische Verllagsanstalt, Hamburg.

Shapland, J. (1996), 'Continuing Professional Development: Burden, Care or Challenge?', The Lord Chancellor's Advisory Committee on Legal Education, *Report of the Proceed-*

ings of the Consultative Conference, pp. 7-14.

Spedding, L.S. (1987), *Transnational Legal Practice in the EEC and the United States*, Transnational Publishing, New York.

Spencer Brown, G. (1969), *Laws of Form*, Allen & Unwin, London.

The Lord Chancellor's Advisory Committee on Legal Education and Conduct (1966), *First Report on Legal Education and Training*, L.C.D., London.

The Lord Chancellor's Advisory Committee in Legal Education and Conduct (1996), *Continuing Professional Development*, L.C.D., London.

The Times Higher Educational Supplement (1992), 'Law Chiefs Abandon Euro Degree Idea', September.

Twining, W. (1989), 'Access to legal education and the legal profession: a Commonwealth perspective', in R. Dhavan, N. Kibble and W. Twining (eds), *Access to Legal Education and the Legal Professions*, Butterworths, London.

Weick, K. (1976), 'Educational Organizations as Loosely Coupled Systems', *Administrative Science Quarterly*, no. 21, pp.1-19.

8 Faculties Under Influence: The Infeudation of Law Schools to the Legal Professions

CLAUDE THOMASSET AND RENÉ LAPERRIÈRE

Introduction

The relations between the law schools and the legal profession are deeply rooted in history. In Quebec and Canada, the law schools are an emanation of professional training: the creation of law faculties dates from the nineteenthth century, and for years represented a formal training totally given and controlled by the legal professions and their members. The modern version of a faculty of law staffed with full-time professors, offering core and optional courses and performing research, dates only from the 1950s and 1960s. Since then, university law schools have slowly gained a certain margin of autonomy — or should we say academic freedom — from the professional schools which they had been since their inception (Arthurs, 1983).[1]

The development of law schools into significant university faculties was stimulated by a constant rise in the numbers of students. While public financing of universities increasingly depended on the numbers of registered students, law faculties were and still are to a great extent considered as easy fund purveyors, since the cost of training a law student is very low and the attraction of the legal professions keeps demand for legal education almost unlimited. Even though conditions of access to the law schools were selective, the wave of democratization of higher education kept pouring large numbers of students into law programs. The consequence was that total undergraduate enrolment in Canadian law schools climbed from 2,896 in 1962-63 to 9,351 in 1976-77 (Arthurs, 1983 p.25). The same tendency was observed in Quebec where the number of lawyers jumped from 3,447 in 1971 to 16,344 in 1995, increasing the proportion of lawyers per 100,000 inhabitants from 56,4 to 222 for the same period (Barreau du Quebec, 1996). No wonder that this inflation of membership became a recurrent subject of recrimination between professional corporations and law schools.[2]

The recruitment of increasing numbers of highly qualified professors brought new expectations into law schools, which were reflected in the curriculum. The academic preoccupations and the full-time status of these professors prompted them to offer novel teachings and to perform scholarly research. Thus a new area of tensions arose with the professional bodies who insisted on controlling the substance, quantity and quality of teaching in these schools that were still considered primarily as dispensers of the future lawyers' training and used as a selective device.

In this chapter, we will examine more closely two aspects of the uneasy relationship between law schools and professional corporations. First, we will describe and assess the influence of the Bar on law schools in Quebec: on their programs, their faculty and their students. Secondly, we will take a close look at what we identify as the principal cause of the persistent infeudation of the law schools to the Bar and the Chamber of Notaries: the existence of legal professional monopolies.[3] We will then be able to expose the case for a change in this relationship away from the professional domination and confinement of legal training and research.

The Influence of the Bar on Law Schools

Any observer of law faculties in Quebec, and in Canada as well, will notice that they belong to a culture which differs from the rest of university departments, and live under the influence of professional corporations. The references to the profession are everywhere: in the programs, the staffing, the teaching methods, the career prospects. It would seem normal that universities and the profession should work together to offer the best training to those who intend to be lawyers, and that influencing each other would bring a benefit to both institutions. But experience has taught us that in fact, the appropriation of the legal field by the professional corporations and mentalities has led to subtle but real forms of implicit or explicit control over the curriculum as well as the faculty members and the students.[4]

Control Over the Curriculum

A law curriculum includes all the courses a student should attend in order to graduate as a bachelor of laws and to be eligible to the law societies' training programs.[5] If the common law schools programs in Canada have already been scrutinized, this is not the case for the Quebec law schools (Cassels and Maloney, 1989). We will thus focus on the Quebec situation and enrich our analysis with the findings from the Canadian enquiries into common law schools' programs.

The main stress put on law programs comes from the law societies in the common law provinces, as well as the Bar and the Notarial profession in Quebec. It affects compulsory courses but has a most pervasive effect on optional courses. It also results in non imaginative ways of evaluating students through standard examinations inspired by the professional societies' exams.

The Bar Prerequisites

The analysis that Jamie Cassels and Maureen Maloney offered on the situation in Canadian common law schools is also valid for Quebec law schools (Cassels and Maloney, 1989 pp107-108). The first year of law school curriculum is compulsory and for the most part identical. In common law schools, property, tort, contract, criminal, and constitutional law belong to that list of compulsory courses, whereas in Quebec, family law, the law of persons and administrative law are usually added to it. A rapid look at Quebec law school curricula will show the identical emphasis put on compulsory courses which are regarded as fundamental for the training of future lawyers.[6] They may be named differently but they cover such matters as persons, family, obligations, civil liability, property and successions, company law, constitutional law, administrative law, criminal law, labour law, judicial law and evidence.

This list is established in conformity with what is now called by the Quebec Bar an 'indicative profile' whose components include: law of persons, family law, matrimonial property law, obligations, contracts, civil liability, property, law of real securities, evidence, civil procedure, constitutional law, criminal law, criminal procedure, administrative law, company law.[7] This list is larger than most of the compulsory courses scheduled in the Quebec law school curricula. It thus affects the optional courses attended by law students in a drastic way.

The Reality of Elective Matters

Jamie Cassels and Maureen Maloney have stigmatized the adverse effects of law societies' training programs on optional courses in common law schools (Cassels and Maloney, 1989 pp107-108). They stressed the attractiveness of those elective matters which belong to the implicit professional profile. They deplored the marginalization of courses dealing with non-lucrative matters or with non-traditional skills.

In an attempt to measure this effect on Quebec law schools, we have tried to analyse the actual practice of law students registering into optional courses in their respective law programs.[8] Over a five year period, we have noticed that most of the optional courses offered by law schools which are well attended by students are among matters required for the Bar examination program, such as matrimonial law property, civil law property, municipal law and land use planning, taxation, contrats, criminal law, and so on.[9] We are also in a position to evaluate the effect of the Quebec Bar's large publicization of its 'indicative profile' in 1993 on the changes which occured in the students choices since that date. Most of the optional classes which were not Bar-oriented have had much difficulty in surviving. To maintain them on the curriculum, some law schools alternate the scheduling of those courses every two or three years in order to find enough students interested in them. Other law schools have decided not to offer those courses altogether. Most of those courses are in domains outside the professional profile such as feminist theory, aboriginal law, social law, housing law, health law, comparative law, sociology of law, and so forth.

The consequences of this pressure from the legal profession on the law school curricula are detrimental to any attempt to develop an alternative approach to law teaching and to alleviate the pressure from the dominant positivist paradigm.[10] It restrains law schools from adopting innovative teaching methods and alternative student assessment.

Teaching Methods and Student Assessment

A good way to evaluate the emphasis put on alternative teaching methods and innovative student assessment is to look at the place occupied by legal research and writing courses in a law student curriculum. All five law schools in Quebec have at least one of these courses which is compulsory and full-time students should take them during their two first years at university. When we take a closer look at the reality of those courses, we find that students get fewer credits for those courses than for other law courses, no regular professor is hired to teach such courses, students are not interested in them, and so forth. Mooting is more exciting for law students than learning a good methodology for legal research. Legal research may also mean the capability to find only statutes, regulations and decisions in legal data banks and nothing else! This may be enough for lawyers-to-be, but it will result in totally deficient training for students aspiring to understand how law works.

But is this question 'how does law work in real life?' a legitimate question in a law school? If not, why worry about alternative ways of teaching law? However, if, as we assume, this question should be asked and answered in law schools, then legal research courses are the back-bone structure in a law student curriculum.[11] In those courses, students should develop tools to learn how to ask good questions about law and how to start finding the answers. However, when one is a Bar-oriented student, one wants to learn how to pass the Bar examination. And those exams do not require students to be minimally critical towards law, since on the contrary bar exams do not allow alternative answers to questions. So, for what purpose should law professors strive to initiate their students into the mysteries of sophisticated research tools if these are not necessary, on the short run, for passing Bar exams? 'Real life' will come later on...

Some law professors have developed strategies to make students understand that, in their own interests, they should seriously learn how to think about law from a broader perspective than merely the one promising success at the Bar exams. A privileged way to achieve this is to offer students the possibility of working in groups.[12] One of the five law schools in Quebec has developed, in a largely hostile environment,[13] a longstanding expertise in group work and has gained a good reputation in this way of training law students.[14] The benefits of working in groups are numerous. Among the most important is the fact that students are in a situation where they need to interact in discussing the legal problems they have to solve. They will be confronted with opposing solutions, just as in real life. They will be in a position to make choices, not according to what is expected to answer a question in a Bar exam, but to what they think should be best according to their own values and conceptions about law. They will learn how to think by themselves and not only through supreme court decisions and mainstream doctrinal works.

Control Over the Faculty

Let us recall that law schools in Quebec, which are officially 'Faculties of Law', arose from a professional demand for training lawyers. In the mid-nineteenth century McGill and Laval universities opened almost simultaneously programs which were oriented towards the training of lawyers.[15]

In the same way as McGill Law Faculty, the Faculty of Law at Laval University was created from the demand in organizing a program to structure the instruction of future lawyers. Up to that time, lawyers had been trained without any formal organization by other lawyers. From then and up until the mid-twentieth century, most of the instructors at the Faculty of Law were practitioners (lawyers and judges). In 1956, the Faculty of Law of Laval University had only four full-time professors.[16]

These origins of the faculties of law in Quebec explain to a great extent the influence of the Bar on their full-time professors. Even if most faculties of law have now more than thirty full-time professors and more than fifty in the biggest ones (Laval and University of Montreal), we feel that law professors form a community whose prime loyalty is towards their legal profession rather than to their university.[17] The influence of the Bar on the faculty members appears through the allocation of teaching responsibilities at the undergraduate level, arrangements concerning external professional work of faculty members and their involvement in teaching at professional training schools.

Who Teaches Law Students?

Even if law professors are now increasingly hired with higher postgraduate diplomas, some of them, at least up to the end of the seventies, possessed only a professional diploma in lieu of a Master's degree.[18] This meant that they had never been confronted with intellectual debates about law. Consequently, they were not in a position to offer their students alternative ways of thinking about law. Is it that different now that a larger number of law professors have completed postgraduate studies and written Ph.D theses? It is very difficult to answer such a question since no survey has been carried out in regards to this new situation. But we remain sceptical, because law programs and law students do not offer the flexibility to teach compulsory courses in a way that would diverge from the requisites of Bar exams.[19] It may be different for elective courses. But, as we have seen previously, elective courses are no longer so different from the compulsory ones since they are also mainly required by the professional examinations.

Another factor reinforces the influence of lawyer-oriented teaching in law schools. Even if the number of law professors has drastically increased during the last thirty years in Quebec, they are usually not in a position to completely cover the teaching demand from law programs. Consequently, most law faculties hire part-time lecturers to fulfil their sessional planning. These can be invited professors from other law schools, but more often they are practitioners bringing into law schools their way of doing things in the 'real life' of lawyers. Most of the time, students are fascinated by such know-how and are inclined to measure the performance of full-time professors by their capacity to give immediate *ad hoc* answers to their questions and to tell lawyers' stories in the same way as practitioners do.

This represents a central issue for law professors whose ambition is to teach students how to learn rather than to be fed with information which will become obsolete soon after they enter the profession. Indeed, many law professors fear that in the classroom they will be unable to answer specific questions in their legal fields or teach students all the items they include. This encyclopedic approach puts constraints on teaching methods, and encourages the dependence of students towards the teacher who claims to know best what students should learn. It prohibits the development of teaching methods which give students responsibility and initiative in their learning process.

Professional Activities of Law Professors

In Quebec law schools, some full-time professors may claim to fulfill their university obligations while being part-time partners or associates in law firms. Most law professors engage in external professional activities without feeling or being considered in conflict of interest with their university duties of research and tutoring post graduate student. Much of the time they are graded higher during the periodic university peer evaluation process because of the 'prestige' they are thought to bring to the image of the law faculty. Even students expect law professors to be practitioners in adequately teaching law. They are most surprised when they hear that law professors are carrying out research not driven by law practice. This lack of a research-oriented tradition in law faculties inhibits the development of a new kind of full-time law professor, dedicated to research and alternative law teaching, contrasting with the mainstream model dominated by the law profession.

Commitment of Law Professors to the Profession

Most law professors insist on keeping up their membership of the legal profession. They participate in the profession by voting and even fill elective positions.[20] They may chair committees and take part in the profession's activities. In keeping their membership for 10 years, they become eligible to be called to the bench.[21] They may also be involved in professional training programs where they teach according to their specialty. In our view, these activities reinforce the intimate links between law professors and the professions and may inhibit their capacity to oppose the profession when their academic interests and those of their students are at stake. Some colleagues may argue to the contrary that their good relations with the profession bring them valuable inside information that will be useful to students and prepare them for the professional exams. This is a short-sighted vision because it implies that the legal professions are the only possible careers for law students and that nothing else other than the professional style of training can prepare law students for the real life after university. Law professors who limit their span of action to the professional environment cannot emancipate their way of thinking and fully become university scholars.

Control Over the Students

One of the paradoxes we have pointed out in recent work about legal education in Quebec (Thomasset, 1996) is that most law students intend to become a lawyer or a notary when they graduate from law schools.[22] But when we looked afterwards at what they had been actually doing with their professional accreditation, about seventy-five percent of graduates were actually practising law.[23] This means that a large proportion of students were engaged in careers not requiring a lawyer's training. This situation reveals the lack of imaginative thinking which dominates the law school ideology. Why do law schools limit legal education to the training of lawyers-to-be? Why can't students imagine anything else than becoming lawyers or notaries when entering law school? We contend that the professional corporations' monopolies on legal practice impose these limitations on any other alternative ways of taking advantage of a legal education. They deeply affect the attitude students develop towards non-lawyer-oriented compulsory courses and in a much more dramatic way, elective subjects, as well as teaching methods.

'Hard' and 'Soft' Law Courses

We have seen earlier that law programs have their core subjects of 'hard law' which reflect the training program of the legal professions. This does not leave much space for other 'soft' compulsory courses about law and history, legal research and writing, international law or legal theory. What is heard from students attending those classes is that they feel they are wasting their time because these courses will not prepare them for their professional career. Most of the time, students will delay their registration up to the last moment when they come to worry about the completion of the program to get their diploma.[24]

The expectations of law students towards those 'soft' law courses are preconditioned by the idealized image of lawyers they receive from the mainstream ideology nurtured on media-built stereotypes and professional magazines.[25] If law students knew when entering law school that a significant proportion of them are bound to really take advantage of their professional training, they might be more inclined to pay attention to other dimensions of legal education. They are seldom informed of other than traditional job opportunities or about developing innovative practices. They never pay attention to these 'alternative' realities and discourses if they are not confronted to 'soft' law compulsory courses.

Elective Matters

With the financial cuts in university budgets, students have come to exercise increasing power on academic authorities in a context where the viability and the scheduling of optional or elective courses depend directly upon the number of registered students in order to balance the law program budget. Now that students are generally considered as clients in the big industry of post-modern universities, focus is brought on client satisfaction. This means that non-compulsory courses which do not get enough clientele are at risk of being cancelled and not rescheduled. According to the professional expectations of a large majority of law students, elective matters directly related to professional training programs are naturally the most popular to the detriment of less profession-oriented courses.

Our survey on three Quebec law programs confirms this trend.[26] Most elective courses of the first kind fill classes of fifty to sixty students (some have more than seventy) and are scheduled at least once a year or even once a semester. However, the elective courses of the second kind, less profession-oriented, attract only twenty or thirty students in a class and are scheduled at best once a year; most of the time they appear on the agenda only once every two or three years. Those elective courses cannot expect to have a great influence on law students' career strategies. Scrutinizing more carefully the figures obtained from one of the Quebec law school allows us to rank the students' choices. Bar-oriented elective courses are always among the five first choices of a majority of students; on the other hand, the other courses appear very occasionally among the first five choices of the majority of students. This means that students are opting for the latter classes not by deliberate choice but for other reasons such as schedule commodity, expected workload or the teacher's reputation, recalling Cassels and Maloney's remarks about holiday resorts and main-and-malestream professional credibility (Cassels and Maloney, 1989).

If elective courses of the second kind are not considered important by students and are not financially supported by the academic authorities, they will disappear from law programs which will then become even more profession-oriented. But students are not helping themselves in so doing because they are endangering their capacity to adapt their careers to matters which do not appear in the professional training profile but which are in real demand for legal services.[27]

Some students have been aware of this danger and have suggested the suppression of the Bar training program, to be replaced by a professional exam after articling (Lambert, 1996). This would give law students the opportunity to stay one more year at university and develop broader perspectives in new domains not strictly related to the traditional practice. Some Australian universities have already taken this direction and are promoting new combined or double programs in law and business, law and computing sciences, law and science, commerce and law, economics and law, civil engineering and law, social science and law, social work and law, and so forth.[28] This trend will affect the way of considering the monopoly on legal practice since new expertise will be gained by those students which may then be affiliated to two or more different professions, for instance law and social work. This could have a destabilizing effect on existing professional monopolies by blurring the frontiers of exclusive fields of practice.

Student Perspective on Teaching Methods

In a period of drastic cuts in university financing, fees are rising fast and in an economic crisis situation more and more students have to earn their own money to pay their studies. This means that they spend less and less time studying law in the law library. They adapt their timetable to attend those classes which fit best with their working schedule. This situation affects teaching methods because what is best adapted to those student realities are lectures and exams. Pressure is put on teachers not to offer alternative ways of teaching which may require more study and more time spent at university. If this situation appears to be generalized for all university students, it is aggravated in law schools where the professional training model is already based on lectures and exams. Students do not expect to deviate from this model. We are convinced that exams and lectures are modeling students to conform to the authority of the teachers who claim to hold the truth. In so doing teachers are confirmed in their position of power and students in their passivity and need for security. Alternative ways of learning, such as group work and small group seminars which require more time from students and teachers, are more readily set aside, even if their positive results are recognized by students who experienced them.[29] Yet these methods essentially provide more autonomy to students in the learning process and allow them to choose where they want to invest their intellectual interests.

The mass of students are not prepared to fight for teaching methods which will impose upon them more initiative and more individual work. On the other hand, as we have seen earlier, most law teachers are measuring their competence as teachers on the basis of their students' results at the Bar exams. One cannot expect too much change in the teaching practices of law schools as long as the profound causes of this situation are not identified and discussed. We must then turn to the basic question: why are law teachers and law programs so infeudated to the legal professions?

The Legal Basis, Extent and Effects of Professional Monopoly

As we have seen, the influence of the Bar and the Chamber of Notaries in Quebec on the law school programmes is considerable. What relationship of power explains this situation? Our contention is that the principal reason lies in the existence of a professional legal monopoly over the practice of law. The law of Quebec establishes a *de jure* monopoly over the main functions of a lawyer or a notary, and this is completed by a *de facto* monopoly of lawyers and notaries on legal jobs or on the field of legal expertise covered by the customary intervention of lawyers.

Origins of Monopoly

Even if the existence and the legal setting of professional monopolies seem axiomatic to members of professional corporations, one must note that they were non-existent at a certain point in time, that they took decades to develop in their present form, and that they remain subject to change. The reverse illusion stems from the extensive character of the monopoly and from the disproportionate social, economic and political power acquired by the professional corporations in the course of their development. Especially in French-speaking Quebec where the traditional elites were clergymen, physicians and lawyers and where the Legislature was dominated by lawyers, these groups were quick to secure their economic position and social status through legislation at any time when it seemed useful to defend or promote their interests.

At an early stage of the practice of law, there existed no formal legal education in Quebec universities; one would become a lawyer through apprenticeship in a legal office and by judicial recognition. The legal profession's monopoly took shape long before formal legal education developed in the universities. Representation of people before the courts was its main element for years; it was completed in 1954 by a monopoly over legal advice and consultation, or in other words legal opinion.[30] Even though the Bar Association was founded in 1849, it was not until 1890 that the protective notion of usurpation of the functions of lawyers was cast in the legislation[31] and not until 1909 that it was extended to include more specific descriptions of the field of practice of lawyers, mostly pertaining to acts related to judicial representation.[32]

Over the years, while some parts of the lawyers' monopoly remained largely undisputed, others (namely, giving legal advice) were vindicated before the courts. Legislative limits over the monopoly were imposed in the 1970's with the creation of a Small Claims Court where legal representation by lawyers was barred; other lucrative matters such as automobile insurance were removed from the jurisdiction of ordinary courts and socialized into administrative law, thus affecting the practical extent of the market for lawyer services.

Nature of Monopoly

The nature of monopoly consists in restricting the offer of services in order to maximize their price. This implies keeping outsiders out of the business and controlling the economic behaviour of members in order to maintain the unequal distribution of income among them. In elite professions, such as medicine or law, monopoly is closely linked to the maintenance of social status, consecrated by a title,[33] by easier access to the media and to political responsibilities or influence, and by a global revenue placing the profession at large in the highest scales of earnings which does not eliminate large income differentials between firms and between individual members.[34] Another feature and condition of status is the preservation of the group's autonomy against the democratic claims of the public or governments which would try to diminish their privileges or their share of the gross national income.

To preserve these economic and social privileges in the long term, the professional corporation as a group must always keep an imbalance between supply and demand for legal services. Thus, the profession has oscillated between a traditional attitude of limiting access to the profession, by way of excessive entrance fees, examinations, length of formal training, articling, and so on, and a more modern approach of increasing demand for legal services and opening new markets, mainly through legislative action requiring additional legal formalities and legal representation. The extension of the welfare state was providential for lawyers, because even if they hated the idea of socialization, they saw the demand for their services increase dramatically over the years and they finally came to understand that the extension of a State acting through legislation and institutions subject to the rule of law would necessarily increase demand for legal work. Nowadays, in the storm of neo-liberal deregulation and public budget cuts, the Bar stands as a valiant advocate of the public good and for the maintenance of those public programs which most benefits its members.[35]

Justification of Monopoly

The ultimate justification for the maintenance of a legal monopoly is the public interest. Law societies must permanently show that the interests of their members coincide with the interests of the public, a transposition of the worn-out motto: 'What is good for G.M. is good for the US'. This blurring of a fundamental social contradiction is so imperative for the preservation of privileges, that it must convince everybody and become paradigmatic. This is why we find invocations to public good repeated *ad nauseam* in the Bar's and the lawyers' speeches, in the legislation and the Charters of Rights and Freedoms (namely with the right to a full legal defence), in the judge-made law (by requirements of due process and natural justice), and as we will see later in the formal training of future lawyers.

The public's interest necessitates the independence and autonomy of lawyers: democracy itself is supposed to rest on the shoulders of lawyers, who jealously preserve their independence in order to defend citizens (and corporations) against abuse by state bureaucracies (according to the common law conception of democracy). As for money, lawyers are untainted by it: as an officer of the court, the lawyer is supposed to work for the realization of justice, not for private interests. Hence, any lawyer can defend any case by almost any means and arguments without being criticised for social partiality or bias. Social privileges are deemed essential for the preservation of independence, otherwise the profession would be given over to venality, corruption and mediocrity. All elite professions follow the same line of reasoning, even university professors, whose tenure and privileges are meant to preserve their academic freedom.

Thus, professional ideology adapts from time to time (generally with a long delay for the more conservative legal professions), to the changing moods of public and corporate policies based on the new social theories of the gurus of our time: the economists. When industrial liberal capitalism was triumphant, monopolies were seen as a natural and legitimate product of profit-seeking. But they hampered the operation of free markets and by killing competition they impeded initiative and progress. When state powers decided to limit them with anti-trust laws, they had to be reaffirmed and established on a legal basis as an exception required for the public good. Now that neo-liberalism is becoming dominant, more justification is required to maintain privileges based on legislation or regulation, and with the shrinking of public domain and activity, the need for legal services may well fall dramatically. Lawyers will then be forced either to restrict their offer of services by limiting the number of admissions, or to aggressively expand their markets and render their services indispensable.

That is the main point that the Quebec Bar's Committee on the Future of the Profession tries to make in its 1996 Report, written with the assistance of a business consultant firm and two economists (Barreau du Quebec, 1996). This report analyses the situation in market terms, describing the profession as an industry, the lawyers as legal service suppliers, and stressing that the Bar should adapt rapidly to the changing social, political, economic, technological and international environments. It recommends the adoption of a 'Singapore-type' scenario of aggressive production and marketing of services in order to face competition, as opposed to the illusory comfort of the *status quo* or an 'Albania-type' scenario of withdrawal and isolation.[36] The discourse on the protection of the public, the fundamental object of any professional corporation according to the *Professional Code*,[37] is totally obliterated;[38] not much reflection is spent on what should be done to define and promote the best interests of the public at large because they still are naturally equated with the best interests of the profession.

The Extent of Monopoly

The delimitation of the extent of a legal monopoly is crucial for the protection of the interests of the profession, especially when it is confronted with competition from other professionals (such as accountants or administrators) or other people or businesses working in areas covered by legal norms, formalities and procedures. The *Bar Act* enumerates a large number of acts reserved for lawyers, and pertaining to the practice of law: for instance, writing legal documents which will become the object of legal procedures, or sending a letter of demand. It also covers legal advice and consultation, in very general terms which inevitably ask for interpretation.[39]

Judicial Interpretation

In economic matters, the courts traditionally held a language of economic liberalism, giving a restrictive interpretation to all monopolies or other devices confering a privilege, at least as a matter of principle.[40] However, this attitude fell short of challenging the monopoly of legal professional corporations on the basis that they would be illegal coalitions restraining commerce and freedom of work.[41] In Quebec, as elsewhere in Canada, judges of superior courts are appointed by the governments in power and chosen exclusively from the pool of lawyers: this would tend to explain the dual attitude of the courts, oscillating between the consecrated rules of restrictive interpretation and the indulgence for the maintenance of the structures, if not the promotion of the interests of their former profession, and by extension of other professional organisations.

The delimitation of boundaries defining the different acts of judicial or other enumerated and reserved forms of legal representation was a long-standing problem for the courts. It involved easy prosecution against people who, according to the Bar Act, could be accused of claiming to be or acting as lawyers. But more difficult battles were waged against other professionals, especially the Bar's war against the notaries.[42] More instability was found in the interpretation of the open-ended monopoly over legal opinion because of the very general — almost generic — description of the reserved field. Theoretically and practically, any person giving his or her opinion on any matter of law falls under the restrictive provision.[43] A strict monopolistic position is untenable here because legal norms and solutions have become pervasive in our society, supposedly governed by 'the rule of law'.

To assert its monopoly and oppose it to others, the Bar had to deal with intruders; in particular, those who challenged most effectively the interests of its members, for instance financial advisors[44] or journalists[45] purporting to perform legal work for their clients or explain law to the general public. It had to live with the practice of accountants and fiscalists, which involve much interpretation of tax law, probably because its membership could not claim much competence over this domain which they had traditionally left over to these specialists in figures. For years, it tolerated the practice of some members buying and reselling with profit the legal opinions of university professors or lawyers from other jurisdictions or countries not belonging to the Quebec Bar, before consenting to recognize their competence and admitting them as legal counsels with limited privileges. It is still watching very closely the development of paralegals, who may be technicians trained at the college level who will help law firms by performing procedural work, or other people having some knowledge of law from their experience and offering services at the margins of customary legal practice.[46]

The Bar also works actively at defusing any internal attempt from its members at changing the boundaries of lawyers' practice by offering traditional services at more competitive prices or new services in a multidisciplinary setting: sufficient pressure comes from the Bar's inspectorate so that generally no disciplinary action is needed. But one of the finest ways of keeping the troops in line, as we will see, is to inculcate in them a traditional training, not only during their attendance at the Bar school, but throughout their legal training at university.

International Comparisons

As it stands, the Quebec Bar's monopoly over legal practice and legal opinion is one of the most pervasive in the Western world.[47] Compared to that of other Canadian provinces, the statutory wording for representational functions may be more precise, but the legal advice clause is unlimited, even by the standard of actual practice (meaning what is usual for a lawyer to do in order to give a legal opinion). A general characteristic of the definitions of the protected field is their vagueness, the practice of law being tautologically defined as what the lawyers actually do in their practice, or even worse by what ideally should be the field of practice of lawyers. However, most laws require that violators offer their services on a regular basis and for remuneration: these restrictions do not exist in Quebec.

In the USA, the situation in the 50 States is comparable to that of the Canadian provinces, and there exists a great disparity of definitions and judicial interpretations. Some law societies are very militant in ascertaining their monopoly, while in other States the courts tend to restrain them.[48] Strict monopoly is far from being established, the ideal for the bar integrationists being the Canadian provinces.[49] In the sixties and seventies, legal monopolies were challenged with success by other professional groups and by governments who sued the Bars for illegal coalitions and deals restraining competition. State Bars still have to fight in court against paralegals and self-help initiatives undercutting their traditional market.

If Canadian lawyers took their model from their US counterparts in order to forward their economic interests by transforming their practice into lucrative businesses, they inherited their elite status from Great Britain. There is no distinction in Canada nor in Quebec between barristers and solicitors: lawyers belong to a single law society, 'the Bar'. From what we gathered, British barristers enjoy a *de facto* monopoly more protected by the common law, judicial custom and their membership in the Inns of Court, than by statute. Solicitors, on the contrary, have to rely more heavily on legislation[50] and litigation[51] in order to assert their more limited monopoly against competing professions or individuals. In 1991 the Courts and Legal Services Act brought an enlargement of the legal field and a relaxing of rules leading to an extension of the privileges of solicitors and a novel form of oligopoly, while a number of acts such as conveyancing were opened to other practitioners under the supervision of a commission. The concern of the neo-liberal ruling class over the restoration of competition did not abolish the aristocratic structure of the legal profession, but it seems to have succeeded in restraining monopoly and favouring more competition at the lower levels of legal practice.

The all-out monopoly over legal opinion enjoyed by Quebec lawyers and notaries appears to be inspired by French style legal writing, freely using general concepts, formulae and terms in order to cover whole fields of activity, whereas English statute law is generally more descriptive and more specific. This cultural factor explains many of the differences we observe between Canado-American law and Quebec law. Yet, in France where universities are quite old and gather at least as much prestige as professional corporations, lawyer monopolies and privileges were from time to time abolished, reinstated, redefined, merged and reseparated. In 1971, the *avoués* were merged to the *avocats*, while a new modern profession was created, that of legal counsel *(conseil juridique)* authorised to give legal advice, mainly in the fiscal, social and corporate fields.[52] This experiment was abandoned in 1990 by the merger of legal counsels to the Bar,[53] and this was found not to be illegal or detrimental to consumers by the Competition Board. However, any university professor, legal professional belonging to another corporation, corporate jurist or member of enumerated regulated professions, and any person having a university degree in law covered by a professional liability insurance and rules of ethics respecting professional secrecy and conflicts of interests, can still give legal opinions on their own. Thus, the lawyers' monopoly is far from being as extensive in France than it is in Quebec.

The Effects of Monopoly on Legal Training and Research

We do not intend to discuss at length the general social effects of monopolies such as the exaggerated prices for services to the public, the obstruction to inventiveness, adaptation and progress. We will try to determine to what extent the professional monopoly explains the overwhelming influence of the Bar on legal education and legal research. In other words, would the picture be much different were it not for the monopoly? The three main effects of professional monopoly, as we observe it, relate to the special status of its members, the constitution of a closed internal control and isolationism from the rest of society.

Elite Status

Monopoly has much to do with the preservation of an elite status for members of professional corporations. Economic privileges stemming from the control of supply and the extension of demand can be acquired only if the services are deemed essential or desirable. Most people would rather dispense with having trouble with the law or having to spend time and money to vindicate their rights; but in many instances it becomes a necessity, just as it may be necessary to consult a medical specialist in order to recover from illness. At a certain period of time, as is still the case in some US states, courts can sentence people to death, hence making indispensable the services of lawyers; in other cases, even trivial ones, courts can imprison people, ruin them or seriously damage their social lives and reputations, or hold the key to correct individual or social injustice. This power of the courts in our political systems explains the power of those who hold control over the access to courts or to legal language and formalities.

This power is used to gain economic advantage, an important ingredient of elite status, which is also founded on specialized knowledge. It also explains the arrogance of elite professionals in general, the feeling of social superiority and the contempt for those who do not detain the same power or knowledge; in the legal field, this arrogance is exacerbated by an adversarial system of justice designed to crush, paralyze or destroy the opponent.[54] Elite status brings social consideration, reflected in titles, and instils conservatism into those who take advantage of it; this conservatism is increased in the case of lawyers because law itself, as a discipline and practice, is vowed to the preservation of social order, of the *status quo*. Law is also based on authority and wields constraint, which are features of power reinforcing the internal cohesion and the social position of the profession.

Internal Corporatism

The monopoly of a group or association such as the Bar is viable if it is not jeopardised by competition amongst its members, not disrupted by political rivalries over the control of the corporation, nor left to contestation over the distribution of power, influence and income. Thus, the exercise of disciplinary powers by the corporation over its members and the surveillance procedures such as the inspectorate are necessary ingredients to keep the membership in line. But, most important, the maintenance and development of monopoly must count on a strong positive feeling of belonging, an *esprit de corps,* which anyone may observe in elite professions. This special feeling, which nurtures corporatism, is the cement which binds the institution: it is imperative that members must identify with the profession, and be proud to do so; this acts as a system of mutual help and protection.

This corporate culture is maintained by associating with peers and frequenting the same places and institutions; but it is forged in the first place by education and training, from which members acquire their system of values and build their personal identity and group attachment. Thus, the corporation's control over the reproduction of its membership through the training of its future members is essential to the perpetuation of its elite position, and conversely the power derived from its monopoly is used to apply selective and conservative pressure on these parts of training performed by independant institutions such as universities.

This entrapment into the lawyers' *esprit de corps* and values is extremely strong among most members, including law teachers, because of another feature of the legal discipline, the search for security: security of rules, security of transactions, and above all security of the person. The fundamental insecurity of most people living from law and desiring to keep on the right side of law, to know law in order to defend himself or herself against legal aggression, explains a good deal of the conservatism of the profession; and the additional security and opportunities offered by one's membership in a powerful monopolistic corporation explains why so many non-practising lawyers (including university professors) still pay their dues (and their respects) to the Bar.[55]

Social Exclusiveness

This search for security and exclusiveness leads to a monopolistic system of protection consisting in insulating law, as a practice and as a discipline, from the rest of social interactions and fields of knowledge. Anyone purporting to give an opinion on law or legal institutions, who does not have legal training, or even who has legal training but does not belong to the corporation, is disqualified as ignorant or irrelevant. This sequestration of law explains the superb isolation of law faculties in higher educational institutions which is materialised in concrete terms on university campuses. It explains why jurists have been so eager to constitute the discipline of law as 'an art and a science', autonomous from humanities or social sciences. It explains why law professors have historically invoked their professional status to form separate trade associations inside universities and claim higher 'market' wages and privileges from their employers, and continued to do research or consultation on a professional basis outside the institution instead of integrating this activity and its overhead-free profits into the development of research infrastructures and programs inside the institution that offers them full-time employment and job security.

Thus we have come full circle: monopoly is the keystone of legal culture; it is the economic foundation of privilege; it is the social instrument of status; it is the legal instrument of appropriation and control. If only lawyers can get access to legal knowledge, legal representation and even legal opinion, and if the Bar controls training, practice and intrusion, and maintains absolute closure on the field of law, then monopoly becomes paradigmatic and practically nobody working in the legal field can imagine another state of affairs.[56] This setting is considered so 'natural' that tautological justifications on the basis of competence and public interest seem fully supported by their simple enunciation. If legal monopoly were to cease forthwith, the ascendancy of professional legal culture would certainly persist for a time, but would be shaken in its foundation and lead to a profound reshaping of legal privileges, institutions, discourse and practice.

The Case for Change

Should law be the exclusive property of legal professions? Different answers will be given according to where one is located on the map of legal services (Duncanson, 1996). From the standpoint of professors of law working in an academic setting, it should be obvious that law is a collective asset. This would mean that the access to legal norms, their interpretation and their use should not be the preservation of any legal profession. The next step would lead to questions such as why do these legal norms exist? To whose benefit? Are they still accurate? These questions are essential to understand the meaning and the effectiveness of legal rules, but they are far different from what the legal professions are expecting the law schools to teach their students.

The confinement of law as a practice and an intellectual discipline has caused much institutional and social discontent and critique. In 1983, the *Arthurs Report* pressed for less predominance of professional concerns and more genuine pluralism in the curriculum to allow for the development of authentic legal scholarship, research on law reform and legal theory.[57] But, being overwhelmingly composed of jurists and having mostly consulted legal actors, the Consultative Group took the professional monopoly for granted and, instead of contesting its social relevance, tried to adapt legal research and education to its requirements, or to circumvent them, while pleading for more openness of mind, an enlargement of orientation and perspective, more cooperation, and more money for law faculties and their members in order to encourage academic research and scholarly writing above professional preoccupations. The Consultative Group's prudent and submissive mentality in the face of professional power and culture derived from monopoly rendered its core recommendations very difficult to implement wherever they touched the profession's interests.[58] As a result, even if some improvement was noticeable in academic research, the problems which were identified in 1983, especially those involving curriculum, are pretty much the same and still define the relationship between legal education and legal professions today.

By contrast, some law schools outside Canada have adopted some quite interesting approaches to legal education, such as that outlined in the 1997 welcoming speech of the University of New South Wales Law Faculty Dean.[59] This approach is based on active learning and on a curriculum composed of a relatively small compulsory core of subjects and a wide choice of elective matters which prepare students for a wide variety of careers. Law Schools are considered part of the great university tradition of scholarship and intellectual inquiry for its own sake. The use of law is aimed at reforming the social orderings and at casting light upon their understanding. Law is seen as being in the service of the community's yearning for justice.

Our assessment of the present situation in Canada leads us to plead for more change along these inspirational lines in order for legal education to gain its autonomy and for law to develop as a fully-fledged academic discipline.

The Necessity of Change

The ongoing discussions on the legitimacy or opportunity of limiting access to the Bar School and the practice of law underline the long-term choices facing the profession: controlling the supply of legal services, as the present Barrister of Quebec has suggested in his 1995 election campaign, or expanding the field of legal services and increasing their value, as advocated by the Bar's Committee on the Future of the Profession. Certainly it appears, even in the ranks of the profession, that change is needed; in any case, change will necessarily occur due to the joint pressure of globalization and technicisation. The logic of globalization combat the maintenance of artificial barriers to the free exchange of services. Technicisation goes still further by extending the dissemination of law through cyberspace, and most importantly by confronting traditional decision-making with novel processing methods under the control of other professionals, usually computer scientists. This technical knowledge holds an enormous symbolic power in a world where technology is seen as the magical means to solve social problems.[60]

In this vast reshuffling of economic, social and political powers, law schools try to keep pace, but mostly to steer clear of confrontation. Yet, they too are facing a major problem with the underfunding of public universities: they must recruit and graduate more and more students in order to maintain their financial viability. Hence, stress is put on quantity to the detriment of quality, on training to the detriment of research. Most students legitimately insist on getting jobs in the legal area after their graduation; with the present extent of monopoly, they are practically forced to prepare and undergo the professional courses and exams, except if they consent never to perform legal representation or opinion, for instance by being content with research or editorial work for legal firms or other institutions.

However, there exist many needs for legal services that are not covered. Back in 1973 a study by Andrée Lajoie and Claude Parizeau revealed that traditional civil law practice was declining in favour of new fields such as social law and labour law (Lajoie, Parizeau et al, 1976).[61] Other fields of practice have developed rapidly since then: immigration law, housing law, human rights law, international law, environment law, and law applying to biotechnologies and information technologies. Moreover, the need for legal services is still present for people not having access to lawyer or notarial services, especially for information purposes and legal advice (Macdonald, 1991). The Bar's 'indicative profile' concentrating on civil law and procedure matters is out of synch with social evolution: it precludes the development of legal services responding to these needs and impedes the training of people who otherwise could eventually find and perform useful work in these fields.

In addition, pressure from the legal professions represents a serious constraint on the constitution of a scholarly or scientific discipline of law, as advocated not so long ago in the *Arthurs Report*. But, interestingly, other institutional pressure may well force the law schools to come out of their isolation, not for the sake of science or out of humanist longings, but because pluridisciplinarity could facilitate institutional savings by enlarging the number of students attending classes, by adding extra subject matters to their curriculum and by lengthening the duration of studies. Budget cuts in universities may well lead to structural changes to institutional settings, merging law schools into larger and more cost-effective units: such developments, however, are no guarantee of more interdisciplinarity, or more scientificity in the legal discipline itself.

The Conditions of Change

We must then consider the conditions under which law schools may acquire more autonomy from the legal professions. In the 1980s the *Arthurs Report* had already seen the development of the public educational sector as a challenge to the professional mentalities, 'intellectual and societal values' dominating law schools, omitting altogether to challenge professional controls (Arthurs, 1983, pp.42-43). First and foremost, there is a need for the affirmation of academic jurists, people with full diplomas and preferably pluridisciplinary backgrounds or sensitivity, whose belonging and loyalty belong primarily to public education, not to professional corporations. This would allow for more transdisciplinarity within the institutions, and hopefully lead to a better understanding of the role of law and legal education in society. In Neil Sargent's terms this academicizing of the law school requires that the law school renounce its primary allegiance to the doctrinal tradition as the pre-eminent source of professional-knowledge claims and favours a confederation of 'knowledges' whose components would tentatively include feminist social theory, cultural anthropology, linguistics, criminology, law and economics, sociology of law, and social psychology (Sargent, 1991, p.21).

Formal training in other disciplines may well help law-professors-to-be evade the imprisonment in law imposed by the legal culture, and to question their own legal training and models acquired from the past. But it is not an easy task without dangers, as Neil Sargent warns (Sargent, 1991, p.15). It involves more than putting researchers trained in different disciplines into a law school environment, or putting them to work on common research projects, because there is a danger that the contribution of social scientists and critical doctrinal scholars to an understanding of law as a social phenomenon will continue to be marginal to the primary purpose of the law school in training legal professionals.

A second condition for change appears to be the better integration of law professors into their educational institution in order to find support for their scholarly yearnings. The universities have become major players on the political scene in Quebec over the last 30 years. The expansion and democratization of education, especially higher education, has become a major economic and social goal, considered essential for the modernisation of Quebec society, at least in the 1960s. It has brought major investments and expenditures in the field of education at all levels.

Universities, especially the traditional ones, had always insisted on preserving their autonomy in the face of government, but they came to depend heavily on public financing and became more and more integrated in the logic and the culture of public bodies. As semi-autonomous bureaucracies, their loyalties tended (to varying degrees) to shift in favour of government away from the private professional corporations which were still trying to preserve a maximum of control over the selection and training of future members. The new political power developed by universities and the education bureaucracy can explain, for instance, why in 1973 the Bar lost control over the accreditation of university programs for admission of graduates to the Bar School and eventually to the practice of law.[62] But the law faculties did not really take advantage of this gradual power shift to assert more autonomy in the face of the professional corporations and integrate themselves better into the academic setting and academic community; on the contrary, they were always tempted to claim for, and often succeeded in obtaining special status and privileges inside their institutions by invoking their professional quality and using their professional alliances.

This infeudation of law schools directly results from the existence of two corporate monopolies over the mainstream practice of law and over any type of legal advice, consultation or opinion. If graduates from law schools could freely offer their services and practice in the fields of their acquired competence (especially those corresponding to new social needs not covered by the Bar's prerequisites) without having to belong to professional corporations, the faculties could claim more autonomy, offer a diversity of training and develop new fields of research opening novel possibilities of legal education and training. The law schools would still have to take into account the recurrent need to train 'traditional' lawyers, but they would not be seriously hindered in their institutional and intellectual development by the requirements of a private corporation given public monopolistic powers.

The logic and logistics of university teaching and research call for pluridisciplinarity, promotion of scientific approaches and methods, internationalization of knowledge, comparative studies, critical analyses and social responsiveness, whereas a professional school traditionally limits itself to monodisciplinary expertise and acquisition of positive knowledge deemed useful for day-to-day efficiency.

As we have seen, a professional monopoly is not only an economic arrangement, but also an institutional setting maintained by an ideological discourse. The pressure of a monopolistic environment naturally works against openness: monopolies must be broken if new fields are to be explored and new methods tried. Thus, a structural change requires the limitation of professional monopoly to the acts that are strictly necessary for the protection of the public, namely those related to judicial representation and only on proof that the members have acquired a real competence to perform them, and this appears to be a *sine qua non* precondition for real change. This is the direction of the reform of professional law already carried out by the province of Ontario in the health care professions,[63] suggested by the Manitoba Law Reform Commission in 1994,[64] and put forward as a privileged 'approach' by the Quebec Professions Board in a 1996 document cautiously entitled 'Approach Towards Reserved and Shared Professional Acts'.[65]

As long as professional corporations remain in the position of doorkeepers holding the keys of professional status and practice, their extravagant influence and even control over law faculties will endure. Moreover, social recognition of the specific value of jurists, as opposed to strict lawyers, will come only if enough space is left for them to offer and promote their services in the marketplace, and if legal work can no longer be equated with exclusive membership in the Bar or the Chamber of Notaries.

The Means of Change

We will not insist for more than a few lines on the diversity of means that can be used in order to realize the proposed changes, because they should be left to discussion about their opportunity and feasibility. It is clear from our preceding arguments that action should first be taken at institutional levels to integrate law schools better into university structures and to break their isolation. Afterwards, efforts should be concentrated on the remodeling of the curriculum in order to offer multiple choices to students.

More diversity is required in terms of approach, contents, methods of learning and evaluation. We cannot insist enough on the necessity of breaking away with the old legal subject-matter classifications inherited from an exegetic and encyclopedic approach deemed necessary in practicing law, and replacing them with methods based on the acquisition of scientific tools and pluralistic approach, the comparison and confrontation of norms and rules belonging to different fields of legal practice, and the development of theoretical and critical scholarship, even in traditional or mainstream subject-matters (Poirier, 1987).

Conclusion

In this paper, we have seen that the influence of legal professions on legal education amounts to a multifaceted control over the curriculum, the faculty and the students at law schools. This pervasive influence on educational institutions reaches much further when it orients 'legal doctrine' and the evolution of the whole discipline of law. We have explained the persistence of this control by the existence of a quasi-absolute monopoly maintaining closure and isolation in spite of increasing competition, invasive technologization and international globalization.

Most analysts whom we have quoted remain pessimistic about the possibilities of a change, almost defeatist in the face of professional domination and the difficulty to find allies sufficiently equipped and interested in contesting the professional culture. The *Arthurs Report* stopped short of confrontation and explicitly refrained from suggesting any change, rather pleading for improvement by accretion. The Quebec Bar, by approving the Report of its Committee on the Future of the Profession, demonstrated that it was sensitive to promote change as far as it could prove profitable for its membership.

We feel that this feudal order of things can be broken by nothing less than a revolution... a cultural revolution, of course. To free the legal discipline from its sequestration, jurists must liberate their minds from their subservience. The precondition for such a move is to become aware of the remote causes and internal characteristics of the paradigmatic monopoly in which they live, work and think. Then, the most difficult effort consists in renouncing that part of their personality modeled on the conditionings inherited from their training or acquired through their socialization into a privileged profession.

Law professors have a structural role to play in this process. Their institutional status provides them with financial independence and academic freedom which should be put to use to criticize social arrangements and propose improvements at the risk of being unpopular or marginalized. Their diversified training and the pluralist milieu in which they work puts them in a privileged position to distance themselves from the biased influence of the profession. Unfortunately, most law teachers, even with the best intentions in the world, do not (or cannot) see any conflict of interests whatsoever between their membership and action in a profession, and their belonging to educational institutions; even those who work for social progress experience much difficulty in escaping from their profession's narrow vision as to the appropriate legal solutions to social problems.

What is needed here is more than a political will to contest monopoly, because it is still an impracticable task to gather a majority in favour of significant change. We believe in the power of ideals and ideas, and in ascribing a historic task to those who work for the liberation of law in a perspective of greater social justice. The role of scholars is to debate ideas and set models of intellectual integrity so that the quality of social participation can improve. This may start in the classroom, but it must also extend to communities of thinkers, whatever their extent. If law professors develop conviction and pride for what they are worth and capable of, instead of lamenting over the success of their professional counterparts, they may well assume leadership, serve as role-models for their students, and become a source of inspiration for those who want to pursue their intellectual quest through post-graduate work or social involvement.

Notes

1. Report by the Consultative Group on Research and Education in Law (chaired by H.A. Arthurs), *Law and Learning*, S.S.H.R.C., Ottawa, 1983 [the 'Arthurs Report']. This was the most thorough study ever undertaken on Canadian legal education and research and their relation to professional bodies and culture. It offered historical notes on the evolution of Canadian legal education, together with a description of curriculum and teaching, faculty size and qualifications, resources and activities of law schools. It pleaded for

many changes to put legal research and education on the rails of progress, addressing its recommendations to the legal community and the public institutions (universities and fund providers).

2. This tendency seems to reverse itself in the last two years, the Quebec law schools receiving less than half their usual numbers of admission requests. But it is still too soon to evaluate the effect of this decrease on the future numbers of graduates and lawyers.
3. In Quebec, the legal professions include lawyers, notaries and the judiciary. In this essay, we will concentrate on the Bar, which is the most numerous corporation, and give only minute attention to the notaries, and leave the judges outside the arena. It is worth mentioning that notaries have the same standing as lawyers, but specialize in matters mainly pertaining to family law and conveyancing; and that judges must be chosen among lawyers of ten years' experience.
4. The authors will draw from 30 years' experience as postgraduate students and academic staff in Quebec law schools, but from different backgrounds. One of them graduated and obtained his doctorate from a Quebec law school and the other graduated from a French law school and obtained both a master's degree in a Quebec law school and a French doctorate in urban studies. They were thus able to confront very different perspectives and conditionings.
5. In Quebec, the Bar is the only professional corporation possessing a publicly-funded school dispensing a 4th year of legal training with exams followed by compulsory articling under lawyer supervision.
6. See the full description of the law programs from the five Quebec law schools (McGill University, Université du Québec à Montréal, Université de Montréal, Université Laval and Université de Sherbrooke) through their home pages on the Internet.
7. See an insert published by the Quebec Bar in *Les carrières du droit, L'annuel de la préparation au marché du travail*, Collection Guides universitaires, Édition 1996, p. 40. The list is introduced by the warning: those subject matters are supposed to be learned before entering the Bar's professional training program [free translation]. This list has been officially publicized for the first time in the 1993 issue of this same magazine. The debate about this 'indicative profile' is as old as the one on legal training outside the university and up to now has never got a satisfactory answer.
8. When writing this paper, only two out of the five law schools had those figures available, but when talking with the deans or the vice-deans, they all agree that they have much difficulty in maintaining optional courses, because of the students' choices and also because of the present drastic university funding cuts.
9. We have collected figures for the last five years: 1991-1992; 1992-1993; 1993-1994;

1994-1995; 1995-1996.

10. On the positivist paradigm, see N. Sargent, 'The Possibilities and Perils of Legal Studies', *CJLS/RCDS* vol. 6 (1991), pp. 1-26; J.-G. Belley, 'Paradigmes et innovation: les professeurs de droit et l'avenir des professions juridiques', *CJLS/RCDS* vol. 9 #2 (1994), pp. 163-179.
11. On critical legal teaching, see C. Thomasset, 'L'enseignement critique du droit et la responsabilité sociale du professeur', in L. Langevin (dir.), *L'enseignement critique du droit: journée d'étude*, GEPTUD, collection Enseignement, Université Laval, Sainte-Foy, 1996, pp.11-23.
12. During the annual meeting of the Canadian Association of Law Teachers at University of Quebec in Montreal, in June 1995, a session was held about group work in law school classes. All panelists were convinced that it represented a serious alternative for student assessments and that it offered a cooperative way of student training.
13. It may become less hostile now that the Bar has adopted a report about its future which proposes, among other solutions to the crisis the profession is experiencing, group work to replace the individual way of working. The new lawyer will have to learn how to work in a group... guess where? at the university, of course! See Barreau du Quebec (1996), pp.112-113.
14. See a pamphlet issued for the 1996-1997 student recruitment campaign by the Département des sciences juridiques at University of Quebec in Montreal, where much emphasis is put on its group work pedagogy. Several alumni attest their appreciation for the success of this alternative way of learning.
15. Excerpts from the Internet home page of the Faculty of Law at McGill University, under the heading: 'History of the Faculty of Law'. Further details of the Faculty's history may be found in S.B. Frost and D.L. Johnston, 'Law at McGill: Past, Present and Future' (1981), 27 *McGill L.J./Rev. Dr. de McGill* 33, as well as in S.B. Frost, 'The Early Days of Law Teaching at McGill' (1984), 9 *Dal. L.J.* 150.
16. Information appearing on the Internet home page of the Faculty of Law of Laval University under the heading: 'Histoire de la faculté de droit'.
17. A good way to measure this loyalty is to enumerate the professors of law faculties who are members of a legal profession compared to those who belong to the Canadian Association of Law Teachers (CALT). In our department for instance, only a minority are members of CALT but a vast majority are members of the Quebec Bar or the Chamber of Notaries. Knowing that the Bar's annual fees amount to nearly seven hundred dollars with an additional thousand dollars for professional insurance, compared to a forty dollars annual subscription to CALT, it is easy to weigh the influence of a professional

belonging among the faculty members!

18. Our university (UQAM) is one of the few universities who impose selection criteria which require the Ph.D degree or the equivalent from all professoral candidates, even law candidates. Since law candidates usually hold a professional degree after their bachelor in laws degree, the Quebec universities have, for a long time, accepted this professional degree as an equivalent to a master's degree. Our university had to accept this fact, since candidates holding a Ph.D in law were still very few in the seventies, when our law program was created. But times are changing and nowadays, to appoint a full-time law professor, our university requires at least two master's degrees or a Ph.D degree. Our department of law has the highest proportion of Ph.D professors among the five Quebec law faculties.
19. See on experimentation of alternative teaching on contracts and on person and family law: J.G. Belley, 'Une expérience d'enseignement critique en droit des contrats' and A. Robinson, 'Expérience d'enseignement féministe en droit des personnes et droit de la famille: l'apport du mouvement féministe dans l'enseignement des cours de base dans les facultés de droit au Québec', in L. Langevin (dir.), *L'enseignement critique du droit: journée d'étude*, GEPTUD, collection Enseignement, Université Laval, Sainte-Foy, 1996, pp. 41-54 and pp. 25-40.
20. The present Quebec Bar president (bâtonnier) is a law professor, the second to occupy that seat since the seventies.
21. Many colleagues were appointed as judges of the Quebec Superior Court, the Quebec Court of Appeal, and the Supreme Court of Canada.
22. According to the figures gathered in the Bar Committee's Report, *supra*, note 3, pages 24 and 26, the percentage of graduate law students registering at the Bar's school climbed from 80% in 1988 to 90% in 1992.
23. The only extensive study about the careers of law graduates was realized in 1973-76 by A. Lajoie, C. Parizeau et al., *La place des juristes dans la société québécoise*, Thémis, Montréal, 1976. It showed that 55% of law graduates had become lawyers, 16.5% notaries, and that almost 25% did not have a traditional practice, of which 38% were administrators, 24% teachers, 11% social scientists, 6% paralegals, and 5% artists and writers (pp. 184 and 186). More recent statistics exist, not on the careers of graduates, but on the fields of practice of members of the Bar. E. Mackaay, *Les Avocats du Québec*, Barreau du Québec, 1991, p.129, shows that 61% of members are in private practice, 8% are attached to a corporation and 31% work in the public or parapublic sector (p. 7). 28% of their work is in matters not figuring in the Bar's indicative profile (p. 36), and 19% does not pertain to acts exclusively reserved for lawyers (p. 42). The latest figures

of the Bar Committee's Report, supra, note 3, p. 21, indicate that in November 1995, 17.6% of registered lawyers do not perform any act reserved for lawyers, 21% are civil servants and 61% belong to private practice or work for corporations.

24. This was experienced by one of the authors (C.T.) when teaching an advanced legal research course which was compulsory among a choice of four activities (but it is no longer the case with the more recent curriculum changes!). What happened with that class is that most of the registering students had had the bad surprise of being told, at the end of their last semester, that they could not get their bachelor in laws degree because this course was missing in their curriculum, thus preventing their registration into the professional training program. What can one think the motivation was in the classroom?
25. Lajoie and Parizeau (1976) demonstrated at p. 304 that the fields of specialization and the income of lawyers were directly related to their socio-economic backgrounds; in spite of the elite image of rich lawyers that attracted many newcomers of modest origin, the statistical reality kept most of them in the lower strata of lawyers' incomes.
26. At the time of writing, we were still waiting for the figures of the two others, who had more difficulty in retrieving those complex figures on actual elective course scheduling and attendance.
27. See A. Lajoie (1976), E. Mackaay (1991) and the 'Macdonald Report': Groupe de travail sur l'accessibilité à la justice (chaired by R.A. Macdonald), *Jalons pour une plus grande accessibilité à la justice*, 1991.
28. See the Internet home page of the Faculty of Law of the University of New South Wales (UNSW, Sydney) and that of the Faculty of Law of the University of Technology of Sydney (UTS). All these new programs started in 1996.
29. During our own long experience of teaching (more than twenty years), we have frequently received acknowledgements from students who recognized that group work and seminars are much more efficient in learning than exams.
30. S. 128 (1) (a) of the *Act respecting the Barreau du Québec* [the 'Bar Act'], R.S.Q., c. B-1, originally adopted in S.Q. 2-3 Eliz. II (1953-54) c. 59, s. 5 (1) (a).
31. S.Q. 1890, c. 32, adding s. 3562a to the Revised Statutes of Quebec, 1888.
32. S.Q. 1909, c. 52, adding ss. 3562a to 3562k to the Revised Statutes of Quebec, 1888.
33. Quebec lawyers insist on being called 'Ma"tre' and the exclusivity of this title is protected by law.
34. The figures of the last Canadian census (1991) indicate, for the year 1990, the differentials between mean annual incomes by occupations: Statistics Canada, series 93-332. The mean annual income for all occupations in Quebec is $23,441 (24,329 for Canada as a whole); lawyers and notaries earn $54,641 in Quebec (69,121 in Canada, largely

because of the business law volumes in Toronto), judges earn $104,333 in Quebec (only 97,258 in Canada). Compared to these figures, social scientists earn $30,584 (Canada: 31,798), managers and administrators $36,969 (40,199), engineers and architects $41,084 (43,638), university teachers $44,375 (46,892) and physicians and surgeons $90,454 (95,728). Income distribution is very unequal inside the legal profession: according to E. Mackaay's 1992 figures on private practitioners, supra, note 29, pp. 43 and 45, the mean annual declared income of non-salaried respondents was $84,640 while that of salaried lawyers was only $45,283.

35. This has seldom been so clear as in the last 25 years, when the Quebec Bar fiercely opposed the creation of Legal Aid in the 1970s, then strategically accepted a twin system by which some lawyers would become salaried members of a Legal Aid public corporation while private practitioners could take mandates and be reimbursed by public funds. In 1996, in the wake of a general decrease in public expenditures, lawyers just as fiercely opposed — this time by strike — budget cuts in Legal Aid, always under the ritual justification of the preservation of the public's absolute and unlimited right to justice through the indispensable services of lawyers.

36. In this newspeak, law must adapt to become a source of production of wealth: the mentality of autonomy and self-control must give way to a better integration of lawyers in the economic circuits, with all the buzz-words of management, human resources, information, technology, globalisation, delocalisation, value-added services, image marketing, and softer conflict resolution methods as opposed to litigation. Of course, there are many good points in this discourse pleading for nothing less than a 'novel culture' to open the bar, take the leadership, rebuild the image of the profession, reconquer and enlarge markets for lawyers henceforth considered as entrepreneurs.

37. R.S.Q., c. C-26.

38. In the *Bar Committee's Report*, the protection of the public is mentioned *pro forma* only at the very last page (128), ranking second in the Bar's mission, next to the defence of its members' interests.

39. On this specific question, see R. Laperrière, 'La communication de l'expertise juridique: un monopole professionnel?' in D. Bourcier and C. Thomasset (eds), *L'écriture du droit face aux technologies de l'information*, Diderot, Paris, 1996, pp. 341-369.

40. See, in two decisions of the Supreme Court of Canada on cases originating from Quebec, opinions of Taschereau J., in *Pauzé* v. *Gauvin* [1954] S.C.R. 15, 18; and of de Grandpré J., in *Laporte* v. *Collège des Pharmaciens* [1976] S.C.R. 101, 102.

41. See a decision of the Supreme Court of Canada originating from British Columbia ['Jabour']: *Attorney General for Canada* v. *Law Society of British Columbia* [1982] 2

S.C.R. 307. In his opinion, Estey J. makes it quite clear that the professional monopoly rests on the public status of lawyers as officers of the courts and the trust that clients and the public must give them individually and collectively because people are not able to evaluate the need for legal services nor the quality or efficiency of services rendered by lawyers.

42. See for instance: *Barreau du Québec* v. *Chambre des notaires du Québec* and *Office des professions du Québec* [1992] R.J.Q. 1954 (C.S., Crépeau J.).
43. For instance, all members of the Bar were warned recently that they were forbidden to give informal legal opinion even to their friends or family if they had not paid their dues and professional insurance premiums.
44. See *Barreau de Montréal* v. *Royal Trust Co.* [1961] C.S. 433, 435 (Trudel J.).
45. See *Jacmond* v. *R. (Barreau de Montréal)*, C.B.R. (crim. on appeal) 26.04.1972, no. 70-33612 (Leblanc J.); and *Barreau de l'Abitibi-Témiscamingue* v. *Guindon*, JE 91-777 (C.Q., Saint-Pierre J.).
46. This phenomenon has developed more in Ontario than in Quebec and was studied by the Ianni Group: see the *Report of the Ontario Working Group on Paralegal Services*, Toronto, 1990, 262 p.
47. On these international developments, see R. Laperrière (1997).
48. The situation of legal monopolies in the USA was well described and analysed by Abel (1989).
49. Halliday (1987), p.53.
50. *Solicitors Act 1974*, c. 47.
51. For instance, see *Green* v. *Hoyle* [1976] 2 All E.R. 633.
52. *Loi 71-1130 du 31 décembre 1971 portant réforme de certaines professions judiciaires et juridiques*, art. 54-79.
53. *Loi 90-1259 du 31 décembre 1990*, in force on January 1, 1992.
54. So pervasive is this attitude that in my [R.L.'s] first administrative law course (2nd year), the first time I heard the latin maxim 'Audi alteram partem' (Hear the other party), I wrote it down 'Odi alteram partem' (Hate the other party), which is pronounced the same in French.
55. Why should a lawyer, or a university professor, be afraid of the Bar? Because the Bar is a powerful corporation, within which the exercise of power is diffuse, as was customary in secret brotherhoods. This inspires a reverential fear of the peers' judgment when one does not conform with the dominant ideology, mentality or even customs. This feeling of anticipated guilt is exacerbated in the legal profession by the very nature of law, which is based on authority and imposed by the threat of constraint and punishment. It

helps to explain why law faculties may occasionally have sudden changes of mood towards the Bar, but do not dare challenge its power and interests.

56. To one of the authors [R.L.] suggesting at a law professors' congress in 1995 that the Bar's monopoly should be relaxed in order for the faculties to assert more autonomy, a law dean replied that the suggestion reflected a standpoint 'from another planet'. Indeed!

57. The Committee noted, at pp. 41-42, that in the opinion of law deans, the legal profession's only substantial area of influence on legal education in the 1980s appeared to be curriculum. We feel that this blindness is rooted in the paradigmatic feature of professional legal culture. The Report recognizes this lack of sensitiveness at p. 42: 'It may be that formal influence is not exerted by the profession, and that its informal influence is not perceived, simply because of a coincidence of values and objectives between the faculty and the profession'. This attitude exemplifies, in our words, enclosure in a common culture.

58. This attitude is best exemplified by this concluding citation, at p. 149 of the *Arthurs Report*, supra, note 1: 'We believe there is, in both the law faculties and elsewhere, a body of opinion that will welcome our proposals. Certainly there is no reason in principle for those who feel otherwise to be upset by them. After all, we are not proposing that anyone be required to change his or her current way of doing things: those who wish to teach or practise how and what they have always done may continue to do so. As we stated earlier, we are only advocating additional emphasis on the scholarly not less emphasis on the professional'. The authors go on, by way of additional excuse comforting our interpretation: 'Is this description of our proposals perhaps a trifle disingenuous? Inevitably, the new emphasis will be seen as an implicit criticism of the old. However, we have not criticized the professional emphasis per se, but rather such an emphasis pursued single-mindedly, and, even in its own terms, not always effectively'.

59. Excerpts from the 1997 welcoming speech of the dean of the University of New South Wales Faculty of Law, Australia, presented on the UNSW Internet Home page.

60. See C. Thomasset (1996a), C. Thomasset, L.-C. Paquin and F. Blanchard (1996), C. Thomasset (1997).

61. The same tendencies were confirmed in 1991 by Mackaay's general survey sponsored by the Bar (Mackaay, 1991).

62. See the *Bar Act*, R.S.Q., c. B-1, s. 43 (1) (c), and regulations under the *Professional Code*, R.S.Q. c. C-26, s. 184.

63. This reform abolished the concept of exclusive fields of practice, and replaced it by a list of 13 categories of acts that can only be performed by authorized professionals; most of these acts are shared between numerous professions: *An Act respecting the regulation of*

Health Professions, S.O. 1991, c. 18, s. 27.

64. Manitoba Law Reform Commission, *Regulating Professions and Occupations*, 1994, 133 p.

65. Office des professions du Québec, *Approche à l'égard de la réserve et du partage d'actes professionnels: Vers un système professionnel plus souple et mieux adapté*, January, 1996, p.22.

References

Abel, R.L. (1989), *American Lawyers*, Oxford University Press, New York.

Arthurs, H.A. (1983), Report by the Consultative Group on Research and Education in Law, *Law and Learning*, S.S.H.R.C., Ottawa [the 'Arthurs Report'].

Barreau du Québec, Comité du Barreau sur l'avenir de la profession (1996), *La pratique du droit au Québec et l'avenir de la profession* [the 'Bar Committee's Report'].

Belley, J-G. (1994), 'Paradigmes et innovation: les professeurs de droit et l'avenir des professions juridiques', *CJLS/RCDS*, vol. 9, no. 2, pp. 163-179.

Belley, J-G. (1996), 'Une expérience d'enseignement critique en droit des contrats' in L. Langevin (ed.), *L'enseignement critique du droit: journée d'étude*, GEPTUD, Collection Enseignement, Université Laval, Sainte-Foy.

Cassels, J. and Maloney, M. (1989), 'Critical Legal Education: Paralysis with a Purpose', *CJLS/RCDS*, vol. 4, pp. 99-138.

Duncanson, I. (1996), 'Degrees of Law: Interdisciplinarity in the Law Discipline', *Griffith Law Review*.

Frost, S.B. (1984), 'The Early Days of Law Teaching at McGill', 9, *Dalhousie Law Journal*, p.150.

Frost, S.B. and Johnston, D.L. (1981), 'Law at McGill: Past, Present and Future', 27, *McGill L.J./Rev. Dr. de McGill*, 33.

Halliday, T.C. (1987), *Beyond Monopoly: Lawyers, State Crises, and Professional Empowerment*, University of Chicago Press, Chicago.

Lajoie, A. and Parizeau, C. et al. (1976), *La place des juristes dans la société québécoise*, Thémis, Montréal.

Lambert, B. (1996), 'École du Barreau 1995-1996, l'an 1 de la réforme', *Journal du Barreau*, Opinion section, June 1st.

Laperrière, R. (1996), 'La communication de l'expertise juridique: un monopole professionnel?', in D. Bourcier and C. Thomasset (eds), *L'écriture du droit face aux tech-*

nologies de l'information, Diderot, Paris, pp. 341-369.

Laperrière, R. (1997), 'L'interprétation du droit et les monopoles des professions juridiques', in C. Thomasset and D. Bourcier (eds), *Interpréter le droit: le sens, l'interprète, la machine*, Bruylant, Bruxelles.

Macdonald, R.A. (Groupe de travail sur l'accessibilité à la justice) (1991), *Jalons pour une plus grande accessibilité à la justice* [the 'Macdonald Report'].

Mackaay, E. (1991), *Les Avocats du Québec*, Barreau du Québec.

Poirier, D. (1987), 'Épistémologie juridique: étape indispensable à la construction de modèles conceptuels en droit', presented at the Canadian Law and Society Association's Annual Meeting, Learned Societies, Hamilton, 3-5 June 1987, 30 p. (microfilmed at the Library of York University).

Robinson, A. (1996), 'Expérience d'enseignement féministe en droit des personnes et droit de la famille: l'apport du mouvement féministe dans l'enseignement des cours de base dans les facultés de droit au Québec', in L. Langevin (dir.), *L'enseignement critique du droit: journée d'étude*, GEPTUD, Collection Enseignement, Université Laval, Sainte-Foy.

Sargent, N. (1991), 'The Possibilities and Perils of Legal Studies', *CJLS/RCDS*, vol. 6, pp. 1-26.

Thomasset, C. (1996), 'L'enseignement critique du droit et la responsabilité sociale du professeur', in L. Langevin (ed.), *L'enseignement critique du droit: journée d'étude*, GEPTUD, Collection Enseignement, Université Laval, Sainte-Foy, pp.11-23.

Thomasset, C. (1996a), 'Law and Computer: A Cultural Revolution?', Paper presented at the 15th Annual Law and History Conference, Griffith University, Faculty of Law, Brisbane, July 1996.

Thomasset, C. (1997), 'L'interprétation du droit: du prétoire au laboratoire', in C. Thomasset and D. Bourcier (eds), Interpreter le droit: le sens, l'interpreté, la machine, Bruylant, Bruxelles.

Thomasset, C., Paquin, L-C. and Blanchard, F. (1996), 'Modélisation et formalisation du savoir juridique: l'emprise des informaticiens sur le droit', in D. Bourcier and C. Thomasset (eds), *L'ecriture du droit face au technologies de l'information*, Diderot, Paris, pp. 371-409.

9 Post-Fordism and the Reformation of Liberal Legal Education

JULIAN WEBB

Introduction

The aims of this paper are twofold. First, it is to suggest that recent changes in higher education can be explained as an attempt to reconstruct university (legal) education through a normalising discourse, posited on a 'post-Fordist' model of education. Secondly, it seeks to explore a number of cultural, epistemic and policy implications of that change for the law school. To do this I will present an argument in three stages. I shall briefly define and justify my adoption of the post-Fordist metaphor; then I shall explore the institutional and process changes which have taken place in British higher education since the late 1980s and consider how these are reflected in the English law school. Finally I will evaluate their effect on the discourse and meanings of legal education, and specifically on our understanding of what constitutes a 'liberal' legal education after ACLEC's First Report on Legal Education and Training (1996).

A Post-Fordist Higher Education System?

The concepts of Fordism and post-Fordism derive originally from the sociological study of business organisation and have been used to offer a grand narrative explaining the changes in industrial organisation under late capitalism (see Piore and Sabel, 1984; Harvey, 1989; Brown and Lauder, 1992). Fordism has been the main organising principle of industrial capitalism from the early 1920s to certainly the end of the 1960s. It is characterised by the production line - whereby a standardised product is constructed by a workforce, with limited and narrowly defined skills, managed according to 'scientific' (Taylorist) principles with mass distribution to a largely undifferentiated market. By contrast, the post-Fordist mode of production requires a shift from mass to flexible 'craft' production systems of design and manufacture. It is facilitated by high technology and tends to rely both on the labour of multi-skilled workers and on the growth of co-operative arrangements between firms (what Webster (1995:148) calls the "vertical disintegration" of organisations). These systems deliver goods and services to the "glocal" (Robertson, 1995:28) niche markets of a powerful, but fragmented, consumerism.

To apply the concepts of Fordism and post-Fordism to education may seem a strange step, and indeed I would not wish to push the analogy too far. Rather, in this paper, I shall use Fordism and Post-Fordism as metaphors for exploring changes in higher education, without committing us wholly to the problematic and overly deterministic narrative of change that post-Fordism implies. Subject to this caveat I suggest the analogy is a valuable one for two reasons.

First, it is because these industrial systems affect far more than just the industrial mode of production. Social theorists writing from both modernist and postmodernist positions have emphasised the links between industrial, aesthetic and epistemic systems and values. Harvey (1989) thus stresses Fordism's role in forging the commodification of aesthetics and culture that constituted the high modernism of the post-War boom years. Similarly Lyotard (1993) has attempted to show how truth claims in the postmodern world have been subverted by the demands that knowledge satisfies conditions of utility (what he calls 'performativity criteria') and 'tradability' which, like Harvey, he identifies as the process of commodification of information.

Second, it can be said that the very act of bringing such 'foreign' concepts into the discourse of education is significant because it emphasises the way in which conventional educational discourse has become "a limiting factor in our self-understanding" (Edwards, 1993:181). I hope that by confronting the way we talk about such educational practices we can begin to uncover more about their meanings and to question more effectively their legitimacy.

The Changing Context

If we are to understand the English law school we need to view it, culturally, as an institution within a wider institution - the university itself. As Twining (1995a:39) has pointed out, most of the major changes in university legal education have reflected changes to higher education more generally rather than changes to legal practice or the legal system.

The university of the 1960s was an institution of high modernity: arising out of the "conjuncture between modernism, techno-science, Fordism and the welfare state" (Scott, 1995:123). The last decade, and more, as we are all too well aware, has been a period of enormous change in higher education policy, culminating (for our present purposes) in the publication of the *Dearing Report* in July 1997.[1] These changes have fundamentally altered the face of British higher education, to the extent that it is now commonly said that the British system has been transformed from an elite to a mass system of higher education (eg, Scott, 1995).

For present purposes it is enough to highlight, briefly, four of these fundamental developments and the way in which they have affected the law schools and their students, since this provides the basic context for the arguments which follow. The elements we will consider are: the numerical and demographic trends in participation; the changes to the regulation and resourcing of British higher education, and the 'globalization' of higher education.

The Numbers Game

One of the key theses to the post-industrial/post-Fordist argument has been the creation of the 'information society' - a service-driven society requiring knowledge-workers with high levels of education and skills. A number of writers (not uncontroversially) particularly emphasise the centrality of professions and professionalisation to the information society (Bell, 1987:33; Perkin, 1990:2). Whether or not this is the case, there is fairly general agreement that demand for higher education has been steadily increasing into the 1990s. In Britain, between 1971 and 1996, the number of students in full-time higher education has virtually trebled, from under 500,000 to nearly 1.5 million. Most striking of all has been the pace of transformation, with most of this increase crammed (literally, as class sizes have threatened to go, if not through the roof, at least into adjacent corridors) into the five years from 1989/90 to 1993/94.

Legal education reflects that process in microcosm. Though undergraduate legal education in the 1960s initially grew less rapidly than the average, it soon caught up by virtue of policies which allowed both the number of law schools, and the number of student places in those schools to increase dramatically. A few statistics serve to give a flavour of the pace of change. Thus, if we start in the early 1960s, Oxbridge and London were still, numerically speaking, the dominant providers of law graduates. By the time of the Ormrod Report (1971),[2] there were 22 university law schools, and 17 other higher education institutions offering law degrees. As a consequence, by 1970, the 'golden triangle' of Oxford, Cambridge and London produced no more than a third of all law graduates. Today there are over seventy universities and university sector institutions offering at least one qualifying[3] law degree scheme, and a seemingly endless number of other degrees in which law is available as a substantial component. If we look at the actual number of students entering law school to read for the LLB, as we would expect, this has also swelled dramatically. In 1980/81, 2,911 students entered the first year of law school in England and Wales - a figure which nearly matched the entire law student population of twenty years earlier.[4] In 1994/95, 8,560 students accepted places on single honours LLB programmes alone (Bermingham *et al,* 1996:16).

One consequence of this has been an increasing mismatch between student career aspirations and actualities (eg, ACLEC, 1996:42-3). While studies since the early 1980s have consistently suggested that around 70% of law students aspire to careers in the legal profession, the profession today simply cannot accommodate all of those who have survived the process of professional training. The implications of this need to be considered in the context of the demographic changes that have taken place in recent years.

The Demographics of Participation

Expansion has been achieved by the increased participation of both traditional (post-school/tertiary education) and non-traditional students in higher education. The policy of improving participation rates in post-compulsory (16-19) education has had two effects. It has sustained a substantial core of A level entrants to higher education and created a new pool of applicants who have followed the so-called 'vocational A level route' provided by General National Vocational Qualifications (GNVQs).[5] Together these have off-set, to some extent, the demographic threat caused by a declining young adult population. The age participation rates for young people in higher education have increased from about 10% to a third over the last two decades. At the same time, participation by the over-25s has also increased substantially, with the 50% barrier (for full-time students) finally being breached in 1993 (Slowey, 1994).

Again, the law school has not been immune to these trends. In crude terms, the chances of an applicant actually entering law school have improved from about 14:1 in 1980/81 (Wilson and Marsh, 1981:6) to 2.5:1 in 1994/95 (Bermingham *et al*, 1996:17). However statistics suggest that the consequent changes to the demographics of the law cohort are less marked than for higher education generally. Thus, A level entry appears still to account for some four-fifths of admissions,[6] while under a quarter of entrants to single honours law courses in 1994/95 were over the age of 21 (Bermingham *et al*, 1996: 21).

Increased participation has been accompanied by significant changes in both the gender and ethnic balance of the student population. Statistically, gender inequalities in access to higher education have generally declined since World War Two (Blackburn and Jarman, 1993). Similarly, participation by British ethnic minority students has also increased to a point where most ethnic minority groups are now proportionately over-represented in higher education.[7] Recent studies suggest legal education has evolved more or less consistently with these trends. Over 50% of undergraduate law students in 1994 were female and some 17% drawn from ethnic minorities, and the proportions of both women and ethnic minorities appear (at least until recently) still to be rising (Halpern, 1994; Bermingham *et al*, 1996).

However, there are aspects of this picture which are less positive than the whole suggests. Research has consistently shown that marked inequalities still exist in legal education (and elsewhere). Ethnic minority students in particular are more likely to obtain places in the post-1992 universities. Many of them are thus placed at the wrong end of a largely unspoken prestige structure, with clearly negative consequences for their employment chances (cf Shiner and Newburn, 1995). The pattern here may well be one of cyclical disadvantage. Non-traditional students are more likely to come from backgrounds where there is a lack of the cultural and material capital necessary to gain access to the elite schools and universities. As graduates from non-elite universities, who may also lack cultural affiliations with the organisations to which they seek access, they are doubly handicapped in the race for professional status.

Regulation and Resourcing

Historically, universities have operated with, in Karl Weick's (1976) phrase, 'loosely coupled systems'. Relatively uncoordinated and externally unregulated, they functioned on the basis of an authority that was, in Weberian terms, more often traditional than bureaucratic, and with little functional congruence between institutional structures and core activities.

This traditional model has been under threat since the late 1970s. A corporatist rhetoric has swept across both sides of the old binary divide, driven partly by the universities' attempts to avoid the same kind of efficiency scrutiny that was imposed on the Civil Service in the mid-1980s (see Scott, 1995:61-70), and by some necessarily defensive manoeuvring following a wave of financial and other managerial crises which assailed some institutions in the 80s and early 90s. These developments have created linked trends towards both devolution and centralisation. More and more universities have moved towards 'atomized' (Schuller, 1990) systems of financial and human resource management, based on departments or schools as budgetary units subject to a variety of performance criteria, with senior academics as line managers. In this way the fragmentation of industrial units is, to a degree, being replicated in academia.

At the same time, central regulation of these individual units has also been increased through the technologies of internal audit and quality control. This pattern is also repeated across the university system as a whole, chiefly through the use of peer review. We now experience a network of such quality control systems through Funding Council, now Quality Assurance Agency (QAA), teaching quality (TQA) and research (RAE) assessments. As Bradney and Cownie (1996:22-3) note, although not all the outcomes of this process are negative, it is certainly arguable that it has hastened the stratification and declining collegiality of academia. Moreover, the central role of the QAA in constructing benchmark standards for higher education anticipated by *Dearing*[8] posits a form of control that could easily step beyond quality assurance *per se* and into a largely state and industry-defined model of the teaching and learning process.

The changing regulatory framework also cannot be separated from the other major trend since the early 1980s: the reform of university funding. Funding now operates through a transformed relationship between the universities, the state and private enterprise which has been created (following the pattern in secondary education) by a quasi-contractualisation of relations. This process has a number of important characteristics.

First, although mainstream undergraduate teaching is still funded by the state through a system of *per capita* funding subject to institutional quotas, the general movement has been to drive costs downwards by Funding Council (ie governmental) demands for 'efficiency gains'. As Rigby (1995) has shown, although the volume of public funding has, inevitably, increased with student numbers (by 23% between 1989 and 1994) this has largely been absorbed by increased demand for student support - in the form of maintenance grants and access funding. By contrast, the *per capita* unit of resource to the teaching institutions has fallen by over 30% since 1980. Many would argue that one of the long-standing problems faced by the law schools, at least until the recent halt in expansion, has been their status as the university milch-cow: low unit costs (at point of delivery) and a high demand for places has made them particularly susceptible to the "stack 'em deep, teach 'em cheap" ethos that has, to some extent, accompanied the massification of British higher education.

Secondly contractualisation has resulted in increased selectivity in the allocation of state funding - a shift from general contracts for teaching and research to what Brownsword (1996:25) has called "bespoke individual contracts" for institutions. In the case of research funding, especially in areas like law where levels of contract research funding are small, this process of selection is now driven chiefly by RAE outcomes.

Thirdly, the decline in state funding has been accompanied by some (but not comparable) growth in non-state funding for both teaching and research functions. This process has been enhanced by both credential inflation in the market place, and by the imposition of recruitment targets which have, latterly, tended to cap expansion of undergraduate numbers and forced universities to look for alternative sources of revenue. The spectacular growth in graduate education, for example, is in large part a response to both these trends.[9]

The transformative nature of these changes should not be underestimated. The processes of audit have tended so far to reinforce the

Matthew effect that has long existed in British higher education, thereby broadly confirming earlier social judgements as to the elite institutions of the system. Despite the widening of access, the contractualisation of higher education, it has been argued, continues the shift towards the 'parentocracy' implied by the reforms to primary and secondary education (Brown, 1990, 1996). Competition for credentials, and especially credentials from the educational elite, is now less than ever determined by merit; rather it is grounded in the market power of potential consumers, because, as Brown (1996:44) puts it: "resources + preference = choice".

Globalization

Globalization is a central tenet of the post-Fordist thesis. As a concept, it refers not just to an internationalisation of markets and production, but to a new social, cultural and political condition (Webster 1995:140). It is evidenced, *inter alia*, by increased migration, global communication and information flows and the creation, largely through the internationalisation of the media, of a commonality of cultural images. Globalization is simultaneously without and within the university; it is a key part of the economic agenda driving change in higher education,[10] and part of the transformative processes within higher education.

The globalization of higher education is at its most obvious in the international character of the student body: in 1993-94 over a fifth of undergraduate and nearly a half of postgraduate law students at British universities were domiciled abroad (Bradney, 1996:50). It can also be seen in the internationalisation of curricula. Even in the English law schools, where, as Wilson (1987:829-33) has argued, the curriculum has long been dominated by a marked insularity, globalization is having an impact on both curriculum content and processes. Thus, we are seeing at the substantive level a (limited) resurgence of comparative legal studies and the interpenetration of the national and supra-national legal orders of the European Union.

More generally, the time-space compression (Harvey, 1989:284) associated with modern systems of communication has made possible considerable changes to the development and dissemination of knowledge. The much heralded 'virtual university' generates not just the potential for greater access to information sources, for distance learning, and for more widely distributed networks of scholarship, it creates a greater heterogeneity of knowledge production. This, among other things, may yet serve to increase the rate at which knowledge development is dispersed away from the universities as physical entities and into the media of hyperspace and the corporate classrooms and R&D divisions of industry.

Underlying this brave new world there are a number of tensions between the global and the local - tensions that have become part of a new phenomenon of 'glocalization' (Robertson, 1995; Scott, 1995:95). Whatever we may think of it linguistically, this concept does usefully emphasise that cultural capital formation is a matter of often complex interaction between the global and the local.

In higher education this may be reflected in a whole range of tensions. At a policy level, there may be dissonance between a university's regional or national definition of its mission and the international aspirations of (some of) its scholarship (cf. Thompson, 1970:163). Globalization also raises the spectre of greater cultural imperialism[11] as the virtual university beckons. Here it is the national and international elite (particularly, one suspects, of Western Europe and North America) who have the most to gain. Will the students of the future, if they have the resources, settle for qualifications from their local university if advanced technology enables them to obtain degrees from Harvard or Oxford or the Sorbonne? At a deeper intellectual level it may involve arguments about discipline boundaries or sub-boundaries, particularly if, as with law, the traditional boundary is connected closely to the geography of the nation-state. There are, for example, those who urge us towards a much more fundamental rethink of the curriculum, with less emphasis on local content and more on either the underlying legal theory (de Groot, 1992) or the transactional skills and processes common to legal operations across geographical boundaries (Daintith, 1991:202-3).

Conclusion: Transforming Education, Transforming Culture

While I intend to pick up a number of more specific points later in this paper, I wish to stress a key idea which emerges from this section. The massification, contractualisation and globalization of higher education are related phenomena and should be seen, jointly, as radical influences on the cultural landscape.

Higher education is no longer simply the mark of a civilised society

(Newman, 1952:51-2), still less is it the right, rather than privilege, that I remember us demanding (clearly without much success) on student demos at the end of the 1970s; it is now commodified as a cultural good. Universities today are valued more for their contribution to the (post-industrial) service economy than for their intellectual or public service. They are a key creator of cultural capital not so much by virtue of the knowledge they generate, but by conferring credentials, and hence occupational status.

The consequences of this are more than simply ideological. While universities as a collectivity may be said to be engaged in creating cultural capital, this is occurring in a context where (a) the divisions between institutions are growing rather than shrinking, leading perhaps to a polarisation of British higher education along American lines (Brown, 1996:44), and (b) universities as a whole are less central to the processes of knowledge creation and dispersal than they were. The relatively few truly elite institutions are, by virtue of their status, most likely to succeed on all fronts: in generating demand for their courses and for their student 'products'; in attracting private resources in the marketplace; in transcending the tensions of glocalization. For others 'success' will be a relative concept, and that is true not just for the institutions themselves but for their graduates, for whom the possession of a degree is no longer a guarantee that the door to a professional, or other high status, occupation will be open.

In short, the shift towards a post-Fordist university system has accentuated existing institutional and social differences and produced a system that is more deeply fractured than anything that has gone before. The implications of this become even more interesting when we consider the consequences of post-Fordism for the teaching and learning processes.

The Educational Process

Post-Fordism in learning emphasises the extent to which notions of education and training are to be harnessed to the demands of the post-industrial economy. In essence, the argument is a simple one: employers need workers with the adaptive, technological, skills (and attitudes) required for a flexible working environment; it is the function of the education system to provide them.[12] This is a model of education that, in policy terms, is commonly traced back to James Callaghan's speech at Ruskin College, Oxford in October 1976, and to the 1977 education Green Paper which followed. The challenge to 'liberal' educationalism has since been taken up by a growing body of policy-makers and eductionalists (see, eg, NIACE, 1990; Duke, 1992), and by the education policy of successive governments of the 1980s and 90s. This pattern of events seems strongly to endorse the post-Fordist version of history: the economic crisis of the 1970s was thus the watershed for a change in (Labour) education policy that was initially carried through into practice because it also resonated with the minimal state/public choice rhetoric of the new Right.[13] There is thus a sense here of a more paradigmatic shift that transcends party politics.

The 'flexibilisation' of employment is in many respects the key to understanding post-Fordism in work and education. Underlying the jargon is a stark reality: people can no longer expect to have a long-term 'career' in the traditional sense. Flexible organisations tend to rely more heavily on a substantial body of peripheral workers, with only a relatively small, relatively secure, core. The greater use of fixed term contracts, sub-contracting and consultancy arrangements all reduce security of employment among peripheral workers. If education is to contribute to economic productivity in this kind of environment, this implies a more utilitarian approach to education and a greater emphasis on what Lyotard (1993) calls 'performativity'. I suggest that performativity in practice emphasises:

- the flexibility of educational processes
- vocationalism
- competence-based learning

as I shall now explain.

Flexibilisation

Performativity and the commodification of education demands that learning is no longer viewed as a discrete stage in life, but as an on-going process of lifelong learning (see, eg, Dearing, 1997. para.2) which is geared to changing occupational demands. This requires that universities develop the capacity to respond flexibly to individual learning needs. The flexible university is emerging through three related processes: the fragmentation of the curriculum, functional diversification and the flexibilisation of modes of study.

At a deep level the reduction in disciplinary coherence and the shifting emphasis from formal to practical knowledge (from 'knowing that' to 'knowing how') can both be seen as a consequence of the emphasis on performativity. Lyotard (1993) argues that 'knowledge' is no longer an absolute to be pursued in the Enlightenment tradition, it has been replaced by a plurality of truths (or knowledges) defined by the practical demands imposed on the university. This is reflected in a variety of epistemic shifts impacting on higher education, eg: the social constructionists' scepticism about scientific positivism (Kuhn, 1970); the rediscovery of philosophical pragmatism (Rorty, 1979) and postmodernism's attack on meta-narrative more generally (eg, Lyotard, 1984). Such shifts have led to a greater uncertainty about what the university should teach, and have influenced new forms of teaching and learning. These are increasingly underpinned by a more phenomenological approach to the idea of knowing - recognising that, for each of us, knowledge of a phenomenon is actually changed through use and experience (Eraut, 1994:50-1; Webb, 1995:192-6).

Functional diversification flows out of both a market model of education[14] and, perhaps, a growing academic confidence in the capacity of universities to be multi-functional places of learning (NCUP, 1996:4-5; Dearing, 1997, para. 3). The law schools, in particular, traditionally adopted what Twining (1994:54-5; 1995b) has called the primary school model of professional education - mostly confining themselves to undergraduate teaching for the LLB, and the forms of scholarship necessary to support that task. This is now manifestly not the case. Academic and professional graduate teaching has greatly expanded, particularly in respect of taught postgraduate and vocational awards. Wilson (1993), for example, reported a 150% increase in taught postgraduate law student numbers in the pre-1992 universities between 1980 and 1990/91. Moreover, the greater willingness of the professional bodies to 'franchise-out' the vocational training courses has also, since 1993, led not just to an expansion in the number of law schools offering such courses, but also to the collapse of one of the historical distinctions between pre- and post-1992 universities, namely that the pre-1992 universities did not engage in vocational training.[15] A rather different blurring of the academic/vocational divide emerges out of the creation of specialist 'professional' masters degrees - taught or research degrees which meet, in essence, both academic and continuing professional development functions.[16]

The scale of such developments is hard to quantify precisely; student numbers at present seem quite small, though I would suggest that such developments are conceptually significant when viewed from within a post-Fordist paradigm. Diversification can also be seen in a number of other features of the modern law school's work: for example, the wider range and greater volume of research activity (as witnessed by the change in RAE outcomes between 1992 and 1996), and the delivery of courses for other non-traditional markets. The chief example here would be the offering of law input to multi-disciplinary and combined studies degrees with other departments, though the degree and rapidity of change here is perhaps less marked than in respect of vocational training.[17]

Flexibility is being introduced into modes of study in a number of ways. There is some evidence generally of an expansion of part-time and particularly open and distance-learning modes of study,[18] and of franchising arrangements, whereby institutions of further and higher education, both in the UK and abroad, are 'licensed' by universities to provide specific awards. Modularisation, credit accumulation and independent study programmes are also being used to lock higher education into the wider systems and demands of a 'learning society' (Ball, 1993; Dearing, 1997).

Modularisation, in theory, provides a cornerstone of the performativity thesis. For example, it is said to facilitate choice and learner autonomy by providing students with greater opportunity to determine their own pattern and mode of study; it can increase access by reducing the temporal and spatial barriers to participation; it can enhance the development of multi- and inter-disciplinary curricula by encouraging the collapse of traditional programme boundaries. However, the impact of modularisation is easily overstated in the British context. Although some modular schemes have existed in the UK for twenty years or so, wholesale modularisation remains a relatively recent phenomenon, with most universities 'going modular' in the last four or five years.[19] This means it is still quite difficult to draw firm conclusions about the process.

Nevertheless there is a feeling that the shift to modularity has generally been poorly managed in the UK. It is commonly considered to have been imposed for economic and managerial rather than educational reasons.[20] Arguably many of the basic principles have been misunderstood or poorly translated from the original US model, and the diversity of approaches to modularity in the UK has meant there is little in the way of a common language and experience on which to build (HEQC, 1996a:16). The picture is also confused in many institutions because modularisation has been accompanied by the semesterisation of the teaching year. Where this has happened it appears to have lead to an increase in the breadth of learning and the volume of assessment,[21] with damaging consequences for the depth of understanding (Harris and Tribe, 1995; Bermingham, *et al*, 1996:45).

Vocationalism and Competence

As Teichler (1996:98-9) notes, internationally, the gap between academic and vocational education has been eroded by the academic drift of the professional and technical schools and the vocational drift of the universities, and is likely to continue to erode (Dearing, 1997, para. 3). Vocational drift, supported by the funding policies of organisations such as the European Union and World Bank, in particular reflects a more utilitarian approach, demanding an emphasis on the economic role of higher education in producing "professionals who perform better" (Lyotard, 1993:6).

This process is apparent in a number of features of British further and higher education, and particularly in the discourse which, since the late 1980s has been associated with the development of occupational competences.[22] This approach has been dominated by the so-called 'standards methodology' of the NCVQ, whereby measurement of learning is defined in terms of criterion-referenced performance outcomes which are derived from the functional analysis of occupations (see Winter, 1996:334-5; Maughan *et al*, 1995:262-4). It is emerging in a not wholly dissimilar form in higher education through attempts to define generic skills and attributes indicative of 'graduateness' (HEQC, 1995, 1996b; Bell, 1996; cf. Dearing, 1997, paras. 41, 43, 49, 51).[23]

It is quite difficult to generalise the position of the law schools in this debate. Skills-based learning is undoubtedly fashionable, though so far it has mostly eschewed the narrow emphasis on competence-based learning (Jones, 1994) identified in other domains. Skills training explicitly underpins the reforms of English vocational training which took place in 1989 and 1992/93. The study by Grimes et al (1996:48) also suggests that the majority of law schools - but especially those in the post-1992 universities - incorporate some element of skills into their undergraduate programmes. These developments have tended to focus on the vocational, lawyering, skills, even within academic programmes (see Grimes et al, 1996:49). This itself has been a matter of some contention between those who see the emphasis on lawyers' skills as an unnecessary and inappropriate response to consumer-led demand for vocationalism in the undergraduate degree, and those who argue that the applied context provides a framework either/both for developing a range of generic skills or/and a mechanism for reflection on the processes of lawyering (cf. Jabbari, 1996; Boon, 1996).

One curious feature of the legal skills movement has been its tendency to treat skills as yet another discrete knowledge area to bolt-on to the curriculum. It is particularly true of the lawyering skills, which are commonly developed through discrete modules on, say, interviewing or advocacy or through distinct clinical programmes, most of which are optional (see Grimes et al, 1996). This tendency has, if anything, been exacerbated by the process of modularisation. To this extent, there has so far been a marked failure by the legal academy to accept, in Bell's words, that skills "is an integral dimension of generating discipline specific competence at graduate level" (1996:9). There are some signs, however, that the emphasis is shifting now more towards the recognition and development of generic and transferable skills throughout the degree stage (see, eg, Jones, 1994; Bell, 1996). Again, the Dearing Report (1997, para. 38), by calling on all higher education programmes to develop the 'key skills' (of communication, numeracy, use of IT and 'learning how to learn') is likely to add considerable impetus to this movement, not least because the key skills are likely to figure in any benchmark standards set by the QAA.

Educating for Process, or Processing Education?

The changes just considered have the potential to make, indeed, have already made, the law schools more intellectually interesting and pluralistic places (both in terms of teaching and research) than they were a decade ago, but this is not without its risks. Diversification, both in teaching, and through the creation of a more competitive research ethos amongst staff may lead to a greater fragmentation of law school culture. The development of standards of competence, while usefully forcing us (as teachers) to reflect on the learning process and its outcomes, also promises another new bureaucracy and, perhaps, the kind of homogenising influence (since standards standardise) that is antithetical to the spirit of enquiry which universities are supposed to foster. More generally, as de Friend notes (1995:132-3), the increasing pressure imposed on the law schools from all sides has resulted in the planning horizon for legal education [becoming] extremely short term and 'cost-benefit' driven. There has been precious little space for visionary thinking...if this is so, what of the future?

ACLEC and Beyond: The Post-Fordist Agenda?

The ACLEC Report (1996) is the first major review of legal education since the Ormrod Report of 1971. It is without doubt a highly significant contribution to the literature on English legal education whose target is, to deliberately misquote the title of Bob Hepple's (1996) inaugural lecture,[24] 'the renewal of liberal legal education'. Its main ideas can be summarised briefly (see paras. 2.2, 2.4 and 2.21-2.24). The Report calls for a system of education and training that is more 'integrated' than at present and capable of delivering greater flexibility while increasing the autonomy of the law schools; that enhances access to legal education by creating multiple entry and exit points, particularly at the vocational stage; that better prepares students for a diversity of occupations; that delivers an education that is more ethically aware than that which exists today. Let us first examine these proposed outcomes in the light, not of the tenets of liberal educationalism, but of the post-Fordist agendas of flexibilisation, vocationalism and skills already described.

Flexibilisation

The ACLEC Report is clearly committed to a more flexible system at both undergraduate and vocational stages. It calls for the removal of subject-based prescription for qualifying law degrees (paras. 4.19, 4.33), provided that such degrees provide the equivalent of at least two years of legal study (para. 4.33). It also recognises that the forms of professional training undertaken by law graduates are likely to become more diverse, making it more difficult to treat the degree as a feeder simply for the legal profession (para. 4.5). At the vocational stage it proposes the breakdown of training into smaller segments (see 1996, chs 5 and 6): a common licentiate stage followed or combined with a shorter Bar or Law Society course. This is intermixed in a number of possible ways with periods of 'on the job' training.

Vocationalism

The Report's commitment to vocationalism is more guarded. As we have seen, it strongly defends the independence of the academic or 'initial' stage of training, but calls also for an 'integration' of the academic and the vocational. In this respect more than any other, the Report appears to follow the Ormrod line (1971, paras. 100, 106). The ACLEC Report defines integrated learning as an approach which allows for progressive learning of analytical and conceptual understanding of both substantive law and procedure and the acquisition of basic professional skills and values (1996, para. 2.16).[25]

Is the ACLEC vision different from what Ormrod proposed? In general, I think not, but there is some shift in emphasis. If anything ACLEC broadens the intellectual basis of the initial stage, particularly by addressing the comparative and ethical perspectives in legal study. It does not necessarily open the door to widespread vocationalism in the LLB - the Report stops short of calling for wholesale integration (ACLEC, 1996, para. 2.21). That said, however, the Report's dominant paradigm remains an occupational one: the exempting law degree, which combines the LLB and the Legal Practice Course in one four year programme at Northumbria University was thus cited as the nearest example to an integrated degree in the English legal system; the problem-solving skills called for by ACLEC are ultimately practice-oriented (para. 1.15); the ethical challenge is described chiefly (though not exclusively) as a challenge to the core values of legal professionalism, rather than to law as an ethical system *per se* (see paras. 1.19-1.20). Once again the law schools are told that they can have a law degree that is independent of the demands of the profession - just so long as it is not too independent.

In this vein, the fact that the law schools are told they should respond to 'the market' in determining their curriculum (para. 4.18) is particularly contentious. Its overall effect may be to undermine the formal independence that ACLEC has otherwise sought to create for the law schools. Reliance on the market potentially ties the law school back into the existing *curriculum* rather than *cognitive* model of academic standards (HEQC, 1996b, paras 10.3-10.6). It potentially requires the law schools to respond to whatever is the latest intellectual, or more likely, professional fad, which is most likely to be defined in terms of subject content. The subject prescriptive approach is deeply embedded in the professional legal psyche,[26] and is perhaps more easily comprehended and policed than a system which relies on some deeper, cognitive, notion of what the curriculum should achieve.

Skills and Competence

Performative criteria appear in the ACLEC Report through references to both skills and outcome/competence measures.

The Report clearly states that one function of the initial stage is to enable students to develop general transferable intellectual skills (paras. 2.4, 4.13).[27] ACLEC, along with the legal professional bodies, is now actively supporting development work in this area through the DfEE Discipline Network for Law (Bell, 1996). This important project may do much to set the agenda for legal skills in the next few years. The signs are reasonably encouraging, insofar as the project appears to be operating within a deeper, cognitive, model of skills-based learning (Bell, 1996:4; cf. Jones, 1994) rather than the narrow functionalism that dominated the early thinking on NVQs (cf. Maughan et al, 1995). Nevertheless, one may still question the underlying *aims* implicit in even this model of skills-based learning. If Bell's paper is indicative of the project's overall approach, the employment agenda clearly ranks highly; the extent to which the university is "not on its own" (Bell, 1996:8) in providing higher level learning appears to be a key theme. The point is a valid one, but it does not answer the significant charge raised by Toddington (1994) that the law schools are potentially left exposed to a 'managerialist' approach - "a conception of legal education as a *passive,* vocational system of supply" (Toddington, 1994:254) for the professions, rather than in a position to determine their own more critical agenda for skills. This is perhaps symptomatic of a wider problem. At the same time as identifying continuities between the university and other adult learning environments, we need to articulate what is (or ought to be) distinctive about university education. This, it seems, is being fudged in the present debates; both ACLEC and Dearing (1997, para. 23) acknowledge and defend many of the traditional features and values of university education, without really questioning whether there may be genuine and significant tensions between liberal and managerialist objectives for higher education. Let us now consider some implications of these developments.

'Liberal' Legal Education and the Consequences of Post-Fordism

Let me start by saying that my aim here is not simply to criticise the ACLEC agenda for legal education. There is much in the Report that I welcome - the move away from subject prescription, the recognition that learning processes are important, the calls for greater intellectual rigour at all stages of legal education, the raising of the ethical agenda. These are all worthy outcomes of the review. Nevertheless, the Report is itself a product of the current tensions facing higher education and needs to be viewed in the light of the wider discursive and policy context, particularly as that context has the potential to subvert many of ACLEC's good intentions, a potential that is increased by some problematic features in the Report's thinking.

The 'Defence' of Liberal Educationalism

The notion of a 'liberal' education has long served a totemic function in debates about legal education, and it is therefore unsurprising that it has been called into service once again by ACLEC. But what exactly is it that we are defending?

Classically, a liberal education treats learning as an end in itself which requires no greater justification than the cultivation of intellectual excellence (Newman, 1959:145; cf. Bradney, 1992). The function of the classical liberal university education is not therefore the transmission of technical, professional knowledge *per se* but of cultural capital in its widest sense (Scott, 1984:30). Through an interesting conjunction of ideas, however, universities have long been deemed appropriate places for the training of professional people, precisely because they are thought capable of engineering the intellectual (trans)formation of the student which is a pre-requisite to vocational training. This is not to say that vocational training *is* liberal education, but it does show how we might begin to blur the distinction.

Classical liberalism has always been something of an ideal type, and has become increasingly problematic as a descriptive model for higher education. It is unashamedly elitist and therefore sits uncomfortably with the current trends towards massification. It also predates the spread of professionalisation across the occupational sphere. This, as Beck (1992:209-10) notes, has fundamentally altered the production, control and transfer of knowledge. Professionalisation has transformed the boundaries of formal knowledge through a theorisation of much that was formally only grounded in practical knowledge ('know-how'). Liberal educationalism, as a result, I suggest, has undergone a number of transformations to become a broad church ideology, capable of accepting that university-based learning has both its own intrinsic merit and a practical and economic value, of combining commitment to intellectual excellence with widening access to higher learning, of transmitting a shared culture while upholding ideals of cultural diversity.[28]

Such boundary shifts in discourse are not unusual. But we do need to ask: when is liberalism no longer liberal? If higher education is undergoing a deeper transformation, let us recognise it as such rather than disguise it as something else. In this spirit, I suggest the boundaries of liberalism drawn by ACLEC are problematic in a number of respects.

First, we should not overlook the fact, discussed above, that the adoption of either a 'graduateness' or (though this now looks increasingly unlikely) NVQ model indicates a marked change in focus from what students *know* (propositional knowledge) to what students can *do* (skills/competence). As a consequence of this it becomes easier to displace academic with vocational aims. As I have argued elsewhere (Webb, 1995) skills development is an appropriate aim for the initial stage, provided such skills-based learning is put to 'liberal' ends: that is, to enable students to acquire a deeper, more personalised, understanding of the propositional knowledge acquired in law school, or to become more critically reflective of the legal professional culture. Underlying my point is the argument that liberal education should enable students not merely to understand the choices they have (the classical liberal endpoint), but to make decisions about those choices and to *act* on them in the social world (Bridges, 1993:44); skills-based learning can play an important part in this process. This agenda, however, as I have tried to indicate above, remains underdeveloped in a technocratic system which largely disregards the normative foundations of our discipline - that law is fundamentally not about what is, but what *ought to be*.

Secondly, the fact that legal education is increasingly being tied-in to a standards model ought to be a matter of some considerable interest to the academic community. The issue is not just one of increasing the transparency and consistency of educational standards (which is laudable enough), it is ultimately about defining the epistemological foundations of higher education: just what is it that should constitute appropriate learning in the university? ACLEC in this respect has been largely overtaken by the Dearing agenda, which will shape the revised quality assurance model that is likely to be imposed on the British university system by the year 2000 or 2001. The benchmarking process and the inclusion of key skills raise important issues. It is to be hoped that the benchmarking exercise will be conducted mindful of the very real difficulties inherent in defining standards (as evidenced by some of the excellent research undertaken for the HEQC Graduate Standards Programme) and the many criticisms of the NVQ standards model. It should not be overlooked that significant doubts remain about the transferability of generic and specific workplace skills from academia to employment (HEQC, 1996b), since, if such skills do not transfer, the main occupational justification for their inclusion falls. Moreover, the behavioural emphasis of the NVQ approach is especially suspect at the higher level. As Barnett (1994:74-5) has noted, the NVQ standards methodology emphasises the performative dimension of skills first and foremost; knowledge is evaluated indirectly, and then only insofar as it is something which underpins a skilled performance and is demonstrable (cf. Debling, 1989:88). The higher cognitive processes involved in 'understanding' barely figure at all. Skills in this model could become the new technical rational knowledge of the law school. The "protective fold of legal formalism" (Le Brun and Johnstone, 1994:11) may thereby be replaced by the security blanket of legal functionalism.

Thirdly, ACLEC's emphasis on integration obscures the fact that, ideologically and epistemologically, academic and vocational legal education are, ultimately, different. We may (and, I suggest, should) legitimately seek to create a more effective continuum between them, and I wonder if this is really all that ACLEC wants; if so, that is not the same thing as integration. The academy's role as a place of learning is, in some respects, antithetical to the profession's objectives for training. One function of the academy should be to turn a critical spotlight on the profession (Arthurs Report, 1983:49). This may - indeed should - generate creative tensions between the academic and professional perspective on ethics, skills and the boundaries of legal knowledge. This sense of distance may be lost if a high level of integration is sought. Equally, if the case for flexibilisation is made out, as ACLEC suggests, on the back of a fragmenting legal profession, then the whole idea of greater integration becomes problematic. What are we meant to be integrating? If we cannot anticipate the occupational routes of most of our students, does that mean we must play safe and go for the lowest common denominator of generic skills? Once again, the agenda begins to smack heavily of NVQism. Deconstructing the vocational stage in the way the Committee proposes might similarly reinforce the generalism of training, particularly at the licentiate stage, and, as Sherr (1996:39) suggests, could actually further reduce the intellectual coherence of legal education and training as a whole.

The Commodification of Legal Education

I have attempted to show in this paper that the discursive terrain in which legal education operates has been transformed by the post-Fordist agenda of a market-driven system of education and employment. As education takes on more of the characteristics of a consumer commodity, this raises a number of challenges at both policy and process levels which cannot be ignored. To say, as Jabbari (1996:224) does, that "university law faculties...are able to formulate models of legal education without the immediate pressure of delivering profitable services" is accurate in one sense, but still woefully misrepresents the situation. For most law schools the lack of significant short-term, or even long-term, profitability has had serious consequences for staff-student ratios, teaching methods, library resources and so on. In discussing curriculum and programme developments in most institutions today among the first questions asked are "can we afford it?" or, "will it make us money?". ACLEC is clearly cognisant of the scarcity of resources and the perceived need this generates for law schools to react effectively to changing markets for education. The ACLEC Report suggests the Committee has, for the most part, responded pragmatically to this situation. However, in so doing, it has perhaps assumed too much.

First, it tends to assume that its newly empowered breed of student consumers will behave rationally in choosing their legal education. Given that information in the marketplace is perhaps distributed unequally and certainly utilised unevenly this is debatable. Moreover, the Report rather assumes that rational decision making will lead students to favour the shiny new liberal law degrees it proposes, rather than any tarnished old (illiberal?)

ones that might survive the reforms relatively unscathed. This assumption may prove false - particularly if those unreformed degrees happen to be located in conventionally high status institutions, or happen to deliver a product that fits the more instrumental objectives of the students.[29]

Secondly, this assumption of rationality also disregards the question of how our students will respond to the teaching they receive once in the academy. The ACLEC Report calls on us to make substantial demands on students: to enable them, through active learning, to attain an understanding of legal principles from a number of perspectives, to develop a range of transferable skills and to acquire a sense of ethical values, all in the context of one the shortest prescribed periods of legal study in the Western world. As one who takes the view that we often underestimate the capacities of our students, I am reasonably sympathetic to that call. I am not sure our students will be. In an environment where (for the time being) they know they will face fierce competition for vocational training places and jobs, and in which teachers are increasingly answerable to both management and students to maintain progression rates and the throughput of 'good', ie upper second class, graduates, considerable pressure may be placed on teachers to play safe, to go for didacticism and to teach to the lowest common denominator.

Thirdly, it assumes that the flexible, skills-based model of education and training, which allows one to jump on and off the conveyor belt at various points in the process, will be attractive to a wide range of employers and will actually enhance the employability of all law graduates. For many students, and especially those from non-elite institutions, this may be something of a false hope. Two examples of what I mean will suffice.

Phillip Brown's (1996) work on cultural capital and social exclusion carries some important lessons for legal education. Brown argues that the flexibilisation of employment has brought with it a re-definition of managerial quality and a movement away from bureaucratic recruitment policies. Credential inflation means that possession of paper credentials *per se* is no longer enough; students need the high-status credentials from the elite institutions, but as part of an appropriate 'personality package' - a combination of "credentials, technical skills and charismatic qualities" (1996:42). My suspicion is that the legal profession, far more than industry, has always sought to appoint, and still appoints, on charismatic rather than bureaucratic criteria.[30] The imbalance between graduate supply and professional demand has simply made the effects of this process more obvious. These effects are, as Brown argues, often anti-meritocratic. Such policies make the social, gender and ethnic origins of applicants more rather than less visible, and reinforce the position of the elite institutions. These, as we have seen, tend to recruit their students disproportionately from the parentocracy - the old middle class who can convert their material capital *via* the market system of education into the necessary cultural capital to secure access to senior managerial and professional careers. As Brown concludes, despite the fact that it is generally the non-elite universities who have responded most to the calls of employers to make their curriculum more employment-related (cf Grimes *et al*, 1996) students at such institutions will still remain disadvantaged in the marketplace.

There is also a danger that the flexibilisation of legal education will create a range of intermediate qualifications that are of uncertain employment value. The licentiate may be a particularly high risk option. As ACLEC acknowledges (1996, para. 5.6), it is not yet clear what the demand for or effect of such a qualification may be. Will it have an impact on the employability of those law graduates who currently enter paralegal or other law-related employment as 'unqualified' persons? Will it limit the employability of those with conventional paralegal qualifications? It may be that the licentiate will be most attractive to those who do not have the material resources or opportunity to complete the full professional training. Ironically, therein lies perhaps the greatest danger. Despite ACLEC's good intentions, the licentiate could become yet another mechanism for legitimating the social exclusion of those who are already discriminated against by the market model.

Conclusions

The recent history of English legal education discloses a period of almost unparalleled activity and upheaval. Institutional and cultural transformations have generated new uncertainties about the nature of the academic discipline and the role of the university. Out of this has emerged a number of significant shifts in educational thinking and practice: from elite to mass provision; from the architectonic to the flexible curriculum; from content to process, and from classical liberal to performative outcomes. Underlying all of these is the influence of post-Fordism, the power of the market and its attempts to commodify education as a symbolic good.

The power of post-Fordism lies in the Darwinian (or Hayekian) evolutionary turn it gives to education and the process of knowledge production (cf. Edwards, 1993:182). It has attempted, with more than a little success, to tie the education system into sustaining its vision of a skilled, flexible, and insecure workforce fragmented into core and peripheral employees. This it has achieved through a number of means. Expanding student numbers demands teaching and learning methods more appropriate to a mass rather than elite system. Expansion has also generated an increase in graduate numbers beyond those that industry and the professions can accommodate as core workers. This adds to the pattern of economic insecurity which fuels the post-Fordist economy and also places greater pressure on academics to deliver according to performative criteria. In this post-Fordism is also supported by the uncertainties of liberal educationalism, the tensions of glocalization and the absence of other totalizing discourses able to accommodate the plural meanings of mass higher education.

Contractualisation, student evaluation, quality assurance and audit mean that universities today are answerable to a multiplicity of constituencies, many of which are driven by economic or vocational agendas quite distinct, perhaps, from the 'liberal' educationalism that has traditionally provided the definitive mission of a university. The decline of collegiality and academic autonomy and the normalizing effects of the quality agenda seem also to have created a loss of confidence among academics: there is a greater sense now that we have to justify our existence in utilitarian terms, and this perhaps also explains academia's apparent willingness to jump on the post-Fordist bandwagon. Since this pressure is not simply an external one; it comes from students concerned about the 'relevance' of their learning and from the new managerialism within the institutions, it is unlikely to be countered simply by a defensive return to classical liberalism. There is little point to raising the drawbridge of your ivory tower (cf. Bradney, 1996) when the attackers are already inside the gate.

Of course, the whole post-Fordist shift is also understandable because there is actually nothing fundamentally *wrong* with higher education making students more employable. Moreover, the skills movement in particular has emerged as a response to a genuine problem, in that there has been much in traditional legal education that has failed to engage and stimulate teachers and students alike (cf ACLEC, 1996, para 4.11). Performativity only becomes problematic when that one idea is presented as the primary function for higher learning. At this point we need to stop and ask some hard questions of the system: is higher education about developing independent, creative and self-reflective people, or about creating the docile bodies demanded by a more Foucauldian disciplinary society?

What is ultimately at issue here, I suggest, is that the post-Fordist agenda wholly fails to address whether, and if so how, we might achieve what I identify as the true liberal 'outcome' for higher education: that it makes our students into better people, not just better workers. This personal developmental agenda is vanishing from the discursive terrain of higher education. If the aims of 'humane professionalism', as espoused by the Arthurs Report and by ACLEC, are to be achieved we need to consider what steps are to be taken, not simply to reverse the trend (since personal development has always been under-emphasised in technocratic legal education) but to incorporate that personal agenda into a distinctive model of legal education for the new millennium. My fear is that the post-Fordist vision has already become so dominant that any alternative is rapidly slipping beyond our reach.

Notes

1. This massive report (sixteen volumes, weighing in at over six kilos) represents the most fundamental review of British higher education for some 30 years. References hereafter to Dearing are to the significantly shorter *Summary Report*, published under the same title.
2. The statistical data which follows is derived from Appendix B of the Report.
3. That is a degree which satisfies the initial stage of training for entry to the legal profession as prescribed by the Law Society and Bar. See currently the *Joint Announcement on Qualifying Law Degrees* (January 1995).
4. Based on figures in Wilson and Marsh (1981:6) and Twining (1994:29) respectively.
5. Although the effect of these has been limited to date, they are generally expected, by the end of the century, to constitute a substantial entry route in higher education (HEQC, 1995: Annex B, para.9).
6. 77.4% of all students (60% in post-1992 universities) in 1993 were A level entrants as against 82.3% of law students entering single honours law courses: cf HEQC, 1995: Annex B, para.9; Bermingham *et al*, 1996:21.
7. In 1995/96, ethnic minority students under the age of 24 constituted 11.5% of university

applicants and 10.8% of acceptances, while constituting only 7.3% of the population of 15-24 year olds (Adia *et al*, 1996:1).

8. See Recommendation 25 in Dearing (1997).
9. The Harris Report (1996:5) notes that the proportion of postgraduates rose from 13% to 21% of the total student population between 1979 and 1994.
10. This point was made strongly by Dr David Potter, Chairman of Psion plc and a member of the Dearing Committee, at the Seminar launching the *Dearing Report* in London, 24 July 1997.
11. I was encouraged to this conclusion by analogy with what Boaventura de Sousa Santos describes as 'globalized localism' (1995:263) - the process whereby (chiefly) core countries globalize their local phenomena (fast food, Japanese cars, American copyright laws etc, etc) by imposing them on weaker, peripheral, states.
12. This argument by itself is, of course, over-simplistic even within a post-Fordist explanation. As Peter Scott (1995:102,109) has noted, a (post)modern higher education system is not just driven by needs to increase economic efficiency, it is itself the product of a service economy that is geared to the provision of desirable lifestyles and their associated symbolic goods.
13. Indeed, there is arguably a more fundamental link than this. Hayekian social philosophy involves what John Gray (1986:134-6) calls the adoption of an "evolutionary epistemology" in which, put simply, (i) it is recognised that theoretical and practical knowledge is generated by social institutions and (ii) assumed that societies which encourage competition between knowledge-bearing institutions will be most effective at producing, disseminating and using knowledge. It is also noteworthy in this context that Hayek's model seems to privilege practical knowledge by emphasising its utility in achieving human purposes.
14. As we have seen, the declining resource for core (undergraduate) teaching has meant that the universities have been obliged to diversify their functions, by tapping into alternative markets for both teaching and research.
15. See, eg, de Friend (1995) for details.
16. Examples include Central Law Training's professional masters' degree/specialist diploma programme validated by De Montfort and Staffordshire Universities; dissertation-based LLM's in Advanced Legal Practice, notably at Westminster and West of England Universities, and the LLM in Advanced Litigation at Nottingham Trent University.
17. For recent data on these elements, see Harris and Jones (1997).
18. The launch of a law degree programme by the Open University is the most obvious example of this.

19. Some 90% of university sector institutions are now reported to have adopted or to be adopting modular schemes - *Times Higher Education Supplement*, 25 October 1996, p.4.
20. *Ibid.*
21. Though it is difficult to generalise, we have seen the 'standard' stage model for the law degree change from one in which students follow four year long courses with some element of periodic and summative (end of year) assessment, to one in which six modules are taught across two semesters (ie a 3 + 3 system), with periodic and summative assessment to be completed within the relevant semester.
22. Most notably in the work of industry-sponsored initiatives like the NCVQ (see Barnett, 1994) and Management Charter Initiative (Barker, 1993).
23. Bell (1996:13) defines graduateness as encompassing (1) Knowledge and understanding (2) Analysis (3) Synthesis (4) Evaluation (5) Creativity (6) Presentation (7) Professionalism and (8) Inter-personal skills.
24. Professor Hepple, a member of ACLEC, is acknowledged as chief architect of the final Report.
25. Interestingly, Hepple (1996:479-84) suggests a more academic bias to integration than I would take from my reading of the Report itself.
26. See, eg, the largely content-led approaches to prescription in both the *Joint Announcement on Qualifying Law Degrees* issued by the Law Society and Council of Legal Education in January 1995 and the Legal Practice Course Board's *Written Standards* (v.4, December 1996) for the LPC.
27. The Report, however, is virtually silent on the appropriateness or otherwise of developing the applied lawyering skills at this stage.
28. Cf the statement of aims and purposes for higher education in Dearing (1997, para.23).
29. Cf Economides (1997) on student instrumentalism and its effects on the law school curriculum.
30. It can be summed up as the tendency for the profession to appoint 'people like us' (cf Goriely and Williams, 1996:29-31).

References

ACLEC (Lord Chancellor's Advisory Committee on Legal Education and Conduct) (1996), *First Report on Legal Education and Training*, ACLEC, London.

Adia, E. with Roberts, D. and Allen, A. (1996), *Higher Education: The Ethnic Minority Stu-*

dent Experience, HEIST, Leeds.

Arthurs Report (1983), *Law and Learning*, Social Sciences and Humanities Research Council of Canada, Ottawa.

Ball, C. (1993), *Towards a Learning Society (London: Royal Society of Arts).*

Barker, D. (1993), 'The Management Charter Initiative: An Interim Assessment', *Assessment and Evaluation in Higher Education*, vol.18, p.125.

Barnett, R. (1994), *The Limits of Competence: Knowledge, Higher Education and Society*, SRHE/Open University Press, Buckingham.

Beck, U. (1992), *Risk Society: Towards a New Modernity*, Sage, London.

Bell, D. (1987), 'The World in 2013', *New Society*, 18 December, p.31.

Bell, J. (1996), 'General Transferable Skills and the Law Curriculum', *Contemporary Issues in Law*, vol.II:2, p.1.

Bermingham, V., Hall, C. and Webb, J. (1996), *Access to and Participation in Undergraduate Legal Education: An Exploratory Study*, Faculty of Law Working Paper No. 2, University of the West of England, Bristol.

Blackburn, R. and Jarman, J. (1993), 'Changing Inequalities in Access to British Universities', *Oxford Review of Education*, vol.19, p.197.

Boon, A. (1996), 'Skills in the Initial Stage of Legal Education: Theory and Practice for Transformation', in Webb, J. and Maughan, C. (eds), *Teaching Lawyers' Skills*, Butterworths, London.

Bradney, A. (1992), 'Ivory Towers and Satanic Mills: Choices for University Law Schools', *Studies in Higher Education*, vol.17, p.5.

Bradney, A. (1996), 'Raising the Drawbridge: Defending University Law Schools', in Allen, M. (ed), *The Web Journal of Current Legal Issues 1995 Yearbook*, Blackstone Press, London.

Bradney, A. and Cownie, F. (1996), 'Working on the Chain Gang?', *Contemporary Issues in Law*, vol.II:2, p.15.

Bridges, D. (1993), 'Transferable Skills: A Philosophical Perspective', *Studies in Higher Education*, vol.18, p.43.

Brown, P. (1990), 'The Third Wave: Education and the Ideology of Parentocracy', *British Journal of Sociology of Education*, vol.11:1, p.65.

Brown, P. (1995), 'Cultural Capital and Social Exclusion: Some Observations on Recent Trends in Education, Employment and the Labour Market', *Work, Employment & Society*, vol.9, p.29.

Brown, P. and Lauder, H. (eds) (1992), *Education for Economic Survival: From Fordism to*

Post-Fordism?, Routledge, London.

Brownsword, R. (1996), 'Where Are All the Law Schools Going?', *Law Teacher*, vol.30, p.1.

Daintith, T. (1991), 'Constructing a Common European Legal Curriculum: Problems and Possibilities', *Panorami: Riflesioni discussioni e proposte sul diritto e l'amministrazione*, vol.3, p.198.

Dearing Report (1997), *Higher Education in the Learning Society: Summary Report*, Stationery Office, London.

Debling, G. (1989), 'The Employment Department/Training Agency Standards Programme and NVQ's: Implications for Education', in Burke, J. (ed), *Competency Based Education and Training*, Falmer Press, Lewes.

de Friend, R. (1995), 'Legal Education and Training in Europe: United Kingdom', *International Journal of the Legal Profession*, vol.2, p.119.

de Groot, G-R. (1992), 'European Education in the 21st Century', in De Witte, B. and Forder, C. (eds), *The Common Law of Europe and the Future of Legal Education*, Kluwer, Deventer.

de Sousa Santos, B. (1995), *Toward a New Common Sense: Law, Science and Politics in Paradigmatic Transition*, Routledge, New York and London.

Duke, C. (1992), *The Learning University: Towards a New Paradigm?*, SRHE/Open University Press, Buckingham.

Economides, K. (1997), 'Cynical Legal Studies' in Cooper, J. and Trubek, L. (eds), *Educating for Justice: Social Values and Legal Education*, Ashgate, Aldershot

Edwards, R. (1993), 'The Inevitable Future? Post-Fordism in Work and Learning', in Edwards, R., Sieminski, S. and Zeldin, D., *Adult Learners, Education and Training*, Routledge, London and New York.

Eraut, M. (1994), *Developing Professional Knowledge and Competence*, Falmer Press, London and Washington.

Goriely, T. and Williams, T. (1996), *The Impact of the New Training Scheme: Report on a Qualitative Study*, The Law Society, London.

Gray, J. (1986), *Hayek on Liberty*, 2nd edition, Blackwell, Oxford.

Grimes, R., Klaff, J. and Smith, C. (1996), 'Legal Skills and Clinical Legal Education - A Survey of Undergraduate Law School Practice', *Law Teacher*, vol. 30, p.44.

Halpern, D. (1994), *Entry into the Legal Professions: The Law Student Cohort Study Years 1 & 2*, The Law Society, London.

Harris, P. and Jones, S. (1997), 'A Survey of Law Schools in the United Kingdom, 1996', *Law Teacher*, vol. 31, p.38.

Harris, P. and Tribe, D. (1995), 'The Impact of Semesterisation and Modularisation on the

Assessment of Law Students', *Law Teacher*, vol.29, p.279.

Harris Report (1996), *Review of Postgraduate Education*, HEFCE, Bristol.

Harvey, D. (1989), *The Condition of Postmodernity*, Blackwell, Oxford.

Hepple, B. (1996), 'The Renewal of the Liberal Law Degree', *Cambridge Law Journal*, p.470.

Higher Education Quality Council (HEQC) (1995), *Graduate Standards Programme: Interim Report*, HEQC, London.

Higher Education Quality Council (HEQC) (1996a), *Understanding Academic Standards in Modular Frameworks*, HEQC, London.

Higher Education Quality Council (HEQC) (1996b), *Academic Standards in the Approval, Review and Classification of Degrees*, HEQC, London.

Jabbari, D. (1996), 'Reform of Undergraduate Legal Education: A Polemic on the Relationship Between Academic Law and Legal Practice', in Buckley, R. (ed), *Legal Structures: Boundary Issues Between Legal Categories*, Wiley, Chichester.

Jones, P. (1994), *Competences, Learning Outcomes and Legal Education*, Institute of Advanced Legal Studies, London.

Kuhn, T. (1970), *The Structure of Scientific Revolutions*, 2nd Edition, University of Chicago Press, Chicago.

Le Brun, M. and Johnstone, R. (1994), *The Quiet (R)evolution: Improving Student Learning in Law*, Law Book Co., Sydney.

Lyotard, J-F. (1984), *The Postmodern Condition: A Report on Knowledge*, Manchester University Press, Manchester.

Lyotard, J-F. (1993), *Political Writings*, UCL Press, London.

Maughan, C., Maughan, M. and Webb, J. (1995), 'Sharpening the Mind or Narrowing It? The Limitations of Outcome and Performance Measures in Legal Education', *Law Teacher*, vol.29, p.255.

National Conference of University Professors (NCUP) (1996), *The Case for Universities*, Policy Document No. 6, NCUP, Swansea.

National Institute for Adult and Continuing Education (NIACE) (1990), *Learning Throughout Adult Life: A Policy Discussion Paper on Continuing Education*, NIACE, Leicester.

Newman, J. (1952), *The Idea of a Liberal Education: A Selection from the Works of Newman*, Tristram, H. (ed), Harrap, London.

Newman, J. (1959), *The Idea of a University*, Doubleday, New York.

Ormrod Report (1971), *Report of the Committee on Legal Education*, Cmnd. 4595, HMSO, London.

Perkin, H. (1989), *The Rise of Professional Society: England Since 1880*, Routledge, London.

Piore, M. and Sabel, C. (1984), *The Second Industrial Divide*, Basic Books, New York.

Rigby, G. (1995), 'Funding a Changing System', in Schuller, T. (ed), *The Changing University*, SRHE/Open University Press, Buckingham.

Robertson, R. (1995), 'Glocalization: Time-Space and Homogeneity-Heterogeneity', in Featherstone, M., Lash, S. and Robertson, R. (eds), *Global Modernities*, Sage, London.

Rorty, R. (1979), *Philosophy and the Mirror of Nature*, Princeton University Press, Princeton, NJ.

Schuller, T. (1990), 'The Exploding Community? The University Idea and the Smashing of the Academic Atom', *Oxford Review of Education*, vol.16:1, p.13.

Scott, P. (1984), *The Crisis of the University*, Croom Helm, Beckenham.

Scott, P. (1995), *The Meanings of Mass Higher Education*, SRHE/Open University Press, Buckingham.

Sherr, A. (1996), 'Vocational Education and Training - A Critique' in ACLEC, *First Report on Legal Education and Training,* Report of the Proceedings of the Conference Held on 8 July 1996, ACLEC, London.

Shiner, M. and Newburn, T. (1995), *Entry into the Legal Professions: The Law Student Cohort Study Year 3*, The Law Society, London.

Slowey, M. (1994), *Changing Conceptions of Continuing Education - The Implications for Higher Education*, CVCP Research Seminar, October.

Teichler, U. (1996), 'The Changing Nature of Higher Education in Western Europe', *Higher Education Policy*, vol.9:2, p.89.

Thompson, E. (1970), *Warwick University Ltd: Industry, Management and the Universities*, Penguin, Harmondsworth.

Toddington, S. (1994), 'Skills "Quality" and the Ideologies of Managerialism', *Law Teacher*, vol.28, p.243.

Twining, W. L. (1994), *Blackstone's Tower: The English Law School*, Sweet & Maxwell, London.

Twining, W.L. (1995a), 'Remembering 1972: The Oxford Centre in the Context of Development in Higher Education and the Discipline of Law', in Galligan, D. (ed), *Socio-Legal Studies in Context: The Oxford Centre Past and Future*, Blackwell, Oxford and Cambridge, MA.

Twining, W.L. (1995b), 'What Are Law Schools For?', *Northern Ireland Legal Quarterly*, vol.46, p.291.

Webb, J. (1995), 'Where the Action Is: Developing Artistry in Legal Education', *International Journal of the Legal Profession*, vol.2, p.189.

Webster, F. (1995), *Theories of the Information Society*, Routledge, London.

Weick, K. (1976), 'Educational Organisations as Loosely-Coupled Systems', *Administrative Science Quarterly*, vol.21:1, 1.

Wilson, G. (1987), 'English Legal Scholarship', *Modern Law Review*, vol.50, p.818.

Wilson, J. (1993), 'A Third Survey of University Legal Education in the United Kingdom', *Legal Studies*, vol.13, p.143.

Wilson, J. and Marsh, S. (1981), *A Second Survey of Legal Education in the United Kingdom: Supplement No. 2*, Institute of Advanced Legal Studies, London.

Winter, R. (1996), 'Outline of a General Theory of Professional Competences', in Webb, J. and Maughan, C. (eds), *Teaching Lawyers' Skills*, Butterworths, London.

For Product Safety Concerns and Information please contact our EU representative GPSR@taylorandfrancis.com Taylor & Francis Verlag GmbH, Kaufingerstraße 24, 80331 München, Germany

Batch number: 10725923

Printed by Printforce, the Netherlands